RELIGIONS AND BELIEFS

© **Editions Didier Millet, 2005**
Published by Archipelago Press *an imprint of* Editions Didier Millet Pte Ltd
121, Telok Ayer Street, #03-01, Singapore 068590
Tel: 65-6324 9260 Fax: 65-6324 9261 E-mail: edm@edmbooks.com.sg

First published 2005

Editions Didier Millet, Kuala Lumpur Office:
25, Jalan Pudu Lama, 50200 Kuala Lumpur, Malaysia
Tel: 03-2031 3805 Fax: 03-2031 6298 E-mail: edmbooks@edmbooks.com.my

Colour separation by United Graphic Pte Ltd
Printed by Star Standard Industries (Pte) Ltd

ISBN 981-3018-51-8

All Rights Reserved. No part of this book may be reproduced, stored in a retrieval system, or transmitted in any form or by any means without permission from the publisher.

Note for Readers
Some dates in this book are followed by the letters CE or BCE, which mean 'Common Era' and 'Before Common Era', respectively. These terms are synonymous with AD Anno Domini (in the year of our Lord) and BC, which means 'Before Christ'.
The transliteration system which is applied in this encyclopedia follows the Dewan Bahasa dan Pustaka Malaysia transliteration system for Arabic words. This system differs from the system adopted by the Library of Congress or the Encyclopedia of Islam (E.J. Brill).

The Publishers wish to thank Wan Abdul Rahim Kamil bin Wan Mohamed Ali for providing additional material on Islamic banking. They also wish to thank Azmi Dato' Dr Mohd Rais, Kamarul Hisham Kamaruddin and Zain and Co. for providing additional material and advice on Islamic law.

CONTRIBUTORS

Dr Abdul Monir bin Yaacob
Institute of Islamic Understanding

Prof. Dr Abdul Samat bin Musa
Kolej Universiti Islam Malaysia

Prof. Dr Abu Bakar Abdul Majeed
Universiti Teknologi Mara

Ahmad Sarji bin Abdul Hamid
Badan Warisan Malaysia

Ang Choo Hong
Buddhist Missionary Society Malaysia

Anuar Talib
Universiti Teknologi Mara

Asst Prof. Dr Edmund K.F. Chia
Catholic Theological Union (Chicago)

Assoc. Prof. Dr Juli Edo
Universiti Malaya

Dr Joseph Fung Jee Vui
Diocesan Ministry of Ecumenical and Inter-Religious Affairs

Dr Ghazali bin Basri
World Council of Muslims for Interfaith Relations

Goh Keat Peng
Christian Federation of Malaysia

Dr Ismail Hamid
Universiti Kebangsaan Malaysia (retired)

R. Seeta Lechumi
Universiti Malaya

Benny Liow Woon Khin
Young Buddhist Association of Malaysia

Prof. Dr M. Kamal Hassan
International Islamic University Malaysia

S. Manimaran
Universiti Malaya

Assoc. Prof. Dr Mizan Hitam
Universiti Teknologi Mara

Prof. Mohamad Abu Bakar
Universiti Malaya

Prof. Emeritus Dr Mohd Taib Osman
Universiti Malaya

(Dr) Muhammad Uthman El-Muhammady
International Islamic University Malaysia

Dr Devapoopathy Nadarajah
Universiti Malaya

Nik Mustapha Haji Nik Hassan
Institute of Islamic Understanding

Dr Ong Seng Huat
Xiao-en Cultural Endowment (Kuala Lumpur)

Dr Bro. Cassian Pappu
Malaysian Catholic Education Council

Dr R. Rajakrishnan
Asian Institute of Medicine, Science and Technology

Prof. Dr M. Rajantheran
Universiti Malaya

Assoc. Prof. Saliha Hassan
Universiti Kebangsaan Malaysia

Vijaya Samarawickrama
Taylor's College

Revd Dr Hermen Shastri
Council of Churches of Malaysia

Dr Sidek Haji Fadhil
Kolej Dar Al-Hikmah

Prof. Emeritus Dr S. Singaravelu
Universiti Malaya

Saran Singh
Author

Prof. Dr Siti Zainon Ismail
Universiti Kebangsaan Malaysia

G. Sivapalan
Universiti Malaya

Assoc. Prof. Dr Soo Khin Wah
Universiti Malaya

Dr K. Thilagawathi
Universiti Malaya (retired)

Revd Dr Albert Sundararaj Walters
Seminari Theoloji Malaysia

Dr Zambry Abdul Kadir
Perak State Executive Committee Member

THE ENCYCLOPEDIA OF
MALAYSIA

Volume 10

RELIGIONS
AND BELIEFS

Volume Editors
Prof. Dr M. Kamal Hassan
International Islamic University Malaysia

Dr Ghazali bin Basri
World Council of Muslims for Interfaith Relations

ARCHIPELAGO PRESS

Contents

A young devotee makes an offering at the Buddhist Maha Vihara, Brickfields, Kuala Lumpur.

Stained glass window, St Mary's Cathedral, Kuala Lumpur.

Masjid Ubudiah, Kuala Kangsar.

Introduction

This terracotta brick, found in the Bujang Valley in Kedah, is inscribed with the Buddhist word 'tra' denoting a Tantric rite in Mahayana Buddhism.

Religion has always been an important part of Malaysian life. A number of historical developments have brought about the religious diversity evident in Malaysian society today, be it the introduction of Hinduism, Buddhism and Islam or the presence of Christianity with the arrival of Western colonial powers. This volume provides a window to the diversity of religious faiths and practices which have enriched Malaysia's pluralism and tempered the materialistic ethos of contemporary business and corporate culture. It introduces the reader to the major religions in Malaysia, as described by specialists and scholars, and shows the extent to which religion has shaped the culture of the Malaysian people.

Prime Minister Dato' Seri Abdullah Ahmad Badawi with leaders of various Christian denominations at an International Ecumenical Christian conference, August 2004, Kuala Lumpur.

A woman devotee at a Thaipusam celebration.

The Buddhist Wesak Day celebration is a national holiday.

RIGHT: A carved *mimbar* (pulpit) of a mosque. Islam has been the major religion in Malaysia since the 15th century.

Religious diversity

The region of Southeast Asia has become home to most of the world religions. Buddhism and Hinduism, introduced mainly by trade and conquest, are the oldest and have proven to be the most enduring in the region, with archaeological evidence dating back to around the 5th century CE for Buddhism and the 11th century CE for Hinduism. By comparison, Islam arrived in the region later, as historical evidence shows that active Islamization of the Malay World took place from the 13th century CE onward, although Muslim traders had been in the region much earlier.

The process of Islamization brought about a major cultural transformation in many parts of Southeast Asia. In the greater part of the Malay World, this religion became such an important influence that Malay culture became synonymous with Islam.

Later, the advent of European colonialism in the 16th century brought Christianity—in this case, Catholicism—as a new religion to the area. Protestantism soon followed in the wake of Dutch and British expansionism.

Religious diversity in Malaysia is closely tied to the immigration of Chinese and Indian peoples during the British administration. As a result of the influx of Chinese communities the existence of Confucianism, Taoism and ancestor worship became more prominent, while the renewed prominence of Hinduism can be attributed to the large numbers of Indian immigrants during the same period. The presence of Sikhism in Malaysia also dates back to the arrival of Sikhs in the Malay Peninsula under the British.

These world religions spread their influence in the coastal settlements and urban areas. However, there were also beliefs that were indigenous to the region, such as animism, which continued to maintain their hold on the lives of the indigenous peoples who traditionally occupied the inner areas of the Malay Peninsula, as well as Sabah and Sarawak in Malaysian Borneo. The beliefs of these indigenous peoples of Malaysia are still very much a part of Malaysian life today.

Although Islam is the official religion of the country, the Malaysian constitution guarantees freedom of worship and the rights of adherents of other religions to practise their beliefs. A visitor to Malaysia will not fail to notice the existence of mosques, churches and Hindu, Buddhist, Taoist and Sikh temples in close vicinity to each other. This harmonious co-existence of so many different ethnic groups and religious beliefs has made Malaysia unique in the region for having the greatest number of public holidays in honour of the religious festivals or historic moments of most world religions, as well as the indigenous religions of Sabah and

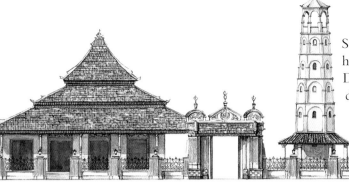

The Terengkera Mosque in Melaka, completed around 1728, has a pagoda-shaped minaret reminiscent of southern China.

A devotee, with his cheeks pierced, taking part in the Taoist Nine Emperor Gods festival in Melaka. This festival, celebrated in Malaysia, is no longer of great significance in China.

Sarawak. So, for example, besides the Muslim holidays, the Chinese New Year, the Hindu Deepavali festival and Christmas have been declared national holidays.

Religion and culture

Although most Malaysians are adherents of major world religions, there is a clear indication that local culture and environment have influenced certain aspects of religion, including rituals and celebrations. For example, the Thaipusam festival, which is celebrated on a grand scale by Hindus in Malaysia, is not a significant celebration in India. There are a number of Hindu and Chinese festivals that are celebrated only in Malaysia. Belief in guardian spirits, called Kong, often worshipped by followers of Chinese religions, is thought to have originated from the worship of nature spirits in indigenous Malaysian culture.

Even some aspects of Islamic institutions have been influenced by local culture. Traditional Malaysian mosques built in the style of local architecture, for example, did not have domes and minarets. In fact, the minarets of early Malaysian mosques show more Chinese than Arab influence. Malay weddings, to some extent, still retain elements that can be traced back to Hindu origins.

The importance of religious values

Religions provide a higher meaning to life while imparting to their adherents transcendent spiritual values and norms of virtuous conduct. As Malaysia forges ahead on the path of economic progress, there has been a perceived religious resurgence, a phenomenon not confined to Islam alone. Though it may be more apparent in the Muslim community, judging by the emphasis on religious education and the call for a return to Islamic values, it can also be observed in other religious communities in Malaysia. It is conceivable that the nation's commitment to high economic growth requires not only a clear moral compass but also the integration of religious and spiritual values in the development of programmes.

Religion and nation-building

The government's policy of Vision 2020 (with the objective of developing Malaysia into a fully developed country by the year 2020) emphasizes that the country's overall progress in the coming decades should be constructed in accordance with 'our own mould'. It reaffirms the need to strengthen the ethico-religious foundation of Malaysia's economic prosperity. Such a futuristic strategy of socio-cultural re-engineering clearly entails greater inculcation of ethical and spiritual consciousness. It is in this way that religions in Malaysia can make their greatest contribution to nation-building.

It is through the awareness of the significance of ethical and spiritual values in nation-building that government leaders have also stressed the concept of 'balanced development' or 'integrated development'. In order to realize this concept, relevant religious and spiritual values are being incorporated in industrialization efforts and processes. This is important to ensure the preservation of a deeply ethical society. The various religions thriving in Malaysia possess the capability of reinforcing the moral fibre of the nation and addressing the challenges of modern technocentric civilization.

A fundamental social institution that has come under great pressure during the process of rapid industrialization and urbanization is the family. Religions are an effective means of nurturing and reinforcing the culture of loving one's parents, respecting one's elders and teachers and caring for the young. The revival of world religions in Malaysia would presumably lead to a rejuvenation of those traditional values.

An Orang Ulu burial post from Sarawak. Malaysia's indigenous peoples have their own beliefs. However, in recent centuries many have converted to other world religions.

Sikhs during the procession celebrating the 400th anniversary of the Sikh Holy book, the Guru Granth Sahib, in Kuala Lumpur, 2004.

7

Chronology

Wooden sculpture depicting the spirits which protect longhouses, Sarawak.

2000–1500 BCE

Indigenous
Ancient ways (animism) passed down and adapted over millennia.

Hinduism
Indus Valley civilization, start of Hinduism.

1500–1000 BCE

Hinduism
Early sacred scriptures—the Veda and Brahmana—first written.

1000–500 BCE

Hinduism
Early Upanishad written.

Jainism
Jainism emerges in India.

Taoism and Confucianism
c. 604–521: Lao Zi founds Taoism.
c. 551–479: Confucius founds Confucianism.

Buddhism
c. 563–483: Gautama Buddha; beginnings of Buddhism.

500–1 BCE

Hinduism
Ramayana and *Mahabharata* epics and Purana written.

1–500 CE

Hinduism
Vaishnavism and Shaivism develop.

Taoism and Confucianism
c. 100: Taoism becomes established in China. The Chinese education system is based on Confucian classics.

Christianity
c. 1–33: Life of Jesus Christ.
Paul and the Apostles organize early Christians.

500–1500 CE

Hinduism
c. 600 onwards: Bhakti movement. Hinduism comes to the Malay Archipelago, via Indian merchants.
1025: Kedah is conquered by the Chola kingdom of South India which exerts a strong Hindu influence.
1100: Decline of Chola and the resurgence of Kedah as an independent state.

Buddhism
Mahayana Buddhism spreads to the Malay Archipelago under influence of the Srivijaya Empire—a centre for Buddhist learning. Buddhism is declared the national religion of Tibet.
900: Theravada Buddhism spreads from Thailand to Kelantan and Terengganu.
1100: Buddhist influence in the Malay Archipelago wanes with the declining power of the Srivijaya Empire.

Bronze statue from the Srivijaya Period (7th–13th century).

Taoism and Confucianism
1400: Arrival of Chinese Hokkien traders in Melaka. They intermarry with locals and eventually become known as Babas and Nonyas.

Islam
c. 570–632: Life of Prophet Muhammad.
622: Prophet's migration (Hijrah) to Yathrib (Medina). Beginning of the Muslim lunar calendar.
660–750: Ummayyad Caliphate (first Arab-Islamic dynasty).
750–1258: Abbasid (Baghdad) Caliphate. Islam is introduced in the Malay-Indonesian Archipelago by Arab and Indian merchants.
1303: Terengganu Stone inscription—first evidence of Islam in Malaysia.

Dome of the Benut Mosque, Pontian, Johor.

1400s: Conversion to Islam of the Ruler of Melaka, Parameswara, later known as Iskandar Shah. Melaka becomes a centre of Islamic learning.

Sikhism
1469–1539: Life of Guru Nanak, the founder of Sikhism.

1500–1800 CE

Taoism and Confucianism
1645: The first Chinese temple is built in Melaka.

Christianity
1511: Portuguese conquer Melaka; the coming of Roman Catholicism to the Malay Archipelago.
1521: Protestantism begins.
1545: St Francis Xavier arrives in Melaka.
1641: The Dutch take Melaka and bring Protestant Christianity to the Malay Archipelago.

Islam
1571–1924: Uthmani (Ottoman) Caliphate.

1800–1900 CE

Hinduism
1850–1900: Indian migrants come to Malaya to work in the plantations, railways and other areas under the British administration. Modern Hinduism comes to Malaya with them.

Woodcut of Chinese Confucian scholars.

Buddhism
1800s: Mahayana Buddhism resurfaces with the arrival of Chinese workers.

Taoism and Confucianism
1850s: Chinese are brought in as labourers in the growing tin mining industry in Malaya. With them they bring their beliefs of Taoism and Confucianism.

Christianity
1805: First chaplain arrives in Penang.
1848: Borneo Church Mission in Sarawak is founded.
1881: Roman Catholic Mission in Sarawak begins with the coming of the Mill Hill Fathers.
1885: Founding of the Methodist Mission in Malaya.

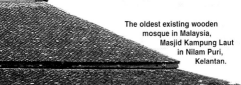
The oldest existing wooden mosque in Malaysia, Masjid Kampung Laut in Nilam Puri, Kelantan.

Islam
1800s onwards: The British control Malaya; however, the sultan of each state remains as the authority on religion and Malay customs.

Sikhism
1870–1880: Sikhs come to Malaya under the British administration to work in the police force and army.

1900–present

Hinduism
1965: Formation of the Malaysia Hindu Sangam.

Buddhism
1995: Formation of the Malaysian Buddhist Sangha Council.

Conch shells are sacred to Hindus as they represent life from the life-giving waters of the ocean.

Christianity
1948: Formation of the Council of Churches of Malaysia (CCM).
1983: Formation of the National Evangelical Christian Fellowship Malaysia (NECF).
1985: Formation of the Christian Federation of Malaysia (CFM).

The Anglican Bishop of West Malaysia, Rt Revd Tan Sri Dr Lim Cheng Ean, officiating at St Mary's Cathedral, Kuala Lumpur.

Islam
1906: A modern Islamic religious school (*madrasah*) is established in Telok Anson (now Teluk Intan) Perak.
1915: The first Islamic Religious Council headed by the Sultan, to oversee all religious affairs in the state, is established in Kelantan.
1955: The first national Islamic religious college (Kolej Islam Malaya) is established by the government in Klang, Selangor.
1960: The first national Islamic welfare organization Pertubuhan Kebajikan Islam Malaysia (PERKIM) is formed.

1962: The Pilgrims Management and Fund Board (Lembaga Urusan Tabung Haji) is formed by the government.
1965: The National Mosque (Masjid Negara) is constructed by the government in Kuala Lumpur.
1968: The National Council for Islamic Affairs, headed by the Yang Di-Pertuan Agong, is established by the Conference of Rulers.

Arabic prayer compass.

1970: The first Faculty of Islamic Studies is set up by the government in Universiti Kebangsaan Malaysia (established in 1970).
1970s: Islamic resurgence of the 1970s and 1980s in Malaysia promotes Islam as a complete way of life.
1971: Angkatan Belia Islam Malaysia (ABIM) (Islamic Youth Movement of Malaysia) is formed.
1980: The Regional Islamic Dakwah Council for Southeast Asia and Pacific (RISEAP) is formed in Kuala Lumpur. PERKIM leaders play a leading role in this new non-governmental organization.
1983: The first Islamic bank is established by the government.
1983: The International Islamic University Malaysia (IIUM) is established by the government.
1992: The government establishes the Institut Kefahaman Islam Malaysia (IKIM) (Malaysian Institute of Islamic Understanding) headed by Tan Sri Ahmad Sarji bin Abdul Hamid.
2003–2006: Malaysia assumes the chairmanship of the Organisation of the Islamic Conference (OIC).

Interfaith
1983: Formation of Malaysian Consultative Council of Buddhism, Christianity, Hinduism and Sikhism (MCCBCHS).

Sikhism
1881: First gurdwara is established in Penang.
1920: Influx of young Sikhs to Malaya searching for a better life.
1988: Formation of the Malaysian Gurdwaras Council.

The sacred Guru Granth Sahib, the Sikh Holy Book. Initially compiled in 1604 by Guru Arjan Dev, this scripture consists of his own compositions as well as those of the preceding Gurus.

1. An *akad nikah* (marriage solemnization) ceremony. In urban areas, such ceremonies are now commonly held at the mosque rather than in the bride's home.

2. A Malay woman wearing a *tudung* (headscarf) in front of the Islamic Affairs Department, Prime Minister's Office, Kuala Lumpur.

3. Muslim schoolboys in *baju Melayu* uniform.

4. The Masjid Zahir in Alor Star, Kedah, is one of the most beautiful old mosques in Malaysia. It was built in 1912, and is the official mosque for the state.

5. At the beginning of any function, formal or informal, Muslims start by reciting a *doa* (supplication).

6. Decorative calligraphy, one of the characteristics of Islamic art, is commonly used in mosques, as seen here at the Federal Territory Mosque in Kuala Lumpur.

ISLAM

The main dome of the Islamic Arts Museum in Kuala Lumpur is beautifully decorated with Islamic art and a verse from the Qur'an.

At the start of the 21st century there were approximately 1.2 billion Muslims worldwide, with approximately 230 million living in Southeast Asia. In Malaysia, an estimated 60 per cent of the population are Muslims, the overwhelming majority of them being ethnic Malays.

Islam was brought to the Malay-Indonesian Archipelago by Arab and Indian merchants over a period stretching from the 10th to the 15th century CE. It is significant to note that the spread of Islam in the region was carried out peacefully. Once Muslim merchants and religious teachers converted local chieftains and rajas, the rest of the population usually followed suit.

The Malay community thus became a part of the universal Muslim *ummah* (community or nation). Those Malays who, for example, performed the hajj (the pilgrimage to Mecca) were then able to experience first-hand the real meaning of universal brotherhood which transcends ethnicity as well as cultural and geographical barriers.

As far as the cardinal beliefs and the pillars of Islam are concerned, Islam in Malaysia is no different from Islam in the Arab world. However, what may be considered unique about Islam in Malaysia by non-Muslims and Westerners is basically the physical and cultural forms—the colourful dress of the Malays, for example, or their indigenous architectural traditions evident in the design of mosques, the manner in which religious festivals are celebrated, the social manifestations of gender relationships and the influence of Malay *adat* (customary law) in Malay weddings, in Islamic inheritance law and in royal ceremonies.

An important feature of Islam as practised in Malaysia is its tolerant and accommodationist spirit, thanks to the fact that Malays have been accustomed to living and interacting with people of various ethnic backgrounds with different religious beliefs for centuries.

Malaysia is one of several Muslim countries in the world in which Islam is the official religion, as enshrined in its constitution, but non-Muslims are permitted to practise their religions freely. The status of Islam as the official religion is thus not a barrier to the harmonious co-existence of other religions in the country.

With increased Islamic awareness from the 1970s, there came a noticeable change in the consciousness of Islamic identity among Malaysian Muslims. This is especially evident today from the large number of financial institutions providing Islamic banking facilities and Islamic educational institutions, the rise in the demand for halal food and products, the popularity of Islamic modes of dress among Muslim women and the growing number of Islamic professional associations involving doctors, scientists and engineers.

In 2004 the government introduced 'Islam Hadhari', an approach which comprises ten principles: faith and piety in Allah; a just and trustworthy government; a free and independent people; vigorous pursuit and mastery of knowledge; balanced and comprehensive economic development; a good quality of life for the people; protection of the rights of minority groups and women; cultural and moral integrity; safeguarding of natural resources and the environment; and strong defence capabilities; for the holistic progress of the Muslim community and the nation.

Islamization of the Malay World and Malaysia

The period of Islamic expansion from the 13th to the 16th century CE is commonly called the 'Islamic period'. The Islamization of the Malay Archipelago brought about a profound cultural change, particularly in Malay letters, art, architecture, dress and marriage customs. Although the spread of Islam slowed down due to Western colonization from the early 16th century, the Malay-Indonesian Archipelago still contains the largest concentration of Muslims in any geographical area of comparable size.

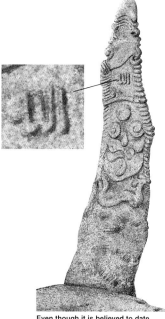

Even though it is believed to date from pre-Islamic times this megalith found in Negeri Sembilan is inscribed with the name of Allah (detail).

A 19th-century embroidered prayer mat made for the Sultan of Perak. The foot of the mat has a concealed pocket for a *songkok* (cap), prayer beads or women's prayer garments.

The spread of Islam

There is no trace of large-scale conversion to Islam among the indigenous people of the Malay Archipelago until the 13th century. Rapid Islamic expansion occurred from the 13th to the 16th century CE. After this time, with the coming of Western powers in the early 16th century, the spread of Islam slowed as local forces were diverted to fighting Western colonization.

There has been much debate among scholars as to the origins of the pioneers of Islamization. At the seminar on 'The Introduction of Islam in Indonesia', in Medan on 20 March 1963, it was concluded that Islam came directly from Mecca. Arab traders, or rather the Arab preachers whom the traders brought along on their voyages, converted many of the people inhabiting the archipelago. It is highly likely that this process of Islamization was continued by local preachers.

The possibility of Malays being converted outside their homeland can also not be ruled out. In one of his manuscripts, Ibn Battuta, the famous 14th-century Arab traveller, mentions the presence of Malays in East Africa and the Malabar coast (India). There, they would have had contact with Muslims.

The impact of Islamization

As a result of Islamization, Malay society became much less hierarchical, and practices in conformity with Islam began to replace earlier Hindu ceremonies. Classical Malay texts indicate that Islam was considered superior to all other religions.

However, cultural elements not contradicting Islamic teachings were retained. For example, the *wayang kulit* (shadow theatre) was used in the initial stages of Islamic expansion by Javanese *wali* (missionaries) as a tool for preaching. A considerable number of words in the Malay language are derived from Arabic, the language of the Qur'an.

Many factors contributed to the success of the Islamization of the Malay-Indonesian Archipelago. For one, Islam brought a new world-view based on one God and the equality of all mankind. Scholars say it was also the result of the wise, persuasive and peaceful approach of Islamization.

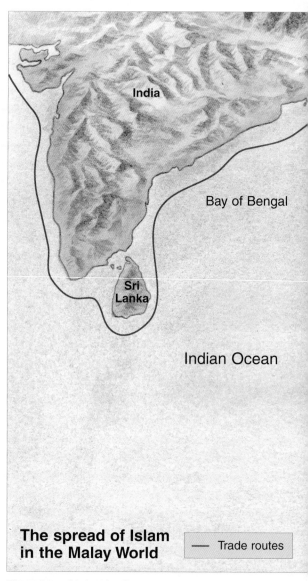

India

Bay of Bengal

Sri Lanka

Indian Ocean

The spread of Islam in the Malay World

—— Trade routes

Theories of Islamization

There are several theories that have been put forward to explain the spread of Islam in the Archipelago. The **trade theory** is the most common explanation. Muslim Arabs introduced Islam in the principalities they visited in their quest for spices and precious metals. Some of them settled permanently and intermarried with local people. It is likely that Indian and Chinese Muslim traders also influenced the spread of Islam in the Malay Archipelago.

The **missionary theory**, referring to the work of learned Muslims who dedicated themselves to preaching and teaching, states that initial conversion by traders was intensified later on by religious teachers. Muslim missionaries also intermarried with the local people and thus spread Islam by marriage.

The **Sufi theory** emphasizes the role of charismatic and mystical Sufi teachers in spreading Islam in Southeast Asia. These Sufis were said to possess supernatural powers and were skilled in the art of healing. They were well accepted by the natives.

The **political theory** suggests that Malay rulers converted to Islam for political leverage and then, in turn, used their power to convert their subjects, who felt oppressed by the strict Hindu-based caste divisions that existed at the time. Islam promised the equality of all human beings.

According to the political theory, the Malay rulers gained political benefits from the conversion in three ways: by becoming Muslims, the Malay rulers, as in the case of Melaka, were assured of the backing and patronage of the powerful Muslim traders; secondly, some coastal chiefs used Islam as a political instrument in their struggle to

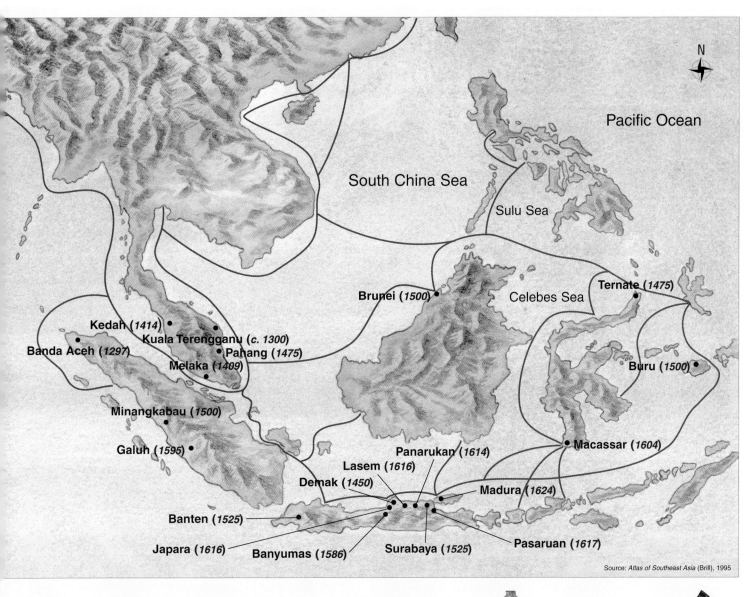

N

Pacific Ocean

South China Sea

Sulu Sea

Celebes Sea

Brunei (*1500*)

Ternate (*1475*)

Kedah (*1414*)

Kuala Terengganu (*c. 1300*)

Banda Aceh (*1297*)

Pahang (*1475*)

Melaka (*1409*)

Buru (*1500*)

Minangkabau (*1500*)

Galuh (*1595*)

Macassar (*1604*)

Panarukan (*1614*)

Lasem (*1616*)

Demak (*1450*)

Madura (*1624*)

Banten (*1525*)

Japara (*1616*)

Banyumas (*1586*)

Surabaya (*1525*)

Pasaruan (*1617*)

Source: *Atlas of Southeast Asia* (Brill), 1995

secure independence from central Hindu authority, as in the case of Majapahit in what is now Indonesia; and lastly, Malay rulers used Islam as a political tool to legitimize their dynasties. The political theory suggests that conversion to Islam enabled Malays to claim that their right to rule derived from Islamic authority.

The political theory also has economic implications because the Malay rulers of coastal principalities were very dependent on taxes imposed on trade at their ports. Conversion meant gaining the support of Muslim traders that was essential in making the ports more prosperous.

All the theories on the Islamization of the Malay World have their limitations. Each theory can only be applied to certain places and certain times. No single theory can adequately explain the whole process of the Islamization of the archipelago. Therefore, the different theories must be seen as complementary.

The earliest verified evidence of Islam in the region dates back to the 13th century CE and is found in Aceh (the gravestone of Sultan Malik-al-Salih of Pasai, northern Sumatra), whereas the Terengganu Stone shows that Terengganu was ruled by a Muslim king in the 14th century CE. From the early 15th century to the first half of the 17th century evidence shows a rapid expansion of Islam in the region covering Melaka (1409), Kedah (1414) and Kuala Terengganu (c. 1300), Demak (1450), Ternate (1475), Pahang (1475), Minangkabau (1500), Brunei (1500), Buru (1500), Banten (1525), Surabaya (1525), Banyumas (1586), Galuh (1595), Macassar (1604), Panarukan (1614), Japara (1616), Lasem (1616), Pasaruan (1617) and Madura (1624).

Early Islamic sites

The earliest Muslim Arab settlement in the Malay-Indonesian Archipelago was Palembang (674 CE). There may also have been an Arab settlement in Kedah as early as the 9th century. A Muslim gravestone found in Pekan, Pahang, dated 1028 CE but written in 14th-century script, remains unverified by scholars.

Literary and archaeological evidence such as these fragments of an Arab *dirham* found in Kedah's Bujang Valley suggests that Islam also came to Kedah in the 15th century CE.

According to the *Hikayat Raja-Raja Pasai*, Islam was introduced and established in the northern part of Sumatra in the middle of the 13th century. The tombstone of the first Muslim ruler of Pasai, Sultan Malik al-Salih, is dated 1297 CE.

East Java was Islamized in the 15th century CE. The Great Mosque of Demak dates back to 1479. The Islamization of Java is mostly ascribed to the propagation activities of Islamic scholars coming from Melaka.

The inscription on a stone discovered at Kuala Berang, Terengganu, dated 1303 CE, indicates early Islamization of the northeast coast of the Malay Peninsula.

The founding of the Malay kingdom of Melaka in the 15th century was a milestone in the history of Islamic expansion in the region. Its ruler embraced Islam in 1409 CE. Under the sultans, Melaka was a centre of Islamic learning and contributed significantly to propagating Islam to other parts of the Malay-Indonesian Archipelago. Seen here is a coin from the Melaka Sultanate.

The Islamization of West Java in the 16th century CE came after the fall of the Melaka Empire to the Portuguese in 1511. In comparison, some cities in East Java such as Lasem, Pasaruan and Madura were Islamized relatively late, in the 17th century CE.

This gravestone, of a Muslim woman named Fatimah binti Maimun bin Habatallah—who may not have been of Indonesian origin—is the oldest known Muslim gravestone in Indonesia. Dated 1082 CE, it was found at Leran, East Java.

13

The Malay Sultanates and Islam

During the Hindu period, the Malay ruler was called a Devaraja, and he was considered a descendant of a Hindu god. This changed when the Malays converted to Islam. The title of the Malay ruler was changed to 'sultan', and he became a head of state without the divine attributes associated with the Devaraja. The sultan is seen as the defender of the faith and head of religion in his state even today, a position guaranteed by the constitution.

Malaysia's earliest dated royal grave, found in Langgar near Pekan, Pahang is the tomb of the Sultan of Pahang, Raja Muhammad. The tombstone records the date of his death as 17 September 1475, and also has an inscription of *sura* Al-Baqarah (Q. 2: 225).

Coins from the Melaka Sultanate are inscribed in Arabic script, showing the influence of Islam on local culture. This coin (1445–59 CE) was issued during the reign of Melaka's fourth ruler Sultan Muzaffar Shah.

Hindu influence

Leadership in Malay society in the pre-Islamic period came under the influence of Hinduism as the religion spread to the Malay-Indonesian world from the 7th century CE. Hinduism became especially important after Kedah was conquered by the Chola kings from southern India in the 11th century.

The Malay Sultanates and Islam

Beginning with some sultanates in northeast Sumatra, such as Perlak and Samudra-Pasai, the Hindu-Buddhist kingdoms in the region, which had been in existence for a millennium, began to be supplanted and replaced by Muslim polities from the 13th and 14th centuries. New states were founded right up to the 18th century CE. While the socio-political structure of these kingdoms remained more or less intact, an Islamic texture, especially in beliefs, world-view and philosophy, began to be woven into the fabric of the populace. Today, the existing sultanates in Malaysia, nine in number, are directly or indirectly descendants of the old sultanate polities. Kedah, Perak, Pahang, Terengganu, Johor and Kelantan can trace their continuity from ancient kingdoms, while Negeri Sembilan, Perlis and Selangor, which are relatively new creations, have also inherited the traditional character of the sultanate polity.

The roles of the sultan and other officials

Since the inception of the sultanate as a polity, the sultan or the ruler was the pivot upon which the polity revolved. In a tradition established by the ruler of Samudra-Pasai, a sultanate in northern Sumatra, the sultan was the embodiment of Islamic belief, world-view, ethos and character. Ibn Battuta, a famous Arab traveller who visited the sultanate in the 14th century CE, described the sultan,

Melaka—a prominent centre of Islamic learning
Like the court of Samudra-Pasai, which served as its model, the royal court in Melaka was a centre for Islamic learning. The sultan often held audience with visitors from the Middle East as depicted here.

The Melaka Sultanate

The Sultanate of Melaka became an important force in propagating Islam among its subjects as well as in the Malay Archipelago. Muslim missionaries from Arabia and Persia succeeded in converting the ruler of Melaka, the son of Melaka's founder Parameswara, to Islam. The newly converted king, who took the name of Iskandar Shah, soon established Melaka as a centre of Islamic learning.

The sultanate introduced a policy of encouraging rulers of other provinces to study Islamic knowledge in Melaka. Sultan Alauddin Riayat Shah invited the rulers of Pahang, Kampar and Inderagiri and their families to study in Melaka. All the sultans of Melaka promoted religious learning, for example, Sultan Muhammad Shah surrounded himself with Muslim theologians.

During the period of the Melaka Sultanate, religious scholars from other Islamic countries were invited to teach its rulers and the people of Melaka about Islam. The *Sejarah Melayu* (Malay Annals) mentions the names of some of the religious teachers who came to Melaka to teach: Makhdum Syed Abdul Aziz, Maulana Abu Bakar, Kadi Yusuf and Maulana Jalaluddin. Some of these theologians were appointed as judges and accorded a high status in the state administration. They were also consulted on various political issues.

Some historians believe that, in the 15th century, the Sultanate of Melaka became the centre of Islamic learning for the whole of the region. Among the missionaries who were trained in Melaka were three well-known Javanese missionaries: Sunan Bonan, Sunan Kalijaga and Shaikh Sutabaris. After completing their studies, they returned home to preach Islam in Java.

In 1511 CE, Melaka fell to the Portuguese and their colonial administration. Subsequently, the Malay sultanates were confronted successively by a number of Western colonial powers. The colonial powers were not meant to interfere in matters of religion and the population remained staunchly Muslim.

The Johor-Riau Sultanate

The Sultanate of Johor-Riau became another centre of Islamic religious learning after Aceh in northern Sumatra declined in importance. Like their predecessors in the other Malay sultanates, its sultans encouraged learning and participated in pursuing religious studies.

Raja Ali Haji of the Johor royal family was educated in an Islamic institution on the island of Penyengat, in the Riau Islands, off the east coast of Sumatra, and became a well-known Muslim scholar in Riau. He was a dedicated instructor who taught various branches of Islamic knowledge, such as theology, law, sufism and Arabic. Besides teaching, Raja Ali Haji wrote books on Islamic knowledge and Malay literature.

〜〜 〜〜 Sultanate of Melaka
━ ━ Sultanate of Johor-Riau

The Melaka empire, which included parts of Sumatra and Johor-Riau, played a crucial role in the spread of Islam in the Malay Archipelago. Many Muslim missionaries originated from Melaka. The map dates from 1762.

Malikul Zahir, as a devout Muslim who loved and promoted learning, and was interested in Islamic jurisprudence, dispensing justice, active in propagating the religion and, above all, remarkably humble.

The sultan was not only a temporal ruler who governed the state, but the leader of the faithful and defender of the faith. He was the head of religion and dispenser of justice to his subjects, as avowed in his title, *Zillullah fil 'alam* (shadow of Allah on earth). The description of the ruler as a shepherd looking after his flock is often repeated in early Malay literature.

Besides the *kadi* (Islamic judge), following the practice started in Pasai and Melaka, Malay royal courts had *ulamak* (religious scholars) who acted as advisors and personal spiritual guides to the ruler.

By the 19th century, in the second tier of state officials (*orang besar delapan*) was an official titled *Orang Kaya-Kaya Imam Paduka Tuan Seri Diraja* in the constitution of Perak. Unlike other courtiers, he derived his income not from the fief he was holding, but from the 'contributions of the pious', which could be the *zakat* (poor tax), one of the sources of revenue for the state.

While the administration of the religious and customary law was mostly in the hands of *kadi*, imams

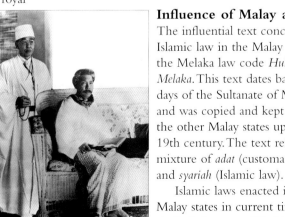

Sultan Alaeddin Suleiman Shah of Selangor (r. 1898–1938) (right) studying religious texts in 1930. Standing is his eldest son Tengku Musa Eddin.

and *penghulu* (village headmen), there was little bureaucracy before the 19th century. Under the colonial administration, a proper infrastructure began to emerge for state religious administration, usually under the auspices of the sultan's office. Although religion and Malay custom remained the sultan's domain, colonial officers tried to interfere right from the beginning. For example, when Sultan Yusuf of Perak issued a proclamation enjoining Muslims to attend prayers at the mosque regularly, or be fined or imprisoned, the British Resident modified it through another official proclamation by deleting the threat of fine and imprisonment.

Influence of Malay adat

The influential text concerning Islamic law in the Malay states is the Melaka law code *Hukum Kanun Melaka*. This text dates back to the days of the Sultanate of Melaka, and was copied and kept in use in the other Malay states up until the 19th century. The text reflects the mixture of *adat* (customary law) and *syariah* (Islamic law).

Islamic laws enacted in the Malay states in current times have similarly been modified by *adat*. This applies especially in matters dealing with everyday affairs such as family law, property and disputes.

An old kris inscribed with Qur'anic verses. Islam had a strong influence on Malay culture.

Islam before the 20th century

Islamic scholars have played an important role in Malay society as leaders ever since the early days of the Malay Sultanates. British rule in the 19th century changed the course of Islamic history in the country. The colonial system of appointing Residents, first introduced in Perak and later in other states, brought British policy-makers and administrators into the mainstream of socio-political life in the country. Islam came face to face with the forces of modernity and secularism.

Early Muslim leaders and scholars

Before the 20th century, the *ulamak* (Islamic religious scholars) played a significant role in practically all important aspects of local life, whether religious, economic or political, as well as in literature and education. They nurtured Malay identity and awakened Malay awareness of the importance of education and provided platforms for the growth of Malay literature and, thus, Malay nationalism. Sheikh Abdul Samad al-Palembani, Raja Ali Haji, Hamzah Fansuri, Nuruddin al-Raniri, Sheikh Muhammad Arshad al-Banjari and Syeikh Daud al-Fatani are only a handful of names that dominated the intellectual scene in the Islamic Malay Peninsula before the 20th century. Al-Banjari's works were widely adopted texts in *madrasah*.

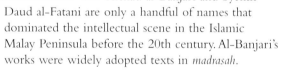

Interior view of the Sultan Abu Bakar Mosque—the most modern of its day.

Islam under the British

In 1874, Perak officially accepted a British Resident whose advice was to be sought on all matters other than Islam and Malay customs. From that date, Muslims had to operate within a milieu partly determined by traditional Islamic values and partly by the process of Westernization. The centralization of the administrative and legal machinery by the British resulted in the curtailment of the role of Islam in the affairs of the country. While the *syariah* (Islamic law) was, in theory, safeguarded by the sultans, the *kadi* (religious judges) had to contend with British rules and regulations enacted by the state legislative councils. As the British extended their hold on the administration and legal bureaucracy, only certain aspects of the *syariah* could be enforced.

Although British colonial rule influenced all aspects of government, private and individual Islamic life remained largely unaffected. Mosques and *surau* (small prayer houses) retained their traditional roles as places of worship and centres of learning; Islamic rituals thrived in the villages; individual religious

The Sultan Abu Bakar Mosque in Johor Bahru built in 1892.

practices such as daily prayers and *puasa* (fasting) were unaffected. Religious schools continued functioning on the periphery of towns and in rural areas, although their position was increasingly challenged by the establishment of government-run Malay schools and English mission schools.

During colonial days, the religious administration was carried out from the sultan's office in some states, while others, including Kedah, Johor, Kelantan and Terengganu, operated as independent departments as part of the state administration.

The Terengganu Constitution, promulgated in 1911, is said to have been the first state constitution in the Peninsula to have a strong Islamic flavour, especially with the provision that the ruling sultan must be an adult male Muslim, intelligent, moral, and devoid of negative characteristics. It provides also for the selection according to *syariah* law of a ruler in the absence of a qualified successor from among the royal descendants. Even the appointment of ministers must fulfil *syariah* law requirements.

While the constitution of the state of Johor did not go as far as Terengganu in declaring itself an Islamic state, it did declare Islam as the religion of the state. In Pahang, the earliest known code of law, which was basically a Melaka code but was augmented substantially by the Muslim code, was first compiled in the late 16th or early 17th century in the reign of Sultan Abdul Ghafar Mahyuddin Shah (1592–1616), but up till the late 19th century

Kampung Hulu Mosque, Melaka, c. 1890.

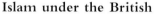

Early Muslim scholars

Muhammad Arshad al-Banjari (1710–1812)

Al-Banjari was born in the small village of Lok Gabang in the area of southern Kalimantan known as Tanah Banjar. As a child, he was named Muhammad Ja'far but on reaching adulthood he was given another name, Muhammad Arshad. Al-Banjari was later added to denote the name of his homeland.

From his early days he excelled in drawing and in calligraphy. When he was seven, his talents attracted the attention of the local sultan. Before long, the sultan took the boy to the palace where he received his early education. Later, the sultan sponsored his studies in Mecca.

Upon reaching adulthood, al-Banjari married a lady named Tuan Bajut. It was on the eve of receiving his first child that he decided to go to Mecca to further his studies.

Five other friends shared his vision and aspirations: Abdul Samad Palembani (from Palembang), Abdul Rahman Mesri al-Bantani

An artist's impression of Muhammad Arshad al-Banjari.

(from Banten), Daud bin Abdullah al-Fatani (from Patani), Abdul Wahab al-Bugisi (from Macassar) and Muhamad Salih Umar al-Samarani (from Semarang).

While in Medina, Muhammad Arshad became a disciple of Sheikh Abdul Karim al-Samman al-Madani, a great Sufi sheikh. Later, in honour of his teacher, Muhammad Arshad introduced the Tariqah Sammaniyyah (a Sufi order) in his homeland.

When Muhammad Arshad returned to his homeland, he had an audience with the Dutch governor, who bestowed on him the title *Tuan Haji Besar* (Great Sheikh) because of his saintly personality.

His approach to *dakwah* (propagation) was holistic in nature, integrating teaching and preaching with deeds such as helping his own people with land irrigation and writing religious books.

He wrote on various aspects of Islam, from rites to theology, astronomy and mysticism. Among his numerous writings, two books are well-known among Muslims in the Malay World: *Perukunan Besar* (A Guidebook for Beginners) which teaches the rituals of worship, and *Sabilal Muhtadin li't Tafaqquh fid-din*, a book of *fiqh* (Islamic jurisprudence) which covers all aspects of Islamic rites. This encyclopedic work which is considered to be al-Banjari's magnum opus, is also known to Muslims in Thailand and Cambodia.

Tok Kenali (1868–1933)

Tok Kenali was born Muhammad Yusof bin Ahmad. Tok is an abbreviation of the term *datuk*, often used politely in the Malay community to address elders. The surname 'Al-Kenali', probably added to his name when he studied in the Middle East, might have been given because he was born in a village known as Kenali near Kubang Kerian in Kelantan.

Tok Kenali became an orphan at the age of five. Subsequently, he was brought up by his grandfather. At 15 he went to the state capital, Kota Bharu, to further his religious education and three years later he went to Mecca to continue his studies.

While pursuing his education in Mecca, he travelled extensively in the Middle East. In Egypt, he had the opportunity to meet the *mufti* (Islamic judge) and reformist, Muhammad Abduh.

After 22 years of study abroad, he returned home and started his own religious

Tok Kenali, a religious leader, was also an early Malay nationalist.

school known as Pondok Kampung Paya. He devoted his time to teaching and *dakwah*. His *dakwah* activities targeted both the religious authorities and the masses. It was in his time that Sultan Muhammad III of Kelantan (r. 1886–89) declared *syariah* (Islamic law) as the basis of all legal procedures in the state. When the state Islamic Religious Council published a magazine, *Pengasuh* (Guide), in the 1920s, Tok Kenali was appointed by Sultan Ismail (r. 1920–44) as both adviser and writer.

Tok Kenali believed that Islam must be practised as a complete way of life. He had a keen interest in politics, which showed in his writings. For him, there was no dichotomy between religion and politics. One of his articles, *Kuasailah Pengetahuan Agama dan Politik* (Master your Religious Knowledge and Politics), a satirical piece of work, shows this belief. In this article, Tok Kenali criticized Muslim scholars who had acquired a good religious knowledge but were ignorant in the ways of re-educating community leaders and, by such means, bringing about change in society.

In his bid to educate the *ummah* (Muslim community), Tok Kenali advocated the idea of not focusing on trivial matters in religion. It was his belief that Muslims should instead concentrate on living in accordance with the Sunni traditions in all acts of worship.

---

it was still observed and adhered to by Sultan Ahmad because its strict *syariah* content had stood Pahang in good stead as a peaceful Muslim society.

In the Unfederated Malay States of Kedah, Kelantan, Terengganu and Perlis, which only accepted British Advisers instead of Residents, Islam remained more firmly entrenched. Opposition to British encroachment into the affairs of the Malay states was represented to the people as opposition to *kafir* (infidels).

Islam in the modern sultanates

The British colonial government, which took over the political power of the Malay sultanates, left the sultans as figureheads overseeing the religion of Islam. The prerogative of the sultan in matters relating to Islam in his state is an established tradition from pre-colonial days. Today, it is enshrined in the state constitutions and guaranteed under the Malaysia Agreement.

The present-day sultanates continue the tradition of the old sultanates; the mosque was in close proximity to the ruler's residence and his audience hall, where the main affairs of the state were conducted, and the market place and harbour, where the economic life was centred. Thus, a modern state

capital not only features a grand state mosque but a religious court house, administration centre, state religious school and other key institutions to ensure an orderly Muslim community life. Even modern Malaysian sultanates take pride in their religious educational institutions, such as Maktab Zainal Abidin in Terengganu and Maktab Mahmud in Kedah. Until religious matters were coordinated by a central institution, the states were quite independent in deciding such matters as organizing the sighting the moon for the fasting month. Even today, the sultan theoretically is the sole authority on religious matters in his state. However, in matters delegated to the central authority, reference is usually made to the consent given by the sultans.

The position of the sultan is not only as head and protector of religion. He also ensures the furtherance of God's word, spiritually and physically through propagation, teaching and the legislation of laws for breaches in religious observances. Historically, there were a number of rulers renowned for their concern in these matters. In more modern times they have included Sultan Senik Mulut Merah of Kelantan, Sultan Zainal Abidin of Terengganu, Sultan Ahmad Tajudin of Kedah, Sultan Alaeddin Suleiman Shah of Selangor and Sultan Idris of Perak.

This 1890 photo shows a female member of a Sarawak Malay family, Daiang Lehut, wearing a veil to cover her hair.

Islam in the 20th century

Prominent Islamic leaders and scholars in the 20th century have included individuals from various fields, particularly education and the law. There have also been a number of Muslim women leaders in Malaysia. The first prime minister of Malaysia, the late Tunku Abdul Rahman Putra, established Malaysia's importance as an Islamic country at the international level when he became the first Secretary General of the Organisation of the Islamic Conference (OIC) in 1971.

Early reform movements

In an attempt to 'modernize' the Malays, several *ulamak* (religious scholars) organized a 'back to the Qur'an and *sunnah*' movement in the 1920s and 1930s. This was known as the Kaum Muda (Young Generation) or Islah (reformist) movement which

effectively exploited the media through their publications, including *Al-Imam* (The Leader) (1906–08), *Neraca* (The Scales) (1911), *Pengasuh* (Guide) (1918) and *Saudara* (Companion) (1928), in spite of repressive British colonial policies. Such publications aimed at bringing about reform in the religious practices of Malays, which were felt by the editors of these publications to contain too many unIslamic aspects. Their leaders included Shaikh Mohd Tahir bin Jalaluddin al-Azhari, Syed Sheikh Ahmad Al-Hadi, Haji Abbas bin Muhammad Taha, Sheikh Mohd. Salim al-Khalili and Zainal Abidin bin Ahmad (Za'ba).

Shaikh Mohd Tahir bin Jalaluddin al-Azhari was one of the early Muslim reformists in the region. He was strongly influenced by Middle Eastern reformists, especially Muhammad Abduh of Egypt.

As a result of contact with other Muslims, particularly in the Middle East, they exhorted Malay Muslims to eradicate practices considered as unIslamic and unnecessary. Some of these were remnants of Hinduism, such as the *mandi safar* (ritual bath in the Islamic month of Safar). The Kaum Muda felt that adherence to such rituals was the root of Malay backwardness. Malay social and economic life was deemed lethargic in comparison with that of the Chinese and Indians. The earliest platform of this movement was social transformation of Malay society through education grounded in progressive Islamic values in order to stimulate the economic development, spiritual strength and political resilience of Malay Muslim society.

The movement was also an indirect criticism of British rule and was aimed at liberating the people from colonialism. Although the efforts of the *ulamak* and other reformist religious leaders had some limited impact on Malay traditional life, the intended cultural revolution did not materialize.

Islamic leaders and Malay nationalism

In the political and nationalist movement that spread in the colonized Malay states, Islamic leaders in the early part of the 20th century who were against the British were Syed Abdul Rahman al-Edrus, Haji Wan Hassan (Tok Janggut) and Haji Abdul Rahman Limbong. Tok Janggut was publicly executed by the British as a rebel. During the Japanese Occupation of British Malaya (1942–5), Islamic leaders who initiated freedom from the Japanese included Haji Ahmad Haji Md Kasim and Dr Burhanuddin al-Helmi.

The Tunku's role in the promulgation of the Federal Constitution

After the Alliance's landslide victory in the first Federal election in July 1955, discussions on self-government and the possibility of independence began. In January 1956, Chief Minister Tunku Abdul Rahman Putra led a second Merdeka mission comprised of four representatives of the Malay rulers and four representatives from the Alliance party to London. There it was decided that an independent Commonwealth Constitutional Commission be appointed to examine the changes needed in the constitution.

When the Reid Commission began inviting written submissions from concerned organizations and individuals in June 1956, the Alliance Party, under the leadership of the Tunku, submitted a detailed plan for the structure of the government. Fundamental rights, citizenship, the special position of the Malays and the religion of Islam were also discussed in the submissions. On the basis of mutual consensus among the three major races—the Malays, Chinese and Indians—the United Malays National Organisation (UMNO) agreed to the principle of jus soli for those born after Independence while in return the non-Malay parties, MCA (Malayan Chinese Association) and MIC (Malayan Indian Congress) accepted the special position of the Malays, Malay as the national language and Islam as the religion of the state. By the principle of jus soli, the non-Malays were given outright citizenship as Malaysians, and in return they agreed with the Tunku's proposal in stipulating Islam as the religion of the Federation as enshrined in Article 3, subject to the freedom of religion as stipulated in Article 11 and the 'special position' of the Malays as stipulated in Article 152 of the Federal Constitution.

Tunku Abdul Rahman Putra contributed significantly to the development of Islam in the country.

Religious schools, for example, the Madrasah Al-Ulum Al-Syariyyah in Perak, produced a number of Malay nationalists.

Other important figures are Hj Fuad Hassan, Hj Ahmad Maliki and Dato Haji Ahmad Badawi bin Sheikh Abdullah Fahim, the father of Dato' Seri Abdullah Ahmad Badawi, the fifth prime minister of Malaysia. Many were also members of the Islamic movement, Hizbul Muslimin, a political organization which was outlawed in 1947 by the British colonial government resulting in several of its leaders being detained.

The war years (1942–1945)

During the war years, when daily life was dominated by the economics of survival, there were few major changes regarding Islam in Malaysia. During the Japanese Occupation, the country was brought under a military regime and the administration of Islam was maintained in a way reminiscent of earlier British rule. Muslims were affected, however, on a day-to-day level. Muslim students were taught Japanese and had to show great respect to the Japanese flag in official ceremonies.

Malay scholar, Zainal Abidin bin Ahmad, commonly known as 'Za'ba', (1895–1972), was part of the early reform movement.

The post-war period

After the war, traditional Islamic life was revived to a certain extent. However, it was circumscribed by the growth of Malay nationalism. When the British returned after the war, they promoted the formation of what they called the Malayan Union, the constitution of which seriously threatened the position of the sultans and Malay sovereignty. The Malays were agitated and strongly rejected the plan. Nationwide protests were held for the first time in the history of the Malay states. As a result, the United Malays National Organisation (UMNO) was formed in 1946 to lead the nationalist campaign against the formation of the Malayan Union.

The anti-Malayan Union struggle engulfed Malays of all political opinions. Over the next few years, Islamic development and reform was sidelined by the fervour of Malay nationalism. One setback for Islamic revival was the banning of the Islamic organization, Hizbul Muslimin, mentioned above.

However, the Alliance government led by Tunku Abdul Rahman Putra made attempts to reactivate some traditional Islamic practices. New mosques were built to enrich the religious life of the Malays. He also founded Pertubuhan Kebajikan Islam Malaysia (PERKIM), the earliest official Islamic body to care for the welfare of Muslim converts. Another important government effort was the setting up of Pusat Islam (Islamic Centre) (later renamed Department of Islamic Development Malaysia (JAKIM)) to regulate matters with regard to Islam. A more systematic and concerted effort to promote Islamic institutions and values in Malaysia was launched by Dr Mahathir Mohamad upon becoming prime minister in 1981.

Ibu Zain (left) was predominantly concerned with education for Muslim women and was influential in Malaysian politics.

Ibu Zain: Malay woman educator

Tan Sri Zainun Munsyi Sulaiman, popularly known as Ibu Zain, was born on 22 January 1903 in Kampong Nyalas, Melaka. Her father, a language teacher, introduced literature to her and was her religious teacher.

Ibu Zain was the first Malay woman to complete her studies in Tengkera Methodist Girls' School in Melaka and passed her Junior Cambridge in 1915. She established her own school in Pasoh Jaya Waras in Negeri Sembilan before assuming a teaching post and later becoming the head teacher of Bandar Maharani Girls' School Muar, Johor. She established the first religious school for girls in the state of Johor and also an association for teachers of Malay and religious schools in Johor. Ibu Zain joined UMNO in 1948 and together with other national leaders she fought for independence. She was elected as a Member of Parliament for the Pontian Selatan constituency, Johor, in 1959. After completing her five-year term as a parliamentarian she decided to go back to education, assuming the post as the Head of Tengku Ampuan Mariam College in Johor Bahru between 1963–89.

In the literary field she contributed immensely, writing on the theme of Malay nationalism. Most of her writing appeared in the *Majalah Guru*, *Lembaran Guru* and *Bulan Melayu* educational magazines. She also took part in the Congress of Malay Language and Letters in 1956 which led to the establishment of Dewan Bahasa dan Pustaka (Institute of Language and Literature) in 1956.

Ibu Zain earned many awards, credentials and titles such as 'Tokoh Guru' (Esteemed Teacher) at the national level and a Masters of Letters from Universiti Kebangsaan Malaysia (UKM) in 1975. Ibu Zain passed away in June 1989 but as an educationist and prolific writer she will always be remembered for her dedicated service to the country. Her famous motto was: '*Agama dididik, moden dibela, dunia dikelek, akhirat dijunjung*' (Religion is to be taught, modernity is to be nurtured, worldly life is to be carried and the hereafter is to be honoured).

Early Muslim political leaders

Among the prominent religious leaders in the 1950s and 1960s was the first PAS (Parti Islam SeMalaysia) president, Haji Ahmad Fuad, who broke ranks from UMNO (United Malays National Organisation) in 1951 to form PAS. He and his supporters strove for a Muslim party with the idea of an Islamic state as its ultimate goal. Haji Ahmad Fuad later left PAS to join the Parti Negara formed by Dato Onn Ja'afar.

Another prominent leader in the 1950s was Dato Haji Ahmad Badawi bin Sheikh Abdullah Fahim, the father of Malaysia's fifth Prime Minister Dato' Seri Abdullah Ahmad Badawi. He excelled in *dakwah* (propagation), education and politics. He was known as a religious figure in UMNO and in 1952 he was elected as the Deputy Head of the party's Youth Movement. He was the head of UMNO Youth between 1957–9 and in 1959 he became a member of the state assembly representing Kepala Batas constituency in Penang. Much of his teaching was channelled through UMNO, specifically the youth. He urged Malay youth to remember the 'five pillars' of mankind; religion, nation, independence, knowledge and economy. To him these five were interdependent; no one was to be ignored, lest the Malays be left behind. He emphasized the issue of sincerity in the struggle to establish Malay identity.

Other notable leaders with similar professional and intellectual credentials were Dr Burhanuddin al-Helmi, Dato Haji Bakar Umar and Dato Mohd Asri. They all strove to establish a morally just and peaceful society.

UMNO leaders Tun Dr Mahathir Mohamad (then Prime Minister), second from left, and Dato' Seri Abdullah Ahmad Badawi (then Deputy Prime Minister), extreme left, during a *doa* (supplication) at an UMNO General Assembly, early 2000s.

Islam as a way of life

The word Islam originates from Arabic and means 'submission', 'surrender', 'obedience' and 'peace'. It implies submission to the will of Allah and obedience to His commandments. Adherents of the religion are called Muslims. From the Muslim perspective, Islam in Malaysia is essentially the same as that practised in the Arab world. The external culture forms, however, vary from country to country. Islam has influenced Malay culture to the extent that the terms 'Muslim' and 'Malay' are often taken to be synonymous.

Masjid Negara in Kuala Lumpur, signifies the position of Islam as the official religion of the country. Malaysian Muslims are predominantly Sunni Muslims belonging to the Shafii School, which is one of the four schools of Islamic jurisprudence.

The words in the centre of this handwoven *songket* are the *bismillah*, a phrase meaning 'in the name of Allah, the most Beneficent, the most Merciful'. Muslims say it whenever they begin a task or an action.

Islam in Malaysia

In Malaysia, Muslims constitute the majority of the population. It is one of several Muslim countries in which Islam is enshrined in the constitution as the official religion but in which other religions are allowed to be practised in peace and harmony.

The pre-eminent status accorded to Islam was a recognition of its dominant role in Malay society and culture in the period before British colonization. Islam has, for a long time, been a major part of Malay culture, to the extent that, in the past, Muslim converts were said to have *masuk Melayu* or 'become Malay'. Even today, the official definition of a Malay includes that he or she must be a Muslim.

Islam also played a major role in the nascent Malay nationalist movement struggling for independence from British rule and it continues to exert a strong influence on post-Independence Malaysian society.

The Islamic resurgence of the 1970s and 1980s pressured the Malay-dominated Malaysian government into giving more attention to Islamic educational, economic, legal and political interests. The notion of Islam as a comprehensive way of life became popular during this period.

Provisions such as breaks for daily prayers, announcement of prayer hours in state-controlled media, time off for Friday prayers and interest-free banking have been made in line with Islamic precepts to enable Muslims in the country to fulfil their religious obligations.

Islam as a complete way of life

Islam has four basic characteristics. Firstly, it is comprehensive, as it covers all aspects of human life—political, economic, social, cultural and moral. Secondly, it is addressed to humanity as a whole. Thirdly, it is practical, meaning that it can be translated, implemented and executed in daily life. Finally, Islam accommodates changing situations in human life through the application of *ijtihad* (reasoning) on all matters not covered by the authoritative revealed texts.

In line with Islamic teachings outlined in the Qur'an and the *sunnah* (traditions of Prophet Muhammad), Muslims adhere to the six principles of faith known as the *rukun iman* (see 'The pillars of faith') and observe the *rukun Islam*, the five pillars of Islam, according to which a Muslim must believe in One God, Allah, and Prophet Muhammad, observe the five daily prayers, pay *zakat* (poor tax), fast during the month of Ramadhan and perform the hajj pilgrimage. The Qur'an states that nobody can atone for another person's sins; therefore each individual is accountable to Allah for his actions.

According to the teachings of Islam, Muslims must abstain from alcohol and gambling, and are

Living according to the Qur'an and the sunnah

The Islamic resurgence in the second half of the 20th century rekindled the aspirations of Muslims to return to the basic sources of Islamic teachings, that is, the Qur'an and practices of the Holy Prophet. These sources provide appropriate rules for every action and for every situation. This is sometimes referred to as establishing Islam as *ad-din* (a complete way of life).

Islam does not permit free mixing of men and women and, therefore, social communication and mixing between opposite sexes is controlled. Muslim society in Malaysia generally frowns upon cohabitation among unmarried couples. Muslims found cohabiting or in suspicious circumstances, for example, in a hotel room, may be charged with *khalwat* (usually translated as 'close proximity') under *syariah* law. A couple found guilty of this offence will be fined. Repeat offenders will be jailed.

Although segregation of the sexes is not as widely practised in Malaysia as in some Muslim countries, there are still instances where the sexes are separated. In places of Islamic worship, women have their own prayer halls and ablutionaries. Although the practice is no longer very common, men and women are sometimes seated separately at wedding feasts.

Muslim women in Malaysia are banned from taking part in beauty pageants. This is in line with the teachings of Islam, according to which beauty contests are not permissible.

This calligraphy in Arabic means 'one who lives by the Qur'an lives a happy life'. It illustrates the importance of adhering to the teachings of the Qur'an.

Ritual cleanliness

There are three types of *najis* (filth) in Islam. The least serious kind of pollution is called *najis mukhaffafah*, which is the urine of a baby boy under the age of two who has been fed on nothing but his mother's milk. The worst kind of pollution is *najis mughalazah*, which is associated with pigs, dogs or animals that have been cross-bred with these. All other kinds of dirt are classified as *najis mutawassitah*.

This classification is important for ritual cleanliness, as a Muslim must be clean, especially when performing prayers or reading the Qur'an. *Najis mukhaffafah* is removed simply by sprinkling clean water on the area. The common types of dirt, *najis mutawassitah*, must be washed with running water till no longer seen, felt or smelled. Removing *najis mughalazah* involves a special ritual washing called *samak* in Malay.

prohibited from eating pork as it is considered to be unclean. Prophet Muhammad's life and conduct are considered as the best model for Muslims to follow. This influence can be felt in many aspects of Malaysian culture. One of these is that Muslims eat using the right hand, since the left hand is normally used for washing the private parts. Following the *sunnah,* a Muslim will usually prefer right over left; as a result, items passed around will normally be passed to the person on the right.

Marriage is also a part of the prophetic tradition. Muslims are encouraged to marry and have families. Premarital sex is strictly *haram* (prohibited).

Although wearing Western-style clothing is very common, some Muslims in Malaysia choose to dress in a manner approximating the Prophet's manner of dress, and as such wear an Arab-style robe called a *jubah* and turban-like headgear known as a *serban*. In line with guidelines from the Qur'an and the *sunnah,* many Muslim women wear clothing that is not revealing and covers the whole body except the hands and the face. Men are prohibited from wearing gold and silk but may wear a small silver ring, in accordance with the example set by the Prophet. Following the example of the Prophet who loved cats, many Muslims in Malaysia keep them as pets—cats are probably the most popular pet in Malaysia.

Top: Religious education is always taken seriously. Here, young girls are taught to read the Qur'an by an *ustazah* (female teacher).

Bottom: In Malaysia it is very common for Muslim women to be involved in business and to hold positions requiring high-level expertise. Dr Jemilah Mahmood, President of Mercy Malaysia, is one such woman.

Sunnis and Shiites

Muslims can be divided into two groups, Sunnis and Shiites. Sunni Muslims, who make up about 90 per cent of Muslims in the world, belong to one of the four schools of *fiqh* (Islamic jurisprudence) known as the mazhab: the Shafii, Maliki, Hanafi and Hanbali schools. Malaysian Muslims are Sunnis and generally belong to the Shafii School, although some Indian Muslims in Malaysia traditionally follow the Hanafi School. The Shiite group is not recognized in Malaysia although in the past some individuals have been known to follow Shiite teachings.

Unlike Shiite Muslims, who reject the first three caliphs, or successors, Sunni

Muslims recognize the authority of the first four caliphs—the 'Rightly Guided Caliphs'—whom they regard as legitimate leaders of the Muslim community after the Prophet Muhammad.

Among the other differences between the two groups are that Sunni Muslims accept the prohibition on temporary marriage by the second caliph, Umar; this is not recognized by the Shiites. Sunnis also accept *ijmak* (consensus) as a source of law.

Muslims in Malaysia are generally Sunni Muslims belonging to the Shafii School, whose interpretations are based on those of Imam as-Shafii.

Balance between this life and the next

The teachings of Islam stress the need for Muslims to practise moderation in their actions. In accordance with the teachings of the Qur'an and the *sunnah,* Muslims must strive to achieve success in this world and in the hereafter.

Muslims are encouraged to participate in trade. In fact, Prophet Muhammad himself was a trader. However, whatever economic activity they participate in it does not mean that religious duties must be put aside. Muslims are still required to fulfil the five pillars of Islam and observe other moral injunctions.

A Muslim should strive both to perform his duties to Allah and fulfil his worldly responsibilities. Muslims are encouraged to ask Allah to grant them 'the good in this world and the good in the hereafter'. They usually end their *doa* (supplication) with this request.

The Prophet's role

The Prophet's role was to convey Allah's message; in the process, his life and conduct became the best model for Muslims to follow in realizing the meaning of Islam.

Some Westerners used to refer to Islam as 'Mohammedanism' and to its followers as 'Mohammedans'. Muslims strongly object to the use of these terms because Islam was not founded by Muhammad. From the Muslim point of view, Prophet Muhammad is considered as the last and final messenger of Allah. He is therefore known as the 'Seal of the Prophets'. However, as much as Muslims revere him as Allah's last and final messenger, they do not worship him. People who have claimed to be prophets after him are considered as heretics in Islam.

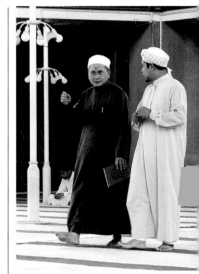

Some Muslim men prefer to wear a robe and *serban* approximating the dress worn by the Prophet.

A female Muslim laboratory technician working in biotechnology research and development at the Forest Research Institute Malaysia.

The pillars of faith

The six rukun iman, *or 'pillars of faith', constitute the cardinal beliefs of Islam. The pillars of faith, based on the* Hadith *(sayings) of the Prophet, provide the foundation for the Muslim outlook on life. Understanding the pillars of faith is critical for all Muslims, not only in Malaysia but the world over, and much basic religious instruction revolves around this.*

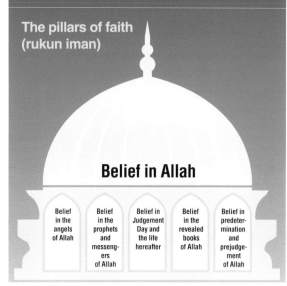

Belief in Allah

Belief in the angels of Allah · Belief in the prophets and messengers of Allah · Belief in Judgement Day and the life hereafter · Belief in the revealed books of Allah · Belief in predetermination and prejudgement of Allah

Calligraphy of the name of Allah from Masjid Negara in Kuala Lumpur. Calligraphy is a common form of decoration in Islamic art as Islam frowns on the representation of living things.

Belief in Allah

The first pillar is to believe that Allah is the one and only God and it is He who created the whole world alone and who is to be worshipped by man.

A person officially becomes a Muslim by making a simple verbal confession or declaration, 'I bear witness that there is no god but Allah and I bear witness that Muhammad is the Messenger of Allah'. This is the confession of faith (*kalimah syahadah*) which encapsulates the Islamic tenet of monotheism: there is only one God who does not manifest His being or attributes in any physical form. This creed of absolute and uncompromising monotheism is known in Islam as *tauhid* (affirmation of the oneness of God). Contravention of this creed is called *syirik* and constitutes the greatest sin in Islam.

The Qur'an says that *tauhid* is the essence of Allah's religion from the beginning of human existence since the time of Prophet Adam but that the originality and purity of the message became distorted over time. Therefore, Allah sent new messengers (*rasul*), such as Noah (Nuh), Abraham (Ibrahim), Solomon (Sulaiman), David (Daud), Moses (Musa) and Jesus (Isa) in different periods of human history to revive the original message. This chain of messengers culminated in the prophethood of Muhammad in the 7th century CE.

Belief in the angels

The second pillar is belief in the existence of angels. Islam teaches that angels were created by Allah to carry out His commandments, among which was the transmission of His message to the prophets.

According to the Qur'an, the angels' loyalty to Allah as their master is undivided. Paradise and hell are in the charge of specific angels. Administering death is the responsibility of the Angel of Death. Gabriel (Jibril), the chief of all angels has the responsibility of conveying Allah's revelations to all human messengers, including Prophet Muhammad.

Although angels are Allah's celestial servants and messengers, it is forbidden to worship them or make offerings to them as this would constitute a form of polytheism. Similarly, it is forbidden to make pictorial representations of angels and of the prophets so as to avoid idolatry, which is a grave sin in Islam.

Belief in the books

The third pillar is to have faith in all the true revelations or books of Allah. These revealed books, in their authentic forms, are believed to represent Allah's guidance for mankind. The Qur'an says that Allah sent His revelations to all earlier messengers such as Abraham, Moses and Jesus in the languages of these messengers. The Qur'an is thus a continuation of Allah's revelation to mankind and as such makes references to the earlier revelations conveyed to Abraham, Moses, David and Jesus. However, it also draws attention to subsequent corruptions of the divine texts, revealed by God from time to time.

Islamic doctrine holds that the Qur'an is the last of the revealed books and that it should remain unchanged from its original form. To safeguard this, the Qur'an is preserved in the language in which it was originally revealed. Muslims are of the opinion that the Qur'an is untranslatable and the closest one

Prophet Muhammad

Prophet Muhammad was born c. 570 CE into a poor clan of the Quraish tribe of Mecca (Makkah). His father died before he was born; his mother died soon after. Muhammad was looked after by his grandfather and then his uncle. As a young man, he was employed by Khadijah, a wealthy widow of aristocratic descent whom he later married.

Although Muhammad spent much time in solitude around the Mount Hira area from the time he married Khadijah, it was not until he was 40 that Jibril appeared before him for the first time. Jibril is said to have brought him the first words of what is now the Qur'an. Being unlettered, Muhammad was reportedly hesitant, but upon the angel's insistence he repeated the words brought to him. From then on, Muhammad received revelations from Allah periodically for 23 years.

The Prophet first shared these revelations with his innermost circle of supporters—his wife Khadijah, his cousin Ali, his friend Abu Bakar, and his freed slave Zaid. Khadijah was one of his strongest supporters until her death. Ali and Abu Bakar later became two of the caliphs entrusted with the leadership of Muslim society.

Before Islam, idol worship was the norm in Arabia. Mecca was the centre for idol worship for the whole region. The pagan beliefs and practices were antithetical to the message of Islam brought by Prophet Muhammad. He preached the worship of one God and deliverance from all forms of bondage to unjust man-made systems. He taught that human beings, as Allah's servants and trustees, were all equal before Him despite their different colours and social origins.

The majority of people in Mecca rejected the message and oppressed Muhammad and his small group of followers. To escape this severe persecution, he emigrated to Medina. Muhammad's migration to Medina in 622 CE is known as the *hijrah* and marks the beginning of the Islamic calendar.

Islam flourished in Medina. A new social order was established and the scope of Islam expanded beyond matters of faith and worship to social, economic and political regulations. After the Prophet's death, Islam spread beyond the frontiers of Arabia.

Calligraphy of the name of Prophet Muhammad from a window of Masjid Negara in Kuala Lumpur.

Muslim men in prayer at a mosque. Islam has a strict creed of monotheism which does not allow the worship of any except Allah.

This *sura* (verse) from the Qur'an unequivocally states that Allah is One.

can come to a translation is to interpret its meaning. For Muslims, the Qur'an, being the word of Allah revealed to Muhammad, is the ultimate authority which distinguishes truth from falsehood, good from evil and right from wrong.

Apart from moral precepts and injunctions, the Qur'an contains guidelines which have a direct bearing on the political, economic, social and cultural life of Muslims. Islamization in Malaysia is inspired by the holistic perspective of the Qur'an. Islam is propagated and practised in Malaysia in a way which does not cause instability in a plural society.

Belief in the prophets and messengers

Faith in all the prophets (*anbiya*) and messengers (*rasul*) of Allah forms the fourth pillar. It is said in the Qur'an that the *rasul* were human beings chosen by Allah to guide mankind to live in accordance

with His will. Allah would raise a new prophet or messenger to restate and revive the message of the oneness of Allah when it became distorted, with modifications in the rules of social conduct to suit changing circumstances.

As it is said that Allah revealed His message in the local languages of the time, the total number of prophets is believed to exceed several thousand, but the Qur'an mentions the names of only 25 of them.

At the end of the chain of prophets and messengers came Muhammad, who was chosen by Allah to complete the mission for which earlier messengers were ordained. Although a Muslim must believe in all of Allah's prophets and messengers, Muhammad enjoys the loftiest position.

Although Prophet Muhammad is not the 'founder' of Islam, Islam reached its climax with his prophethood. Muslims reject any claims of prophethood in Islam after Prophet Muhammad. He is thus also known as 'the Seal of the Prophets'.

One of the pillars of faith is the belief in the revealed books of Allah. For Muslims, the Qur'an is the final revelation.

Belief in Judgement Day

The fifth pillar of faith is to believe in Judgement Day and the life hereafter. The Qur'an explains that on Judgement Day, the record of a person's actions will be brought before Allah. In the life hereafter, the good will be rewarded with a place in paradise with Allah, while the bad will be banished to hell.

Heaven and hell both consist of several levels. One attains paradise or is banished to hell after being judged by Allah for all the deeds performed during one's lifetime. The court of Allah's judgement will be the most just court and no one will be unjustly rewarded or punished. One who dies as a *syahid* (martyr) is guaranteed paradise and is exempted from the trial on Judgement Day.

The belief in the hereafter is based on the Islamic conception of Allah's absolute justice and is thought to strengthen people's sense of ultimate accountability to Allah.

Belief in predetermination and prejudgement

The sixth and final pillar of faith is belief in Allah's predetermination and prejudgement of all that is good and all that is evil. This means accepting Allah's judgement of good and bad in everything to direct one's life.

According to the Qur'an, Allah is omniscient and omnipotent. Nothing happens without His knowledge or will but individuals are free to choose their path of action. Ultimately, people are responsible for their choices which may lead them to do good or evil. It is everyone's duty to strive, but the results of their actions are beyond their control or knowledge. As for Allah, nothing is beyond His power or knowledge or intervention.

The 25 Messengers of Allah

Muslims believe that Allah sent prophets and messengers as guides to people at different times. Prophets are those who lived exemplary lives in order to act as guides. Messengers, on the other hand, were obliged to spread the word of Allah and lead societies.

Although the exact number of prophets and messengers is unknown, Muslims must believe in all of them and recognize the names of the 25 messengers of Allah.

1. ADAM	10. YAAQUB	19. SULAIMAN
2. IDRIS	11. YUSUF	20. ILYAS
3. NUH	12. AYUB	21. YUNUS
4. HUD	13. SYUAIB	22. ZAKARIA
5. SALEH	14. HARUN	23. YAHYA
6. IBRAHIM	15. MUSA	24. ISA
7. LUT	16. ILYASA'	25. MUHAMMAD
8. ISHAK	17. ZULKIFLI	
9. ISMAIL	18. DAUD	

The Ulul Azmi

These five messengers of Allah are held in the greatest esteem for having been subject to intense persecution during their lifetime.

1. MUHAMMAD 2. IBRAHIM 3. MUSA 4. ISA 5. NUH

Misinterpretation of the belief in predetermination

The sixth pillar of faith, the belief in predetermination, is not to be mistaken with fatalism. Muslims should not believe that they need not make any effort. According to Islam, everyone must strive to succeed in their lives while at the same time acknowledging that they are not able to control the outcome of their actions. Allah alone knows and determines the outcome.

Muslims in Malaysia have been urged by their leaders to abandon this belief in fatalism. They are constantly reminded of the Qur'anic verse that 'God does not change the condition of people until they change what is in themselves' (Q. 12: 11).

However, through one's effort and *doa* (supplication), it is possible to influence some aspects of one's fate, if Allah permits.

A worshipper reciting a *doa* (supplication) after his prayers.

The pillars of Islam: Confession of faith and prayer

The first of the five rukun *Islam (pillars of Islam) is the confession of faith. A Muslim professes to the Muslim faith by pronouncing the* kalimah syahadah *(confession of faith), by which he accepts the oneness of God. Prayer or* solat *(sembahyang in Malay) constitutes the second pillar of Islam. Praying is* fardhu *(obligatory) for every Muslim, as frequently mentioned in the Qur'an.*

Written in Arabic, the *kalimah syahadah* states: 'There no god but Allah and Muhammad is Allah's Messenger.'

The most important part of the conversion ceremony is saying the *kalimah syahadah*. Here, an Orang Asli converts to Islam.

Muslims taking *wuduk* (minor ablutions) at Masjid Negara (National Mosque) in Kuala Lumpur.

Confession of faith

The first pillar of Islam is professing the *kalimah syahadah*. This is a confession that 'there is no god but Allah, and Muhammad is His Messenger'. Pronouncing the *kalimah syahadah* is also a part of the conversion process since a person becomes a Muslim through testifying to the oneness of God and believing that Muhammad is His Messenger. The focus of Islam is worship of Allah, and the religion calls for the organization of one's life in accordance with His commandments.

Pronouncing the *kalimah syahadah* signifies the individual's acceptance of Allah as the one God to be worshipped. The *kalimah syahadah* is included in the sermons during Friday prayers and forms a part of the daily prayers as well as being a part of the *azan* (call to prayer), which shows its importance to Muslims. The first thing a baby born to Muslim parents hears is the *azan*, which includes the *kalimah syahadah*, whispered into its ear at birth.

Pronouncing the *kalimah syahadah* is also included in the last *rakaat* (prayer sequence) of the five daily prayers. The Muslim is thus reminded of the first pillar of Islam several times during the day and night. Indirectly, this signifies the renewal of the Muslim's primordial covenant with Allah.

The importance of prayer

The Qur'an highlights the importance of prayer many times. One of the verses that prescribes prayer for Muslims reads: 'Glorify God when it is evening and morning, and to Him be praise in the heaven and the earth, and at afternoon and at noontide' (Q. 30: 17–18).

Prophet Muhammad called prayer 'the pillar of religion'. He also said that performance of prayer made a person a true believer.

Wuduk

Before a Muslim prays, he must first be ritually clean. Thus, before performing their prayers, Muslims must take *wuduk* (minor ablutions), a ritual washing to clean those parts of the body that are normally exposed, i.e. the hands, arms, face, head and feet. Every mosque, *surau* (small prayer house) or prayer room has an ablutionary—an area with taps or a large pool where worshippers may perform their ablutions.

Kiblat

The *kiblat* (direction of prayer) is the direction of the Kaabah in Mecca (see 'Pillars of Islam: The hajj'). This is the direction that a worshipper has to face when praying. Initially, the direction of prayer was Jerusalem until Allah commanded Muslims to pray facing Mecca. Having been the first *kiblat*, and the site of other significant events in Islam, Jerusalem is therefore still a holy city for Muslims.

The five obligatory prayers

In the beginning of Prophet Muhammad's prophethood, the number of prayers was not fixed. It was only after the incident of the night journey and ascension (Israk Mikraj) that the five prayer times were established. The five obligatory prayers are the morning prayer (*subuh*), noon prayer (*zohor*), afternoon prayer (*asar*), evening prayer (*maghrib*) and night prayer (*isyak*).

The morning prayer is to be performed between dawn and sunrise. When the sun has risen, the time for the morning prayer has passed. It is a prayer of two *rakaat* (prayer sequences). The time for the noon prayer begins from the inclination of the sun towards the west, and ends when a shadow is of the same length as the object making it. This prayer consists of four *rakaat*. The afternoon prayer, consisting of four *rakaat*, is observed after the noon prayer until just before sunset. The evening prayer consisting of three *rakaat* is to be performed from the time after sunset until the sky is no longer red at the horizon. The night prayer is to be performed at any time after the evening prayer but before the morning prayer is due. It consists of four *rakaat*.

Although these prayers may be observed at any time of their respective hours, it is highly recommended in the Hadith (traditions of the Prophet) that Muslims pray at the earliest time.

Friday prayers

The Friday prayer is a congregational noon prayer. It is performed instead of the noon prayer. A sermon is delivered before the prayer. The person delivering the sermon is called a *khatib*, and the sermon itself is called the *khutbah*.

Although taking the place of the noon prayer, which consists of four *rakaat*, the Friday prayer

---

The call to prayer

The *azan* (call to prayer) by the muezzin, known to Malaysians as the *bilal*, marks the time of the obligatory prayer. Traditionally, the call was made by the *bilal* from the minaret of the mosque. Now, microphones are used and the *azan* is heard through loudspeakers fixed on the roof or minaret of a mosque. Some local radio and television stations also broadcast the *azan*.

The words of the *azan* are, 'Allah is greater. Allah is greater. I testify that there is no god but Allah. I testify that Muhammad is the Messenger of Allah. Come to prayer. Come to prayer. Come to prosperity. Come to prosperity. Allah is great. Allah is great. There is no god but Allah.'

The call to prayer is made before every one of the five obligatory prayers. However, for the morning prayer (*subuh*), the sentence 'prayer is better than sleep' is inserted after the call to prosperity, and repeated twice.

Nowadays, the *bilal* makes the call to prayer with the aid of a microphone and loudspeakers.

consists of only two *rakaat* because the sermon that precedes it is considered equivalent to two *rakaat*.

The Friday prayer is obligatory only for Muslim men and must be performed by a congregation consisting of at least 40 men who reside in the area. This is in accordance with the view of the Shafii *mazhab* (school of jurisprudence) which is followed in Malaysia.

Other prayers

Besides the obligatory prayers, there are other kinds of prayers which are recommended. These include the non-obligatory prayers: the *witir* (odd-numbered) prayer performed after the evening prayer or as the last prayer of the night; and the *dhuha* (late morning) prayer. Others include the *tahajjud* prayer, which is performed late at night; the *tarawih* prayer, performed during the fasting month; and the highly recommended prayers performed on the two feast days, Hari Raya Aidilfitri and Hari Raya Aidiladha.

The prayer on the morning of Aidilfitri marks the end of Ramadhan, the fasting month, and the beginning of the month of Syawal. It is a congregational prayer of two *rakaat* performed after the sun has risen above the horizon. The manner in which it is conducted is the same as the Friday congregational prayer, with the exception that the *khutbah* is delivered after, not before, the prayer.

The prayer on the morning of Hari Raya Aidiladha marks the Feast of the Sacrifices which falls on the tenth day of Zulhijjah (the month of the pilgrimage). The manner of performing this prayer is the same as that on Hari Raya Aidilfitri.

Muslim ladies wearing *telekung* (white over-garment) while at prayer.

The *khutbah* (sermon) is a part of the congregational Friday prayer.

Performing prayer

Although there are slight differences to be observed by male and female worshippers when praying, the basic prayer positions remain the same. Both males and females who intend to perform prayer must first take *wuduk* (minor ablutions) by washing the exposed areas of the body. Women usually wear a special white garment called a *telekung* over their everyday clothes. Men often wear the sarong and *baju Melayu* (Malay shirt) for prayer.

1 Declaration of intent

2 'Allah is great'.

3 Reciting the *al-Fatihah*

4 Praise of Allah's majesty

5 Standing erect in prayer

1 Except in the case of disability, a worshipper must stand up for prayer. Standing upright facing in the direction of the *kiblat* (the direction of Mecca), the worshipper declares his *niat* (intention) to perform prayer in a low voice.

2 He raises his hands, with the fingers slightly spread, to shoulder level with the thumbs nearly touching the ear lobes, and the palm of the hands facing the *kiblat*. In this position, he recites the *takbir* (praises to Allah). This, the *takbiratul ihram* (*takbir* of prohibition) marks the beginning of concentration, prohibiting the worshipper from saying or doing anything outside prayer.

3 He then puts his arms across his midriff, placing the palm of the right hand over the back of the left, stretching out the fore and the middle fingers, and seizing the wrist of the left hand with the thumb and little finger. While so standing, he recites the opening invocation (*doa iftitah*), followed by the reciting of the *sura al-Fatihah*. After reciting this *sura*, he recites another *sura* or a portion of the Qur'an consisting of at least three verses.

4 Having done this, the worshipper performs the *rukuk* (single bow) by inclining the upper part of the body at a right angle and places his hands upon his knees, separating the fingers a little. Praises to Allah are repeated three times.

5 After this, he stands up straight.

6 He then prostrates himself on the ground so that his knees, the toes of his feet, the palms of his hands (with the fingers close to each other), the nose and the forehead touch the ground. While prostrating, he says praises to Allah three times.

7 Then, he raises his head and body, sinks backwards on his heels, and thus half-sitting, half-kneeling on his thighs, he recites, 'O my Lord, forgive me and have mercy on upon me, and grant me my portion and guide me…'.

6 First prostration

7 First sitting position

8 Second prostration

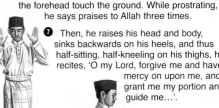
9 'Allah is great'.

10 Second sitting position

8 Following this, he repeats the prostration with the same recitation as above.

9 He then rises and stands erect once again, thus completing one *rakaat* (prayer sequence).

10 Having completed the first *rakaat*, he now performs the second in the same manner as the first beginning with the *sura al-Fatihah*. After every two *rakaat*, or after the last *rakaat* in prayer, instead of rising, he remains sitting on the left foot, placing his hands on his knees and says the *tahiyyat* (salutation) and says the *syahadah*, which is the declaration that there is no god but Allah, and that Muhammad is the Messenger of Allah.

11 Third sitting position

12a First *salam*

12b Second *salam*

11 At the end of all the *rakaat*, an additional recitation is added which includes blessings (*selawat*) for the Holy Prophet and his descendants. This is then followed by salutations (*salam*) made to the right (**12a**) and left (**12b**) which end the prayer.

The pillars of Islam: Zakat and fasting

According to the third and fourth rukun Islam *(pillars of Islam) it is obligatory for a Muslim to pay* zakat *(poor tax) and to fast. Muslims pay a share of their accumulated wealth as* zakat. *This is collected and distributed by the state religious departments; distribution is to the poor and needy. With certain limited exceptions, Muslims fast from dawn until sunset each day during the month of Ramadhan. This collective experience culminates with the celebration of Hari Raya Aidilfitri.*

Gotong royong is a form of communal cooperation which involves all members of the community, young and old, in certain tasks for the benefit of all. The above shows villagers during *gotong royong* for *buka puasa* (breaking of fast).

Zakat

Paying *zakat* is the third fundamental religious obligation of Muslims. It signifies the annual amount in cash or kind which a Muslim with means must distribute to those who are less privileged. The paying of a part of one's accumulated wealth to the needy and the poor is believed to purify one's wealth and possessions.

The most common forms of *zakat* collected from individuals in Malaysia are the taxes on financial savings and salaries, and on harvests such as rice.

Every Muslim, male and female who, at the end of the year, possesses a certain amount of cash or articles of trade exceeding a minimum amount (around RM2500) after meeting all lawful expenses, is obliged to contribute *zakat* at the minimum of 2.5 per cent. There is no upper limit, except that one should not deprive oneself and one's dependents from meeting needs that are considered legitimate in Islam. When a person has wealth in business stocks or trade goods, he or she must evaluate his or her wealth at the end of the year and give *zakat* at the same rate of 2.5 per cent of the total value of the wealth. The rates of *zakat* for cattle, cash and agricultural produce vary.

In Malaysia, the state religious departments are responsible for the collection and distribution of *zakat*. The income tax policy in Malaysia, which makes *zakat* contributions tax deductible, has encouraged many Muslims to make yearly *zakat* payments. The government has also been studying the possibility of making at-source *zakat* deductions from the salaries of Muslim employees. Some government departments have already implemented this new method of collecting *zakat*. In Kuala

---

Types of zakat

There are two types of *zakat* that need to be paid by a Muslim. The first is *zakat harta*, that is, *zakat* paid on one's possessions and business assets while the other type is a fixed amount tax paid by individuals and their dependents, known as *zakat fitrah*.

Zakat harta is paid on assets including income and business earnings, shares and financial savings, grazing animals kept for the purposes of trade and agricultural produce. *Zakat fitrah* must be paid by every Muslim who is alive on the eve of the first day of the month of Syawal. The amount to be paid is calculated according to the cost of approximately 2.25 kg of the staple grain in Malaysia—rice. Payment can be made in the form of cash, in which case the cost is worked out by the religious department of the respective state according to the cost of rice locally. *Zakat fitrah* is distributed to the poor and needy during the months of Ramadhan and Syawal.

Paying *zakat fitrah* at the mosque. *Zakat* was traditionally collected at mosques and *surau* (small prayer houses).

Distributing zakat

An official *zakat* distribution ceremony. *Zakat* collected is distributed to a number of categories of entitled people including pilgrims and the poor.

The pie chart shows *zakat* distribution in the state of Selangor by category.

How zakat is divided

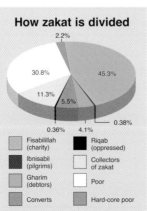

- 45.3%
- 2.2%
- 30.8%
- 11.3%
- 5.5%
- 0.36%
- 4.1%
- 0.38%

Legend:
- Fisabilillah (charity)
- Ibnisabil (pilgrims)
- Gharim (debtors)
- Converts
- Riqab (oppressed)
- Collectors of zakat
- Poor
- Hard-core poor

Zakat collections for the state of Selangor in 2004 totalled RM100,780,665.

Apart from income and savings, one of the items for which a Muslim must pay *zakat* is gold jewellery, provided it exceeds a certain minimum amount.

The modern method of paying *zakat* is via counter payments at specified institutions, such as the Pusat Pungutan Zakat (Zakat Collection Centre) located in each state.

Ramadhan—the fasting month

Fasting during Ramadhan

During the whole month of Ramadhan, Muslims must abstain from eating, drinking, smoking and sexual intimacy from sunrise until sunset. Fasting is not, however, a time for resting. During the day, Muslims go about their usual duties. Throughout Ramadhan, Malaysian Muslim families wake up before dawn to eat a meal (*sahur*) and prepare for the *subuh* (dawn) prayer before going about their daily routine.

In the Muslim community, particularly among Malays, fasting is observed as a collective experience. Therefore, children are trained at around seven years of age to fast, beginning with fasting for half a day until they are older. By the time they reach the age of 12, children are usually expected to fast the whole day as do the adults.

Muslims waiting to break fast at the end of the day during the fasting month.

In Malaysia, to respect the fasting month, Muslims are prohibited from eating in public during the day, even if they are exempted from fasting for valid reasons. In several states, Muslim adults who are found deliberately defying this religious obligation and eating in public may be apprehended by state religious officials and fined if found guilty.

Lumpur and Selangor, *zakat* collection has become very efficient through computerization and well-managed collection offices.

Fasting

Puasa is the Malay word for 'fast' or 'fasting'. During the month of Ramadhan, the ninth month of the Muslim calendar, Muslims are enjoined by the Qur'an to fast. Fasting is meant to instil self-discipline, rejuvenate spirituality, create concern for the poor and needy, and strengthen consciousness of God.

To achieve this, Muslims are not permitted to eat, drink, smoke or have sexual intercourse during the day although they are allowed to do these activities from the time of breaking fast at sunset until the next dawn.

There are several categories of people who are exempted from fasting: the sick, the old and menstruating women. However, they are still not permitted to eat in public during the day.

The fasting month ends with the festival known in Malaysia as Hari Raya Aidilfitri or Hari Raya Puasa. Preparations for this festival are usually made during the month of Ramadhan. A new trend in preparing for this festival is the *Bazar Ramadhan*, a temporary bazaar resembling the Malaysian *pasar malam* (night markets). Everything necessary for the festive season, from *kuih raya* (biscuits served during the festive season) and decorative items to tablecloths and clothes are sold at this bazaar. Certain areas, like Jalan Masjid India in Kuala Lumpur, are well known for this kind of bazaar and attract traders from all over the country.

Buka puasa (breaking fast) buffets are common during the fasting month.

In the fasting month, stalls selling cooked food for breaking fast are set up late in the afternoon.

Buka puasa

Maghrib, the time of the evening prayer, is the time for *buka puasa* (breaking fast). Having fasted the whole day, Muslims may once again eat and enjoy normal activities. Some restaurants make an announcement or play recordings of the *azan* (call to prayer) to mark the time for *buka puasa*. Many hotels allocate a special area or room as a prayer room.

After breaking fast, Muslims are encouraged to perform the evening prayer in congregation. It is a custom among Muslims in Malaysia to invite friends and relatives over to their homes for breaking fast and to perform the *tarawih* prayer, a special prayer, afterwards. Mosques also organize *buka puasa* for congregants who perform prayer there, usually with food donations from members of the community.

Muslim-owned restaurants and food stalls are usually closed during the day for the whole month of Ramadhan. However, throughout the fasting month, stalls selling a variety of food are set up at certain areas in the late afternoon. Hotels and restaurants usually also offer special buffets for *buka puasa*. These are not restricted to Muslims alone, but are also popular among the non-Muslim population.

Tarawih prayer

This prayer is performed immediately after the *isyak* (night) prayer. *Tarawih* means 'pause' and the prayer is so named because worshippers rest after each pair of salutations. It is a prayer consisting of as many as 20 *rakaat* (prayer sequences). In certain Muslim countries, the imam, or prayer leader, will recite one whole *juzuk* (part) of the Qur'an from memory in one night, so that the whole of the Qur'an will be concluded on the last night of Ramadhan.

In Malaysia, the *tarawih* prayer is unique because, unlike other congregational prayers, women and children can go to the mosque to take part in this congregational prayer.

Many Malaysian Muslims prefer to observe *tarawih* in a fairly speedy manner, whereby only short verses are recited by the imam, and there is no rest period between the two *rakaat*. Malaysian mosques also serve refreshments and a variety of home-made cakes, usually donated by members of the congregation, after the *tarawih* prayers.

The *tarawih* prayer is held at night during the fasting month.

The pillars of Islam: The hajj

The hajj or pilgrimage to Mecca is the fifth pillar of Islam. Every Muslim must perform this pilgrimage once in their lifetime (if able). The tradition of the pilgrimage dates back to Prophet Ibrahim and involves a number of rituals. Besides the hajj, there is another pilgrimage called the umrah, which is sometimes referred to as the 'lesser pilgrimage'. This can be performed at any time except the eighth, ninth or tenth of Zulhijjah, which are the days fixed for the hajj, the great pilgrimage.

Malaysian pilgrims during a preparatory course practising the *tawaf* (circumambulation) with a model of the Kaabah.

The meaning and significance of the hajj

The word hajj means 'pilgrimage' or the religious journey to Mecca during the month of Zulhijjah. The pilgrimage to Mecca is the fifth pillar of Islam and is therefore obligatory for all Muslims, men and women, once in a lifetime. The hajj must be undertaken by all Muslim adults who have the strength and financial means to do so.

The hajj provides an opportunity for Muslims from all over the world to meet and to get to know one another. Besides establishing friendships, they may make professional contacts. In short, the hajj offers not only spiritual benefit but also socio-political and economic benefits.

The importance of the Kaabah

The Kaabah, an almost cube-shaped building, was a sacred site even in pre-Muhammad days. The Qur'an states that 'The first house of worship appointed for humankind was that at Bakkah [Mecca], full of blessings and of guidance for all the worlds' (Q. 3: 96). Allah, through His angels, showed Prophet Adam and, later, Prophet Ibrahim, exactly where to erect the house. The prophet and his followers were then instructed by Allah to circumambulate it in praise of Allah.

In the time of Prophet Nuh (Noah), the Kaabah was completely destroyed and its location could no longer be traced. It was rebuilt by Ibrahim. It is narrated that Allah directed the angels to help Ibrahim build the Kaabah by gathering and laying the stones, including the Hajar Aswad (Black Stone), which is a part of the Kaabah. The Kaabah is now situated in an open courtyard in the centre of the Masjidil Haram (Sacred Mosque).

Events during the life of Prophet Ibrahim

The hajj is a form of worship that dates back to the life of Prophet Ibrahim. Most rituals performed during the hajj are related to the events that took place during the lifetime of Ibrahim and his son Isma'il (Ishmael).

Ibrahim was married to Sarah but they were childless. At Sarah's suggestion, Ibrahim married Hajar (Hagar), a virtuous girl, who bore him a son, Isma'il. Allah then commanded Ibrahim to leave Hajar and the infant Isma'il at a barren, deserted valley then called Bakkah.

Hajar's first worry was to find water. When she sighted two small hills, now known as Safa and Marwah, she quickly ran to the nearest, hoping she might get a view over the surrounding land and spot water. As she could not find any, she ran to the other

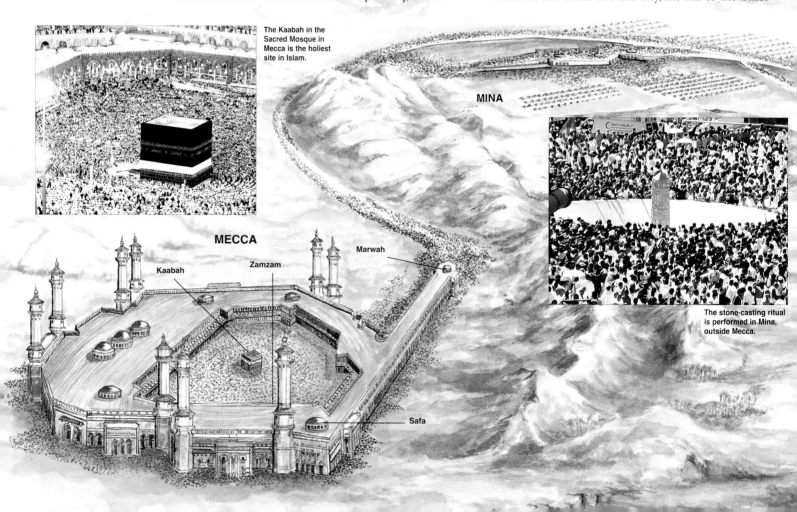

The Kaabah in the Sacred Mosque in Mecca is the holiest site in Islam.

MINA

MECCA

Kaabah

Zamzam

Marwah

Safa

The stone-casting ritual is performed in Mina, outside Mecca.

hill. She hastened back and forth between these hills seven times. Unable to locate water, she returned to her baby. There she found that a spring had appeared at a spot where the baby had kicked the sand. This spring, called Zamzam, still exists in Mecca today and has never run dry.

Next, Ibrahim had a dream in which Allah asked him to sacrifice his son Isma'il. Satan tried to dissuade him by reminding the prophet of how difficult it had been to get this son. At a place outside Mecca, now called Mina, Ibrahim and his son hurled stones at Satan to drive him away. Just as Ibrahim was about to sacrifice Isma'il, a voice from above ordered him to stop. Instead, a sacrificial ram was offered. This event is remembered by Muslims during the Feast of Sacrifice (Aidiladha).

Malay cultural influences

Before leaving for the hajj Malay Muslims usually hold a *kenduri doa selamat* (feast for safe passage) to which neighbours, close friends and relatives are invited. It is held two or three days before departure.

Performing the hajj requires a stay in Saudi Arabia of from 10 to 45 days. After returning, pilgrims usually stay at home for a week or more to allow neighbours, friends and relatives to visit them in their homes.

Men who have performed the hajj are called 'Haji' and the women, 'Hajjah'. The pilgrims usually relate their experiences during the pilgrimage to their visitors. Water from the Zamzam spring, as well as dried fruit and nuts brought back from the pilgrimage, are usually served. As the visitors leave, they are often presented with a small gift, such as skull-caps, prayer beads or prayer mats purchased in Mecca or Medina as a sign of sharing the *barakah* (blessings) of Allah.

The umrah

The *umrah* or 'lesser pilgrimage' is considered a commendable act in imitation of the prophet's example. The *umrah* can be performed at any time except on the eighth, ninth and tenth of Zulhijjah, which are fixed for the hajj. It can be performed before, after or together with the hajj. Malaysians who perform the *umrah* normally stay in Saudi Arabia for a week to a fortnight, although the actual ritual can be finished within three hours. The rest of the time is spent in mosques at Mecca and Medina.

Although the *umrah* is not compulsory, many Malaysians like to perform it. Performing the *umrah* is more economical than the hajj, and there are fewer restrictions from the authorities. The number of Malaysians performing this pilgrimage is increasing annually.

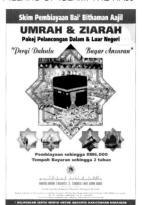

An advertisement by a local travel agency offering '*umrah* packages'. The increased number of Malaysians performing the *umrah* may be a reflection of a return to religious values.

Lembaga Urusan Tabung Haji

Lembaga Urusan Tabung Haji (Pilgrims Management and Fund Board) is the only Islamic organization in the world whose core business is hajj management and is regarded by Islamic countries as a role model for establishing similar organizations. Contributing to the fund enables Muslims to save gradually over a period of time for the performance of the hajj. The organization plans and implements the management and operation of the hajj in Malaysia and in Saudi Arabia. All pilgrims must register with them and once this is done a thorough medical check-up is conducted. The pilgrims also undergo a comprehensive three-level hajj course which is conducted at mosques or other suitable venues throughout the country. Lembaga Urusan Tabung Haji also helps with the issuance of hajj passports and visas and arranges chartered flights with the assistance of Malaysian Airlines. Working in conjunction with the Saudi Arabian Government, it facilitates the arrival and departure at King Abdul Aziz International Airport, Jeddah, arranges internal transportation in Saudi Arabia, provides medical facilities, housing facilities, food and counselling services. A welfare and medical team awaits the pilgrims in Saudi Arabia and is on hand during the hajj period to provide services if necessary.

Pilgrims waiting to board their flight for the hajj at the Kuala Lumpur International Airport.

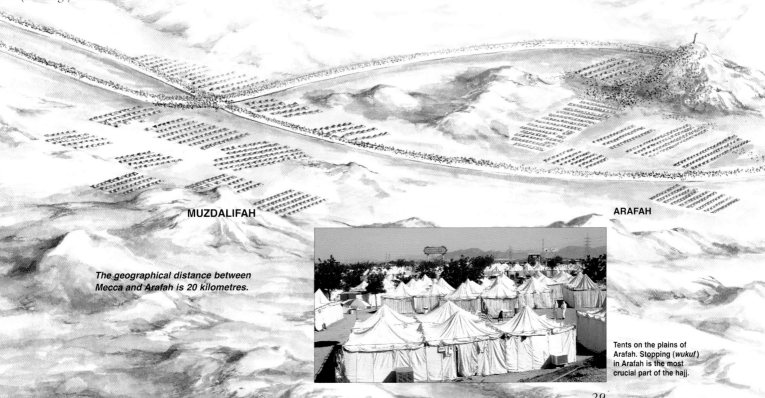

MUZDALIFAH

ARAFAH

The geographical distance between Mecca and Arafah is 20 kilometres.

Tents on the plains of Arafah. Stopping (*wukuf*) in Arafah is the most crucial part of the hajj.

The Qur'an and the Hadith

The Qur'an commands the Muslim's highest veneration as the book of complete guidance revealed by Allah to His Prophet and Messenger Muhammad. It is divided into chapters called sura. *Muslims believe that the Qur'an is the complete and unaltered word of Allah, which is universally applicable. Thus, the Qur'an is a suitable guide for all mankind till the Day of Judgement. The Hadith are the collected sayings of Prophet Muhammad that supplement and elaborate the teachings of the Qur'an.*

The hand-painted markers which demarcate the ends of a Qur'anic verse are examples of the glorious design of the Al-Qur'an Mushaf Malaysia.

Sources of guidance

The highest authoritative sources of divine guidance in Islam are the Qur'an and the *sunnah* (traditions) of Prophet Muhammad. Muslims in Malaysia, as in other parts of the world, consider the Qur'an the book of complete guidance revealed by Allah to His final Messenger Muhammad. To Muslims it is the complete and unaltered Word of Allah which is universally applicable till the Day of Judgement.

The Qur'an consists of 114 *sura* (chapters) that deal with a wide variety of topics. All in all, it is a comprehensive guide for people to live as true servants of God. The Hadith are the collected sayings of Prophet Muhammad that supplement and elaborate the teachings of the Qur'an to guide Muslims in their everyday lives. Muslims believe that the Qur'an is the final revelation from Allah which concludes the series of divine revelations from time immemorial. All aspects of a Muslim's life are governed by principles and norms from the Qur'an and the *sunnah* of the Prophet, or interpretations based on these two principal sources. In Malaysia, numerous books and magazines, published largely in Malay, offer elaborate guidance for day-to-day applications of the principles of the Qur'an and the *sunnah*, interpreted by both classical and modern scholars.

A mother teaching her son to read the Qur'an.

Occasions for Qur'anic recitation

When a child is born, the *azan*, or call to prayer, is uttered into the newborn's ear. The *al-Fatihah* (opening *sura*), *al-Falaq* (*sura* of daybreak) and *an-Nas* (*sura* of mankind) may also be recited to a newborn for divine grace and protection.

Muslims in Malaysia, as in other parts of the world, read or recite the Qur'an, either in whole *sura* or in part, on various occasions. For instance, after performing *solat* (the obligatory five daily prayers), pious Muslims may recite the *al-Fatihah*, the *al-Falaq* and the *an-Nas*, followed by portions of other *sura*.

Sickness is a time when Muslims tend to recite the Qur'an extensively to bring solace and spiritual strength to the ailing. The *sura* most usually read when someone is ill are the *al-Fatihah*, *al-Falaq*,

Studying and respecting the Qur'an

As the Qur'an is Allah's Word, a Malaysian Muslim child begins learning to read it in Arabic at around six or seven years of age. The child often receives this instruction at the house of a religious teacher. In villages, it is more likely that this is the imam (religious leader) of the local mosque or a *guru Qur'an* (Qur'an teacher). Traditionally, a child would be introduced to the teacher by its father with a gift of food (often a bowl of glutinous rice) or a nominal amount of money. Nowadays, most parents give money to the teachers.

One of the first things a Muslim boy or girl is taught in Malaysia is the *adab*, or spiritually correct manner of handling the Qur'an. The most important rule is not to touch the Qur'an in an unclean state, that is, without first performing ablutions. The Qur'an should be picked up, then placed against the forehead, kissed and then held against the breast as an expression of adoration before being opened to be read. The Qur'an is usually placed on a *rehal*, a special bookstand made of wood or plastic, for reading, so that it does not touch the floor. After reading, the Qur'an is closed, placed against the forehead, held against the breast and then returned to its usual storage place.

After learning the Arabic alphabet, the child is first taught Qur'anic reading from the *Muqaddam*, a booklet containing the last 30 *sura* of the Qur'an which are short and easy to learn. Gradually, the pupil is taught to read the entire Qur'an. When the child has finished learning this, a ceremony called *khatam Qur'an* (conclusion ceremony) is held to mark the occasion.

The Qur'an is always treated with the utmost respect. Children are first taught the correct manner of handling the Qur'an. Before reading, the Qur'an is placed against the head, kissed and lastly held against the breast and then returned to its bookstand.

Khatam Qur'an

A *khatam Qur'an* ceremony held during Ramadhan, November 2004 at Masjid Negara, Kuala Lumpur.

When a child has finished learning to read the whole of the Qur'an, a ceremony is usually conducted to celebrate this achievement. This is the *khatam Qur'an* (conclusion ceremony). This ceremony is usually held at the pupil's house or at the local mosque, where the teacher, other pupils and invitees sit in a circle and each one recites a *sura* of the Qur'an from memory. The student for whom the *khatam Qur'an* is being held will then repeat these verses and show his or her mastery of the Qur'an. An imam, usually from the mosque where the child received Qur'an lessons, often officiates. In Malay society, *khatam Qur'an* are often held in conjunction with weddings.

The *khatam Qur'an* does not signify the end of a person's Qur'anic learning. Most continue with Qur'anic lessons in school or private classes.

an-Nas and *al-Ma'arij*. *Ya Sin*, the 36th *sura* in the Qur'an, is read for solace during the trials and tribulations in one's life. The verses of this *sura* are credited with spiritual healing qualities. This particular *sura* is also read in the presence of the dying as it is believed that with its recitation, the soul of the dying will be able to leave the body with ease. Above all the Qur'an is the highest source of personal, civil and criminal laws for Muslim society. Muslim scholars, judges, educationists and preachers use the Qur'an extensively as the primary reference in their professions.

The Hadith

Hadith literally means a narrative or report but in English it is best translated as 'tradition'. It refers to the record of the actions and sayings of Prophet Muhammad. The traditions of the Prophet are called the *sunnah*, and refer to the specific customs, habits and actions of the Prophet. The terms Hadith and *sunnah* are often used interchangeably although they are not synonymous. Strictly speaking, *sunnah* denotes the actual actions, practices and sayings of the Prophet, while Hadith means the narration, account and record of his actions, practices and sayings.

The correct plural form of the term Hadith is *ahadith*, which refers to whole collections of traditions such as those recorded by al-Bukhari, Muslim or Abu Daud. The *ahadith* are the secondary source of Islamic law, and next in importance to the Qur'an.

It is generally concluded by jurists and scholars that there are three aspects that constitute the *ahadith*: *qawli* (the *sunnah* of sayings of the Prophet), *fi'li* (the *sunnah* of actions), which includes the customs and practices of the Prophet, and *taqrir* (the *sunnah* of approbation), which is the Prophet's tacit approval of certain acts.

The *ahadith* were orally transmitted in the beginning and later committed to writing. It was during the time of 'Umar bin Abdul Aziz, the eighth Caliph of the Ummayyad Dynasty (99–101 AH/ 717–720 CE), that the *ahadith* were collected and properly recorded on his orders. Later, more systematic efforts were made. Famous Hadith collections are the *sunan* (compilations) of the six imams: al-Bukhari, Muslim, Abu Daud, al-Tirmizi, al-Nasa'i and Ibn Majah. Their collections are considered the most authentic, and they are popularly known as *al-kutub al-sittah* (the six books) or *sunan sittah* (the six compilations).

Ahadith are often more detailed descriptions or explanations of divine prescriptions made in the Qur'an. Collectors of the *ahadith* were meticulous in tracing the chain of narrators to ensure that the *ahadith* they transmitted were authentic sayings of the Prophet. The narrator who attested the correctness of the *ahadith* was called the *rawi* (relater)

The Al-Qur'an Mushaf Malaysia
The Al-Qur'an Mushaf Malaysia project was officially launched on 26 January 1997, coinciding with Nuzul al-Qur'an, the anniversary in the month of Ramadhan that marks the first revelation of the Qur'an. The outcome of the project is a fully illuminated Qur'an, first published in the year 2000.

The designs used are based on traditional motifs found in Malay crafts and architecture. For the calligraphy itself, the traditional writing tool, the *handam*, was used to retain the authenticity and beauty of traditional calligraphy.

The opening *sura* (*al-Fatihah*) and the first page of the *sura* of The Cow (*al-Baqarah*) of this splendidly illuminated Qur'an.

Qur'an reading competitions
In the 1960s, the first Prime Minister, Tunku Abdul Rahman Putra, introduced the annual *musabaqah* (Qur'an reading competition) during Ramadhan, which is the month when the Qur'an was first revealed to Prophet Muhammad. The winning *qari* and *qariah* (male and female reciters) from the national competition represent Malaysia in the International Qur'an Reading Competition which attracts participants from all over the Muslim world. Today Malaysia is well known for this event in the Muslim world.

Musabaqah are also held on a smaller scale at school level. The staff of some organizations and companies also organize *musabaqah*. These Qur'anic recitation events educate Muslims and non-Muslims alike to the poetry and rhythm of the language of the Qur'an.

The winner of the Annual International Qur'an Reading Competition being presented a prize by the King in October 2004, Kuala Lumpur.

and his version is called the *riwaya*. There are several thousand *ahadith*. Imam al-Bukhari, for example, collected and authenticated 7275 *ahadith*, while Imam Muslim and Imam Abu Daud each compiled about 4000. Each one of their works was given a name, for example: *Sahih al-Bukhari, Sahih Muslim, Sunan Abu Daud.*

Following the *sunnah* of Prophet Muhammad is a duty for every *mukmin* (believer), in line with the Qur'anic injunction which states, 'O you who believe, obey Allah and obey the Messenger and those charged with authority amongst you' (Q. 4: 59).

The Qur'an is available in high-tech versions, on CD and DVD.

Translations of the Hadith are published for Malay readers.

Islamic rites of passage

The first and most important rite of passage for a Muslim is the azan (call to prayer) that is recited into a newborn's ear. Another important rite of passage for Muslim boys is circumcision, which is performed before boys reach puberty. Marriage is considered as a prophetic tradition or sunnah, and thus Muslims consider marriage to be a praiseworthy undertaking that will increase the size of the ummah (Muslim community). It is also the duty of a Muslim to attend the funeral of another Muslim and perform the special prayer for the dead.

RIGHT: A traditional circumcision. In the past, circumcisions were performed by the *tok mudin*, or village circumciser.
ABOVE: Nowadays, most parents in both urban and rural areas choose to have their sons circumcised at hospitals or clinics.

In Malaysia, guests at a Malay wedding were traditionally given a *bunga telur* (literally, egg flower) as a token of appreciation. Nowadays, a small gift is often given.

Influences

In the pre-Hindu period, the Malays observed various rites during the different stages of life to appease the spirits they worshipped. Later, rites and rituals were performed to Hindu gods. After the mass conversion of the Malays to Islam, Islamic rites were introduced in Malay culture although vestiges of the former Hindu heritage remained until the Islamic resurgence in the 1970s largely removed most if not all traces.

Birth

The first call to prayer is one of the most important rites of passage among Muslims. When a baby is born, the *azan* is recited into the baby's ear to ensure that the first words heard by the baby in this world are Allah's name and divinely inspired words proclaiming Him as the only God.

A few days or weeks after the birth, it is usual to hold a ceremony in which dates and water from the Zamzam well in Mecca are fed to the baby. It often begins with *berzanji* (recitation of verses in praise of the Prophet). Following prophetic tradition, the baby's head is often shaved. This practice is now changing, and it is fairly common nowadays to cut off only a few locks of hair.

Circumcision

Circumcision for boys is highly recommended in Islam. The Prophet himself is said to have been born naturally circumcised. Therefore, Muslims regard circumcision to be a commendable prophetic tradition. The age of circumcision varies, but it must be performed before the boy reaches puberty. Some parents now have their sons circumcised at birth in the hospitals where they were born.

Traditionally, circumcision involved a ceremony in which a few boys were circumcised together. The circumcision was marked by a big feast for relatives and friends. The boys were given a ritual bath before the ceremony, and the circumcision itself, performed by the *tok mudin* (circumciser), would take place in a house. This is no longer common practice as parents prefer circumcisions to be performed hygienically at modern clinics or hospitals. The circumcision feast is also no longer common.

Marriage

Traditionally, marriages were arranged by parents for their children. In Malay custom, the bride or bridegroom's parents asked relatives and friends if they knew of a suitable match. The bridegroom's family would then formally ask for the girl's hand in marriage. An engagement ceremony followed, to which only close relatives and friends would be invited. The bridegroom's family would present a ring and other gifts to the bride. Matters such as the *hantaran* (gifts), the length of the engagement and the wedding date would be discussed. Nowadays, most young people choose their own partners but engagement ceremonies are still the norm.

One of the most important aspects of the *akad nikah* (solemnizing of the marriage contract) is the *mas kahwin* (dowry). This is a sum of money that the bridegroom gives to the bride. In Malaysia, the minimum amount is fixed by the religious authorities of the state, but the bridegroom or his family usually give more than the minimum. *Mas kahwin* is different from *wang hantaran*, a sum of money that forms part of the gifts the bridegroom gives to the bride. While giving *mas kahwin* is obligatory for the groom, the giving of *wang hantaran* is in accordance with Malay tradition. The amount of *wang hantaran* is often several times greater than that of the *mas kahwin*. The bride may use the *mas kahwin* as she wishes, while traditionally the *wang hantaran* was often used by the bride's parents to pay for the wedding feast.

After the solemnizing ceremony, which may take place in the mosque, the bridegroom is led in a procession to the bride's house where the wedding feast is held. Nowadays, the feast may also be held a day or more after the solemnizing of the marriage.

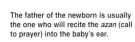

The father of the newborn is usually the one who will recite the *azan* (call to prayer) into the baby's ear.

The akad nikah
Since the 1990s, Muslim couples planning to get married in Malaysia have been obliged, in most states, to first attend a marriage course in which the religious views of marriage and the duties of each partner according to Islamic teachings are emphasized. However, two things have changed little: the *akad nikah* (solemnization of the marriage contract) and the wedding feast. For the *akad* (marriage contract) to be lawful, it must be performed with the participation of (**1**) the groom; (**2**) the *jurunikah* (solemnizer); (**3**) the bride's *wali* (guardian); and (**4**) two male witnesses. The *akad nikah* is performed in the presence of the *wali* by the *jurunikah*, who is usually the imam of the local mosque, or a *kadi* (Islamic judge). The *wali* is usually the bride's father, brother or uncle.

The bride is not required to attend but the *jurunikah* and the witnesses have to hear her consent beforehand. Malaysian Islamic laws require the bride's signature on all marriage documents. If the ceremony takes place in the bride's house, as illustrated here, the bride will wait in another room.

A Malay wedding ceremony (*akad nikah*). The *pelamin* (dais) with the two chairs in the background is for the *bersanding* (sitting-in-state) ceremony, which is Hindu in origin.

The wedding feast is an elaborate affair complete with a variety of dishes. A *berzanji* (Malay cultural performance) may be held to add to the celebration. There are two wedding feasts, the first in the bride's house and the second in the groom's. The feast in the groom's house is not usually held on the same day; it may take place several days later. Although weddings are traditionally held in the homes of the bride's and groom's parents, in urban areas it is common for weddings to be held in community halls or hotels.

Under Malaysian Islamic law, a non-Muslim in Malaysia who wishes to marry a Muslim must first convert to Islam.

Death
Whenever there is a sign that death is approaching, verses from the Qur'an are recited by relatives attending to the dying person. Upon the death of the person, all relatives and friends are notified. The body is then prepared for burial (usually with 24 hours) by bathing it in a mixture of water, and camphor. The arms are then folded as if in prayer, after which the body is wrapped in the white burial shroud. The actual funeral, which is usually held at the family home, involves a prayer and Qur'anic recitation, in which all who have gathered participate. A special prayer may also be held in the nearest mosque.

Before the body of the deceased is taken from the house to the graveyard, the imam may recite the *al-Fatihah*, the first chapter of the Qur'an, three times.

In memory of the deceased, many Malay families hold *tahlil* (special prayers) for three to seven nights, and in some cases also on the 40th day after death, although this is not obligatory.

After the body has been prepared for burial and wrapped in the shroud, a special prayer is performed for the deceased. Even if there is no body, the prayer for the dead should still be performed. This prayer is the most important religious requirement for the dead. The body cannot be buried until this prayer has been performed.

Muslims do not cremate the dead body. The enshrouded corpse is laid on its side at the bottom of the grave with the face facing in the direction of Mecca. In some places the local custom prefers the body to be laid within a bottomless wooden enclosure with a cover on top to prevent soil from falling on the face of the deceased when the grave is filled. It is also customary in some states in Malaysia to place the body in an enclosure dug within the wall of the grave. A wooden plank is then used to cover the enclosure, after which the grave is filled.

Islamic festivals and celebrations

The two main Islamic festivals in Malaysia are Hari Raya Aidilfitri and Hari Raya Aidiladha. Hari Raya, literally 'great day', can be translated simply as 'festival'. Other Islamic festivals celebrated include Maal Hijrah (the first day of the Muslim calendar), Maulidur Rasul (the Prophet's birthday), Nuzul al-Qur'an (commemorating the first revelation of the Qur'an) and Israk Mikraj (the Day of Ascension). The scale of celebration for Nuzul al-Qur'an and Israk Mikraj varies between the states, but the others are national holidays.

Ketupat is traditional food served on Hari Raya. This triangular *ketupat* of glutinous rice, wrapped in palm leaves, is more common in the northern states of Peninsular Malaysia.

The Islamic festival calendar

Festivals celebrated by Malaysian Muslims are more or less the same as those celebrated by Muslims the world over, with minor differences due to the influence of Malay culture and local conditions. A Malaysian Hari Raya would not be complete without *ketupat* (rice cooked in palm leaf cases) and *rendang*, a meat dish. Muslim families in urban areas also commonly hold 'open house' at Hari Raya, to which they invite both Muslim and non-Muslim relatives and friends.

Among the other Islamic festivals celebrated is Maulidur Rasul, commemorating the birth of Prophet Muhammad in 570 CE, though the celebrations are not as grand as in some other Muslim countries. Although Malaysians adhere to the Western calendar, Muslims also celebrate the Islamic new year on the first day of Muharram.

The Islamic Year

The *hijrah*, the Prophet's emigration from Mecca to Medina in 622 CE is the reference point of the Islamic system of dating as it marks the first year in the Islamic calendar which is based on the lunar month. Hence, a year in the Islamic calendar is also called a *hijrah* year. The year 2000 was 1421 in the Islamic dating system.

A signboard indicating one of the locations for the official sighting of the moon, according to which the dates of Ramadhan and Syawal (the beginning and the end of the fasting month) are fixed.

Months	Festival/celebration
MUHARRAM	**Maal Hijrah**–Commemorating the Prophet's emigration from Mecca to Medina in 622 CE, Maal Hijrah is the first day of the Islamic year.
	Hari Asyura–This celebration on the tenth of Muharram commemorates the ordeals and hardships faced by the *ummah* (Muslim community) at various times in history.
SAFAR	No celebration
RABIULAWWAL	**Maulidur Rasul**–The Prophet's birthday falls on the 12th day of this month.
RABIULAKHIR JAMADILAWAL JAMADILAKHIR	No celebration
REJAB	**Israk Mikraj**–The Prophet's Ascension is commemorated on the 27th day of this month.
SYAABAN	**Nisfu Syaaban**–Fasting is recommended on the 15th day of this month, which is just before the fasting month.
RAMADHAN	**Nuzul al-Qur'an**–The revelation of the Qur'an to Muhammad is celebrated on the 17th day of Ramadhan.
SYAWAL	**Hari Raya Puasa/Aidilfitri**–This festival is held on the first day of Syawal which marks the end of the month of fasting.
ZULKAEDAH	No celebration
ZULHIJJAH	**Hari Raya Aidiladha**–This festival is held on the tenth day on the month. Pilgrims gather in Mina, near Mecca, to throw stones at symbols of Satan and undertake the sacrifice of animals.

Maal Hijrah

This festival marks the first day of the Islamic year and is a public holiday in Malaysia. Maal Hijrah (commemoration of the Prophet's emigration) celebrations include state ceremonies to confer awards to Malaysians who have contributed to the advancement of Islam. The award at national level carries the title *Tokoh Maal Hijrah*. Pictured are recipients of the award since its inception in 1987.

1408 AH/1987: Syeikh Mohd Idris bin Abdul Rauf Marbawi

1409 AH/1988: Prof. Tan Sri Datuk Ahmad bin Mohamed Ibrahim

1410 AH/1989: Tan Sri Datu S. O. K. Ubaidullah

1411 AH/1990: Tan Sri Prof. Dr Muhammad M. Abdul Rauf

1413 AH/1991: Tan Sri Haji Mohd Asri bin Haji Muda

1414 AH/1993: Raja Tun Mohar bin Raja Badiozaman

1415 AH/1994: Haji Munawir Sjadzali

1416 AH/1995: Tun Dato' Seri (Dr) Haji Hamdan bin Sheikh Tahir

1418 AH/1997: Prof. Diraja Ungku Aziz bin Ungku Abdul Hamid

1420 AH/1999: Tan Sri Dato' Seri (Dr) Ahmad Sarji bin Abdul Hamid

1421 AH/2000: Tan Sri Ainuddin bin Wahid

1422 AH/2001: Dato' Dr Ismail bin Ibrahim

1423 AH/2002: Datuk Haji Hassan bin Azahari

1424 AH/2003: Dato' Setia Jaya Dato' Paduka Sheikh Abdul Majid bin Mohd Noor

1425 AH/2004: Dato' Dr Halim bin Haji Ismail

1426 AH/2005: Ustaz Muhammad Uthman El-Muhammady

Hari Asyura

The celebration of Hari Asyura falls on the tenth day of Muharram. Muslims commemorate the struggles of the *ummah* (Muslim community) at various periods of history on this day. The celebrations include the cooking of *bubur asyura*, a kind of porridge made with ingredients donated by the whole community.

The mosque in Kampung Baru, Kuala Lumpur, is famous for its tasty *bubur* and often there is a long queue of people outside the mosque for the porridge, which is given free of charge. This takes place in the evening.

Distributing *bubur* at the Kampung Baru mosque during Hari Asyura.

Celebrating Hari Raya

In many west coast states *pelita* (small oil lamps) are placed outside homes in the last week of Ramadhan.

Hari Raya refers to the two main festivals in the Islamic calendar. 'Aidilfitri' is the Malaysianized form of the Arabic name for the celebration that marks the end of the fasting month. It is also known in Malay as Hari Raya Puasa, *puasa* meaning 'fasting'. Hari Raya Aidiladha is also called Hari Raya Haji (Hajj Festival) or Hari Raya Korban (Festival of Sacrifice).

Hari Raya Aidilfitri

The fasting month ends with the festival known as Hari Raya Aidilfitri or Hari Raya Puasa. Particularly in the west coast states of Peninsular Malaysia, this is the most important religious festival in the Islamic calendar. Hari Raya Aidilfitri is celebrated immediately after Ramadhan on the first day of Syawal, the tenth month of the Muslim calendar.

As it is a prophetic tradition to wear new clothing on this day, Muslims in Malaysia often make new purchases for the celebration. It is customary for Malaysian Muslims to wear the traditional Malay dress on this day, even if they do not commonly wear it at other times. Muslim dress such as *tudung* (headscarves), *jubah* (robes) and Malay traditional clothing are much sought-after at this time.

Muslims pay *zakat fitrah*, or alms, to help the poor and needy in the month of Ramadhan. The contribution can be made in the form of either rice or cash. The cash amount is the value of one measure of rice, approximately 2.25 kilograms. The equivalent monetary amount is decided in each state by the Religious Council and varies from state to state. The contribution has to be made before the special prayers on the morning of Aidilfitri. Traditionally, *zakat fitrah* was paid

Balik kampung—returning to one's home town—is common among urban Malaysians. City dwellers head home for Hari Raya Aidilfitri and at other important festival times.

Sending Hari Raya cards is a tradition begun after Independence. Today, electronic greeting cards are becoming popular.

Three generations celebrate Hari Raya Aidilfitri. As a sign of respect to their elders, youngsters kneel before them to kiss their hands and ask for forgiveness for any wrongdoings during the year. To mark the special day, new clothes are worn.

at the mosque but it is now becoming common to find special payment counters set up at public places like shopping centres. Prophet Muhammad prohibited Muslims from fasting on Hari Raya Aidilfitri and instead they were instructed to partake of the cheer and goodwill of the occasion with their families and neighbours.

One tradition taken seriously, particularly by the Malay community, is that of asking forgiveness. In conjunction with this feast day, Muslims ask each other's forgiveness for any act or utterance which may have offended another. '*Maaf zahir batin*', the wording in Hari Raya cards, means 'heartfelt request for forgiveness'. Children usually take the hands of elders and kiss them to ask for forgiveness.

On the morning of Hari Raya Aidilfitri, Muslims perform a special prayer at the mosque. Next, they often visit the graves of deceased family members to pay their respects and to remember ancestors on this day of celebration. This reflects the Muslim belief in the next life. In smaller towns and villages, some Muslims get together with other families to recite the *takbir* (glorification of Allah) on the night of Hari Raya Puasa by moving in groups from house to house.

Hari Raya Aidiladha

Hari Raya Aidiladha, or Hari Raya Haji, is the feast day that marks the sacrifice of the hajj pilgrimage. This festival is celebrated with somewhat less excitement than Hari Raya Puasa. For one, it is a one-day public holiday in most states except in the states of Kelantan, Terengganu, Kedah and Perak, which allocate two days for it.

This festival is more vigorously celebrated in the east coast states of Peninsular Malaysia, which tend to have a more religious orientation. Known also as Hari Raya Korban (Festival of Sacrifice), it commemorates Prophet Ibrahim's unquestioning obedience to Allah in willingly sacrificing his son Isma'il. Satisfied with Ibrahim's implicit faith, Allah ordered him to sacrifice a ram instead.

Although a variety of hoofed animals can be sacrificed, Muslims in Malaysia usually slaughter either

goats or cows. The meat of the slaughtered animals is then given away to the poor of the Muslim community in the area.

The slaughter of sacrificial animals is usually performed at a suitable location by villagers, or in an urban area by members of the community who have contributed to the purchasing of the animals to be slaughtered. Some farms now even specialize in providing animals for slaughter on this feast day. A more recent phenomenon is the importation of camels for slaughter at Hari Raya Haji. Although other livestock animals, including camels, may be slaughtered for this purpose, the fact that they are not native to Malaysia meant that, in the past, camel meat was never eaten by Malays. This new development may be due to a renewed interest in wider Arab-Islamic culture.

Cows, goats and even camels are sacrificed at Hari Raya Haji and the meat distributed to the needy.

Israk Mikraj

This is a celebration of the Day of Ascension which falls on the 27th of Rejab in the Islamic calendar. Muslims believe that on this day Prophet Muhammad was miraculously taken on a journey throughout the night to heaven and received the instruction that Muslims must perform five daily prayers.

Celebrating this festival is a fairly recent phenomenon and celebrations involve holding *ceramah* (lectures) on relevant religious topics in mosques either on the day itself or on the following weekend. Israk Mikraj is a public holiday in the states of Kedah, Negeri Sembilan and Perlis.

In commemoration of the Day of Ascension, lectures are held in mosques.

Nuzul al-Qur'an

While in retreat on Mount Hira, the Prophet was awakened one night by the angel Jibril. The angel embraced the Prophet and commanded him to read. The unlettered Prophet explained that he could not read. Upon the angel's insistence, the Prophet reluctantly asked what he was to read. The angel said, 'Read in the name of your Lord'. He then read the rest of what forms the *sura al-'Alaq (Q. 96)*, the first *sura* to be revealed.

To commemorate this first revelation, Muslims celebrate Nuzul al-Qur'an on the 17th day of Ramadhan. In most West Malaysian states it is a public holiday.

The winner of the Wilayah Tilawah al-Qur'an 2004 competition reading the Qur'an on Nuzul al-Qur'an, Masjid Negara, October 2004.

Mosques

The Malay word masjid *(mosque) comes from Arabic and literally means 'the place for prostration'. Universally, mosques have large prayer halls with separate prayer areas for women and separate ablutionaries. In some mosques, a courtyard with a fountain or pool serves as the ablutionary. While the traditional Malay mosque resembled the Malay house and was adapted to the local climate, some contemporary modern mosques have air-conditioned prayer halls. Mosques in Malaysia have evolved into various styles over the centuries.*

To prevent damage from floodwaters and a disintegrating riverbank, Masjid Kampung Laut, the oldest surviving wooden mosque in Malaysia, was moved from Kampung Laut to Nilam Puri, Kelantan in 1968.

The mosque as a building

Mosques designed during the early days of Islamic propagation were very simple and domestic. The Prophet's Mosque in Medina, Masjid Nabawi, consisted of a group of domestic-scale buildings with a courtyard, prayer hall and adjoining quarters for Prophet Muhammad's family. The trend of Grand mosque designs can be traced back to the third Caliph, Umar.

Though mosques vary in size, the smallest mosque must be able to accommodate worshippers for the five daily prayers and at least 40 congregants for Friday prayer, according to the Shafii School. In its simplest form, a mosque is a building erected around the single horizontal axis, the *kiblat* (direction of prayer), which passes invisibly down the middle of the floor, issuing from the frontmost wall. Ultimately the axis terminates at the Kaabah in Mecca. Reduced to its essentials, a mosque is no more than a wall at right angle to the *kiblat* axis.

Not all mosques in the Malay Archipelago have minarets, which traditionally

The Federal Territory Mosque, Kuala Lumpur

➊ The entrance
The entrance to the mosque marks the transition between the 'impure' street and the 'pure' mosque precinct. At this barrier the congregants remove their footwear.

The main entrance is the focal point of the façade, worthy of the house of God. Men and women usually have separate entrances.

The *iwan* (porch) is a form developed by the Persians and is found in mosques in Iran, Central Asia and throughout the Indian subcontinent. It is usually located at the main entrance of the mosque and at the courtyard sanctuary, where four *iwan* face each other.

➋ Ablutionary (tempat berwuduk)
Ablutionaries are usually located near the entrance so that those who have taken their ablutions can walk barefoot to the prayer hall without dirtying their feet. Ablutionaries may be taps, fountains or pools. Women have separate ablutionary facilities.

➌ Prayer hall
The prayer hall is the site of congregation. It is the most sacred space in the mosque, containing the dome and the *mihrab* (prayer niche). It may also comprise a courtyard which is open to the sky.

The prayer hall is preferably rectangular, with the longer side facing the *kiblat*, as worshippers pray in *saf* (rows) behind the imam (prayer leader). The nearer the row is to the imam, the more meritorious the prayer. Prayer halls for men have to be large to accommodate all the male worshippers on Fridays. The congregational Friday prayer is obligatory for Muslim men only, not women.

Women have their own separate prayer hall, usually on an upper floor. A separate ablutionary is also provided.

➍ The dome
It is common for the main dome not to be located in a central position over the prayer hall and instead it is usually near to the *kiblat* wall.

In the Islamic tradition, the dome is the cosmic symbol representing the vault of the heavens. The colours traditionally used on dome exteriors were sky blue, white, green, blue-green, turquoise, gold, or neutral-toned tile work, brickwork and plaster, or muted combinations of these colours.

➎ The courtyard
The courtyard is a feature taken from Middle Eastern mosques. Here the courtyard, was meant to cool the prayer hall and act as a source of light.

Tombs in the Royal Mausoleum at Kampung Langgar, Kota Bharu, Kelantan.

served as the place from which the *bilal* (muezzin) called the *azan* (call to prayer). In mosques without minarets, loudspeakers fixed on the roof of the mosque serve this purpose. Generally, the minarets of mosques in Malaysia now have loudspeakers to amplify the call of the *bilal*.

Many early mosques in Malaysia did not have domes as they were constructed using indigenous architectural styles and were therefore better adapted to the local climate. In recent years, mosque design in Malaysia has been influenced by styles from the Middle East and other Islamic countries. Examples include the Federal Territory Mosque and the Putra Mosque in Putrajaya, and Masjid Tengku Tengah

Zaharah, outside Kuala Terengganu. These modern mosques are air-conditioned.

The purpose of the mosque in Islam

The mosque is the nucleus of Muslim community life and the place of worship. Although architectural styles vary, the basic elements are the same the world over. The ablutionary is located immediately next to the entrance. The *mihrab* (prayer niche) is found on the *kiblat* (direction of prayer) wall to clearly indicate the direction of prayer (facing Mecca).

Mosques traditionally have cemeteries adjacent to their compounds. In Malaysia, some mosques include the mausoleums of royal families or statesmen.

Modern Malaysian mosques

Malaysian mosques have been designed in a variety of styles over the years. Islamic architecture with a distinct Middle Eastern style (domes and minarets) has become increasingly popular since the 1980s.

1950s and 1960s

Old State Mosque Sarawak (1968). Standing on the banks of the Sarawak River, this mosque with golden domes was built on the site of Masjid Besar (1852), an old wooden mosque, when there was a need for a larger mosque.

Masjid Negara (1965). This mosque was the first of the early post-independence mosques built in a modernist style. Its roof is modelled after a royal *payung* (umbrella) and its minaret after the royal spear worn as part of the sovereign's regalia.

1970s and early 1980s

Masjid Tun Abdul Aziz is situated in the centre of Petaling Jaya, Selangor. It was built in 1973 and was considered at the time to be modern as it was the only circular mosque in the world.

The Sabah State Mosque was built in 1976. This resplendent structure, with its majestic domes and gold inlay motifs, is a more traditional Malay design than others built during the same era.

Mid- to late 1980s

The design of the Melaka state mosque, Masjid Al-Azim, was based on designs of early Malay mosques and reflected the renewed interest in the 1980s in indigenous architecture.

The Sultan Salahuddin Abdul Aziz Shah Mosque in Shah Alam with its large dome, reminiscent of the Middle East, ushered in a new era in Malaysian mosque design.

1990s

Masjid Tengku Tengah Zaharah in Terengganu is beside the sea and appears to be floating on water. Its design echoes that of many old mosques in the Islamic world.

The futuristic modern style of Masjid Asy-Syakirin at the Petronas Twin Towers, in Kuala Lumpur, blends well with the architecture of the surrounding buildings.

21st century

The Putra Mosque was designed in the style of Persian mosques and also combines Malaysian and Arab-Islamic architecture. Its 116-metre-high minaret is reminiscent of the Sheikh Omar Mosque in Baghdad.

Masjid Bukhary in Alor Star, built by the Bukhary Foundation, shows a distinct Middle Eastern influence. Like many modern Malaysian mosques, it has modern amenities for the comfort of the worshippers.

In a unique lighting system, the chandelier reflects light from prisms in the main dome and thus illuminates the prayer hall.

The *mihrab* wall, which indicates the direction of prayer, is ornamented with calligraphy.

❻ The kiblat wall and mihrab
The *kiblat* is the direction pointing to the Kaabah that the faithful must face when praying. A mosque must have its *kiblat* wall perpendicular to the direction of the Kaabah.

The *kiblat* should be obvious to worshippers immediately upon entering the prayer hall. The *mihrab* (prayer niche) indicates the *kiblat* wall. The *mihrab* is also the station where the imam performs prayer in front of rows of worshippers who repeat his gestures.

❼ Library
Apart from worship, mosques are also used for religious and spiritual education. Therefore some mosques have a library.

❽ The minaret
The word minaret comes from an Arabic word meaning 'the place where fire burns' or 'the place where light shines'. The vertical dimension of the minaret represents the link between man and God, while the horizontal dimension represents the relationship between man and his environment.

❾ Classrooms
A school and a kindergarten may form part of the mosque complex.

The role of Islamic places of worship

Muslim places of worship are of several types. These include surau *(small prayer houses),* madrasah *(Islamic schools) and mosques. The mosque serves as a spiritual, educational, social and cultural centre, especially in villages. Even in urban areas, Muslim men are required to perform their Friday prayers, known as* sembahyang Jumaat *in Malay, at the mosque. Muslim men are also encouraged to go to the mosque or* surau *for the five daily prayers.*

The Tabung Haji Mosque in Kuala Lumpur was originally a *surau*. The upgrade to the status of a mosque means that Friday prayers are now performed there.

Individual worship

For individual prayer and worship a Muslim does not require any special place or furniture. What he/she requires is a clean space on the floor for the prayer to be performed. A prayer mat or a clean cloth is needed for kneeling and prostrating oneself on so that the forehead touches the ground.

A *madrasah* is a religious school that usually has a mosque or a *surau*.

However, congregational prayer is highly recommended for both men and women. For this purpose a larger space with appropriate amenities and facilities becomes a necessity. During Aidilfitri or Aidiladha prayers, it is common to have prayers in public courtyards and large open spaces or fields.

Surau and madrasah

Surau is a Malay word that can be defined as 'chapel' or 'small mosque'. The morphology of the word *surau* suggests that it was originally used to describe a sanctuary of pagan worship in the Malay-Indonesian Archipelago. The concept of a sanctuary remained, but it now refers to a purely Islamic place of worship. The *surau* was traditionally a small hut with separate prayer areas for men and women. The term is often used synonymously with *musolla*, a place for prayer in a building, often a partitioned room. *Surau* can be found in public buildings, and most shopping complexes in urban areas now have one for the convenience of Muslim shoppers. They are usually funded by the local community in which they are located.

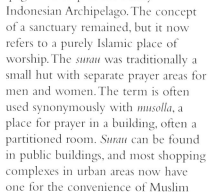
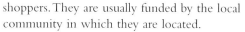

Surau are small community prayer halls or houses usually found in housing areas and in government offices.

A *madrasah* is an Islamic school that may also be used for prayers while the *surau* is a small prayer area, much smaller than the mosque or *madrasah* and not intended for Friday prayers. *Madrasah*, like the Madrasah Al-Masyhur in Penang, were important in the past as centres of Islamic education. Modern *madrasah* are private schools which teach regular subjects with additional religious subjects. As private religious schools *madrasah* generally subsist on the school fees paid by parents of pupils or the generosity of community members.

Mosques as a community focus

The mosque (*masjid*) is the designated place for the congregational Friday prayers, where men from the whole community come together.

In a traditional kampong, the mosque is usually built at a central location. Besides being a place for prayer and religious classes, the community mosque is also the place where religious rites such as death and marriage rites, *korban* (animal sacrifices for the poor), *zakat* (poor tax) payment and other rites are performed. It is common to have burial grounds in or next to the mosque compound and the tombs of local religious leaders may be found in front of or behind the mosque.

Developers of suburban housing areas have taken this central community role into consideration and have allowed for the construction of mosques within modern housing developments.

Occasionally, some places of worship originally designated as *surau*, such as those at the Lembaga Urusan Tabung Haji Building and the old Dewan Bahasa dan Pustaka Building in Kuala Lumpur, have been converted into mosques. Permission must be obtained from the relevant religious authorities for this change in status. This conversion from *surau to* mosque takes place to cater for the changing needs of Muslim communities as urban areas grow and populations move.

In Malaysia, each town or city traditionally had a central mosque known as the *masjid jamek* (congregation), which was the focal point for Friday prayers. Today, however, Muslims assemble in any one of the numerous mosques convenient to them.

There are occasions when members of the congregation request the imam to perform special prayers asking Allah to grant their wishes for the benefit of the community. This is called *sembahyang hajat* or *solat hajat*. If there is a severe drought, the community may assemble at the local mosque on the advice of the imam to perform the *sembahyang istisqa*, a special prayer to ask for rain.

The oldest existing wooden mosque in Malaysia is believed to be the Masjid Kampung Laut in Kelantan. The current structure is said to date back to the early 18th century CE.

The many roles of a mosque

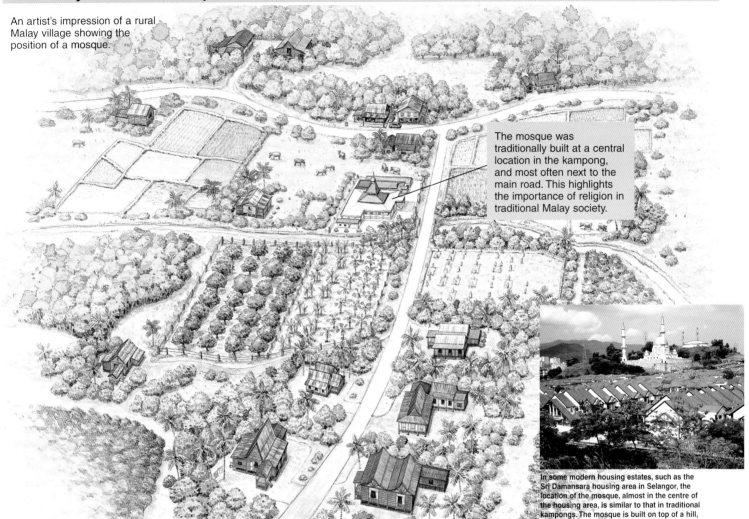

An artist's impression of a rural Malay village showing the position of a mosque.

The mosque was traditionally built at a central location in the kampong, and most often next to the main road. This highlights the importance of religion in traditional Malay society.

In some modern housing estates, such as the Sri Damansara housing area in Selangor, the location of the mosque, almost in the centre of the housing area, is similar to that in traditional kampongs. The mosque is built on top of a hill, and thus acts as a landmark.

The village mosque is primarily used for community worship.

The mosque as a house of prayer

Congregational prayer is valued highly in Islam as the religion emphasizes the sense of community (*ummah*). Worship is seen as a communal act. This is evident in such things as the fixed hours of *solat* or *sembahyang* (prayers) and a common prayer direction, facing the Kaabah in Mecca.

Muslims also perform their annual festival prayers at mosques, such as on Hari Raya Haji and Hari Raya Aidilfitri.

Modern-day mosques still function as educational centres for the community.

The mosque as an educational centre

Mosques traditionally also function as formal and informal educational centres. Some have primary schools attached to them. The Federal Territory Mosque in Kuala Lumpur has a library and a kindergarten.

In recent years, the mosque has become a centre for training pilgrims going to Mecca. A few weeks before the hajj (pilgrimage), major mosques in the country hold courses for pilgrims on the rites that need to be performed during the hajj.

The mosque as a community centre

Muslims, particularly those living in villages, converge at the mosque for social events such as *akad nikah* (marriage ceremonies) and community meetings. Occasionally, visiting dignitaries are asked to address the local community there. Important events such as Maal Hijrah (commemoration of the Prophet's emigration from Mecca to Medina) and Maulidur Rasul (the Prophet's birthday) are also celebrated at the mosque.

Some mosques have clinics, shops, libraries and schools attached to them to serve the needs of the community. Such clinics usually provide treatment based on Islamic principles of medicine, at a low cost. Shops sell articles catering to the religious needs of the community, such as *telekung* (prayer clothing for women), prayer caps for men, prayer beads, plaques and recordings of Qur'anic verses, books on the interpretation of the Qur'an and copies of the Qur'an. In the 1990s, the government started a socio-religious youth programme called *Rakan Masjid* (Friends of the Mosque) to involve urban youth in the activities of their local mosques.

An *akad nikah* (marriage solemnization) at a mosque.

People having a meal after prayers at a mosque.

Islam as the official religion of Malaysia

Since Independence in 1957, the official status of Islam in the Malaysian Federal Constitution is based on a single provision which states that 'Islam is the official religion of the Federation'. However, the legal system of the country is not completely governed by syariah or Islamic law. The provision is also not meant to interfere with the powers of the Malay Rulers as the traditional heads and guardians of Islam in their respective states, nor is it intended to restrict freedom of religion and worship, or to affect the lawful interests of non-Muslims. Nevertheless, as it is the official religion, certain privileges are accorded to Islam.

The impressive Putra Mosque stands as a firm symbol of Islam at Putrajaya (the futuristic administrative centre of the Federal Government of Malaysia).

Constitutional background

Islam is the official religion of Malaysia. The position of Islam as 'the religion of the Federation', as mentioned in Article 3 of the Federal Constitution, is by no means a new provision in the constitutional history of Malaysia. Islam was the official religion of the Malay states—and accorded this status in their respective constitutions, whether written or unwritten—ever since the 15th century CE, when the founder of the Melaka Sultanate converted to Islam.

The earliest written constitutions which name Islam as the state religion are the Constitution of the State of Johor (1895) and the Constitution of the State of Terengganu (1911). These constitutions also guaranteed freedom of religion.

When Islam was designated as the official religion by the Government, which was entrusted with reviewing the proposed constitution by the Reid Commission in 1956, it was made clear that such a provision should not restrict other religious faiths or affect the civil rights of non-Muslims.

The crescent moon in the Malaysian flag is the symbol of Islam as the official religion in Malaysia.

The scope of Article 3

As noted by the Malaysian Supreme Court in 1988, the framers of the independence (Merdeka) Constitution did not intend to have Islamic law applied to the entire justice system in the country. Only Muslims in the country come under the jurisdiction of the *syariah*, and this only where personal and family laws are concerned. Non-Muslims, on the other hand, are governed by civil law. The criminal justice system for the whole Federation is administered by a common penal code for both Muslims and non-Muslims.

Islam and the Malay Rulers

All matters pertaining to Islam and the *syariah* constitutionally fall within the purview of each individual state in the Malaysian federal system, except for the Federal Territories of Kuala Lumpur, Labuan and Putrajaya, which come under the Federal Government. Article 3 does not interfere with the position of each Malay Ruler as the head and guardian of Islam in his state. Thus, the Yang di-Pertuan Agong—the federal monarch elected every five years from among the nine Malay Rulers—is not the head of Islam for the whole country. While continuing to serve as the head of Islam in his own state, he is also the head of Islam in the states and territories that have no monarchs, namely, Melaka, Penang, Sabah, Sarawak and the Federal Territories of Kuala Lumpur, Labuan and Putrajaya.

In theory, each Malay Ruler, as the head of Islamic religion in his state, can act independently on religious matters. In practice, however, each state legislature has created the Majlis Agama Islam which is variously known as Islamic Religious Council to aid and advise their respective rulers on religious matters. These religious councils are concerned solely with the religious affairs of Muslims and do not have the mandate to intervene in any way with the affairs of other religious groups. To coordinate the administration of Islamic affairs,

Islam and royal ceremonies

Even though the ceremonies connected with the sultans, such as the installation, royal birthdays and funerary rites, still include age-old Malay royal customs (*adat*), the Islamic element is surmounting and dominant.

No royal ceremony is complete without a *doa* (supplication), even if the rest of the proceedings are still imbued with the observance of the Malay *adat*. The installation of a ruler still features the custom of ablution, known by the Malay term *bersiram*, and sitting-in-state on a five- or nine-tiered structure known as *panca persada*, but the sultan is not properly acclaimed as the ruler until he is blessed in the name of Allah.

In royal funerary rites, the remains of the ruler are borne to the royal mausoleum on a multi-tiered structure called a *raja diraja*, which literally means 'royal king', but he is not properly put to rest unless the *talkin*, a ritual involving a religious message, is read over his grave.

Similarly, while the term *puja umur*—blessing one's age—may sound unIslamic, the state usually marks the birthday of its sultan in a strictly Islamic fashion by giving thanks with a *doa selamat* (supplication of gratitude).

The installation of the Yang di-Pertuan Agong includes the ritual of kissing the Qur'an and the ceremonial kris.

The Malay Rulers and the Majlis Agama Islam

With the formation of the Federation of Malaya (succeeded later by Malaysia), the component Malay sultanates streamlined their religious infrastructure by having a religious council (the Majlis Agama Islam), *syariah* courts and the Mufti Department.

This religious council oversees Islamic policy matters in general such as promoting Islamic education

A meeting of the Conference of Rulers (the Majlis Raja-Raja) in Putrajaya, 2004.

and the administration of *zakat* (religious tax), while the *syariah* courts deal with marriage and divorce, legal altercations, disputes or property matters. The Mufti Department deals with issuing *fatwa* (Islamic religious rulings).

While bodies have been established to coordinate some of the affairs at the federal level, such as the Department of Islamic Development Malaysia (JAKIM) and the National Fatwa Council, especially with a view to solving social problems arising amongst the Muslims in the country, the states, under the individual sultans, assert state prerogative with regard to Islamic matters and maintain that the administration of Islamic law remains the right of each state. The character of the traditional sultanate as a Muslim polity is being preserved despite the need to liaise with other component states of the federation at the national level.

the Conference of Rulers, of which all nine Malay Rulers are members, established a National Council for Islamic Affairs on 17 October 1968.

This council was formed to advise and make recommendations to the Conference of Rulers, state governments and Islamic religious councils on matters concerning Islamic law or the administration of Islam and education.

However, this national council has no power over the position, rights, privileges and sovereignty of the ruler as the head of Islam in his state.

The implications of Islam as the official religion

There are certain privileges given to Islam, and undoubtedly the religion has great influence on Malaysian cultural, economic, social and political affairs. The basis of this influence is not only constitutional, but also historical as the tradition of the supremacy of Islam was handed down from the early Malay sultanates. However, the special status that Islam enjoys does not affect religious freedom for non-Muslims in the country.

Some articles written into the constitution protect this freedom. For instance, Article 11(2) of the constitution protects a person against payment of any tax the proceeds of which are specially allocated in whole or in part for the purposes of a religion other than his own. Moreover, the constitution does not permit any discrimination against citizens on the grounds of religion in the appointment to any public office or employment in government. This includes discrimination in the administration of any educational institution maintained by a public authority, and, in particular, the admission of pupils or students, and the payment of academic fees.

Article 12(1) of the constitution does not permit discrimination in the disbursement of financial aid for the maintenance or education of students in any public educational institution.

However, Article 153 gives the responsibility to the Yang di-Pertuan Agong to safeguard the special

position of the Malays and the natives of Sabah and Sarawak and the legitimate interests of other communities. This does not affect the constitutional and lawful rights enjoyed by other races.

Limits of religious freedom

The Federal Constitution protects freedom of religion. However, freedom of religion is not without some limits, imposed constitutionally, which aim to ensure public interest and religious harmony. Article 11 is intended to protect the religious beliefs of the people, but the fifth clause of that article clearly forbids any act, in the exercising of religious practice, which may lead to public disorder, affect public health or affect morality. This clause is normally interpreted as meaning that a person cannot go beyond what can customarily be regarded as professing and practising one's religion. Another agreed constitutional protection for Muslims is that state or federal law may control or restrict the propagation of any religious doctrine or belief other than Islam among Muslims.

Financial support

In Article 12(2) of the constitution, it is lawful for both the federal and state governments to establish, maintain and assist Islamic institutions and to provide, or assist in providing, instruction in Islam.

It was in pursuance of this constitutional provision, for example, under the Education Act 1961, that any school receiving grants from the government was required to provide Islamic religious instruction to Muslim pupils provided that the number of such pupils in that school was not fewer than 15. Under the new, more recent Education Act 1996, Islamic religious teaching must be provided if there are five or more Muslim students in such educational institutions. The government is in the process of developing a wider and improved Islamic curriculum in government schools for Muslim pupils as an alternative to the private religious schools.

These stamps were issued in 1997 to commemorate a century since the first Conference of Rulers (1897). At each conference, the nine Malay Rulers—of Kedah, Perlis, Negeri Sembilan, Perak, Selangor, Pahang, Johor, Terengganu and Kelantan—meet as heads of Islam of their respective states and deliberate on issues pertaining to Islam.

The crescent moon at the gable end of this building is an indicator that the owner is a Muslim.

The administration of Islam and Islamic law

The Malay Sultanates were largely governed by syariah, or Islamic law, and Malay customs. British administration changed the face of the legal system by curtailing the application of syariah in the Malay states and creating two separate systems. At Independence, the administration of Islam and Islamic law was governed by the Federal Constitution of Malaya (now Malaysia). The status of syariah courts has now been generally upgraded compared to their position before Independence.

Enactments of Islamic law from various states.

Islam and Islamic law in Malaysia

British treaties with the Malay Rulers provided that the advice of British administrators should be followed and, in accordance with such advice, the civil courts applying English common law were also established. The application of English law was later confirmed and expanded through legislation. The legal position of civil law continued after Malaysia's Independence in 1957.

In the Malaysian Federal Constitution, Article 3 proclaims Islam to be the official religion of the federation, while Article 4 states that the Constitution shall be the supreme law of the federation. Nevertheless, Islam and Islamic law hold a special place in the constitution. Attempts have been made to inculcate Islamic values in the general administration of the country. In the State List in the Federal Constitution, there are provisions concerning Islamic personal law matters that may be legislated exclusively by each state. Due to the territorial nature of each state's Islamic provisions, questions of enforceability and execution have been major issues. The problem is compounded by the dual legal system of the country. This has led to jurisdictional conflict between civil and *syariah* courts. In 1988 the constitution was amended, with the effect that civil courts have no jurisdiction in matters that fall within the exclusive jurisdiction of the *syariah* (Islamic law) courts. However, it appears that the power of the civil courts to hear cases which have some bearing on Islamic law is not totally eliminated. For example, in the cases of guardianship and interpretation of wills, especially when one of the parties involved is a non-Muslim.

The administration of Islam

The JAKIM building at Putrajaya. JAKIM was initially a secretariat responsible for ensuring that Islamic teachings were not influenced by deviant teachings.

JAKIM

While the Majlis Agama Islam (Religious Council) of each state is responsible for advising the sultans in overseeing developments and implementation of religious laws, the administration of Islam in the country falls under the Jabatan Kemajuan Islam (JAKIM—Department of Islamic Development Malaysia) which is a department in the Prime Minister's Office.

This department is responsible for policies regarding Islamic matters and enacting standardized laws and procedures. It also coordinates implementation in all states and oversees the administration of Islamic education in religious schools.

JAKIM was formed as a result of a decision of the Conference of Rulers, which in 1968 decided that there was a need for a body that would be responsible for the development of Islam in the country. Its first chairman was Tunku Abdul Rahman Putra, who was also the prime minister at the time.

A secretariat was then established to ensure that the sanctity and purity of Islamic teachings were preserved. This secretariat then became the Religious Division of the Prime Minister's Department, and was later again upgraded to form the Bahagian Hal-Ehwal Islam (Islamic Affairs Division) or BAHEIS. In January 1997, JAKIM was established as a separate department and took over the role previously played by BAHEIS.

The department's duties, include formulating policies for the advancement of Islamic affairs throughout the country, to aid in the drafting and streamlining of laws and regulations and to evaluate and coordinate the implementation of existing laws and administration. It is also responsible for acting as a centre of information on Islamic affairs and monitors Islamic affairs programmes implemented throughout the country.

Islamic officers

Mufti

A *mufti* is a scholar of *fiqh* (Islamic jurisprudence) who issues legal opinions, and is appointed by the sultan, or the Agong. One *mufti* is appointed for each state and for the federal territories. States and Federal Territories have their own *fatwa* committees. All *mufti* are members of the National Fatwa Council which is responsible for handling religious rulings on the national level.

Kadi/Syariah judges

A *kadi* (Hakim Syar'i) is a judge who decides disputes in the *syariah* courts. Each district of the state *syariah* court has one *kadi*. Judges of the *syariah* courts must have certain qualifications. The power to appoint *syariah* judges is vested in the rulers in the respective states. Methods of appointment vary in respect of the Federal Territories and states which have no ruler.

Imam

An imam is a religious officer appointed by the state government under the Jabatan Agama Islam. He leads prayer and conducts religious rites apart from fulfilling some administrative duties such as collecting *zakat* (poor tax) during Ramadhan.

The imam of Masjid Negara, Datuk Kamaruddin Zakaria, recites prayers for Maal Hijrah celebration, February 2005.

Administration of Islamic law

The law in Islam
In Islam, Allah is the supreme lawmaker and the *syariah* is His ordained code of conduct. One of the distinguishing features of Islam is that it offers detailed rules on all aspects of life and these precepts constitute a divine ordinance for human conduct. In certain matters there is, however, room for interpretation which creates different schools of laws.

The four Sunni schools of Islamic jurisprudence (*mazhab*) are the Hanafi, Maliki, Shafii and Hanbali schools, The dominant school in the Malay-Indonesian Archipelago is the Shafii School of jurisprudence and religious rulings are predominantly made in light of the interpretations of this school.

Syariah in the Malay states
The earliest evidence of an Islamic code of punishment in Malaysia comes from an archaeological discovery popularly known as the Terengganu Stone, which is dated 1303 CE. The inscription on the stone includes Islamic laws modified for use in the sultanate.

The Terengganu Stone (1303 CE) shows Islamic law was operating in the Malay Sultanate.

However, it was not until the Melaka Sultanate had become an Islamic state in the 15th century that Islam and its customs became significant in the Malay Peninsula. Although the details of the administration of Islamic law in Melaka have not been clearly established by historians, a comparative study of the Melaka Legal Digest, a manuscript written around 1450 CE, and the laws enforced in such states as Terengganu, Kelantan, Kedah and Perlis, suggests that these states modelled their legal system on the one adopted in Melaka. Johor also adopted aspects of the Ottoman Majalle at the turn of the 19th century.

After British intervention in several states from 1874, the Malay Rulers, who were formerly the supreme political heads of their respective states, were reduced to being guardians of Islam and Malay customs. The Malay Rulers still retain this function today. It was the colonial administration which largely shaped the precursor of the existing dual legal system.

After Merdeka
There is no specific legislation governing Islamic law in Malaysia as a whole, but each state has its own legislation. For example in the Federal Territories of Kuala Lumpur and Labuan it is the Administration of Islamic Law Enactment (Federal Territories) Act of 1993. In Sarawak, Islamic law is governed by the Majlis Islam Ordinance of 1978. Kelantan has the Kelantan Evidence Enactment of the Syariah Court 1991 for evidence law. Each state may enact additional laws related to specific aspects of Islamic law; the power to do so is invested in the respective legislative assemblies except for the Federal Territories. In criminal matters, the state is not allowed to create offences or impose punishments beyond what is authorized by Acts of Parliament.

The syariah courts
Syariah courts in Malaysia do not have criminal jurisdiction over certain Islamic criminal offences such as *hudud* or *qisas* (specific or fixed criminal offences or punishment stipulated in the Qur'an or Hadith). The jurisdiction of *syariah* courts in Malaysia is restricted to personal and family law. In Peninsular Malaysia, the *syariah* system consists of the court of the *kadi besar* (chief judge), the court of the *kadi* and a court of appeals made up of the Appeals Committee that hears *jenayah* (criminal) and *mal* (civil) appeals.

Hukum Kanun Melaka (Melaka Legal Digest), produced during the 15th century, was probably the first constitution which followed Islamic law.

In Sabah, under the Administration of Muslim Law Enactment 1977, *syariah* law was separated from customary law. Islamic matters now fall under the jurisdiction of the courts of the *kadi besar* and the *kadi*. Some of the Islamic laws were codified into the *Undang-Undang Mahkamah Adat Orang Islam* (Court Laws for Muslims). This code is meant to cover areas of personal and family law such as marriage, divorce and inheritance.

The Majlis Islam Ordinance of 1978 spells out the administration of Islamic law in Sarawak. *Syariah* courts in Sarawak have not only the jurisdiction to try cases specified in the Majlis Islam Ordinance but also in the *Undang-Undang Mahkamah Melayu Sarawak* (Laws of the Malay Courts of Sarawak). Thus the establishment of the *syariah* courts has brought Sabah and Sarawak into the general pattern practised in Peninsular Malaysia.

Syariah lawyers with their certificates of appointment.

In order to ensure justice in the *syariah* courts, parties can be represented by *peguam syarie* (syariah lawyers). Their admission and qualifications are governed by the respective state and federal laws. In 1986, the government agreed to restructure the *syariah* courts. They have now been reorganized into a three-tier hierarchy, namely the Syariah Subordinate Court, Syariah High Court and Syariah Appeal Court. The setting up of this hierarchy is a significant development providing a parallel system of *syariah* courts existing side-by-side with civil courts. The *syariah* court system is now completely separated from *mufti* and Islamic administration departments.

However, under the present administration of *syariah* law, there is no single common mechanism of appeal. There has been a call for the centralization of the *syariah* courts under the federal umbrella so that the implementation of Islamic law, which varies from state to state, will be uniform throughout the country. There is also a call for a specific body to govern the ethics of *peguam syarie*. The Federal Government agreed in 1996 to establish the Malaysian Department of Islamic Judiciary (JKSM). One of the main objectives is to improve and upgrade the administration of Islamic law throughout Malaysia.

Islamic law in the civil courts
The supremacy of the civil courts in the administration of any law, Islamic or otherwise, has been recognized in parliamentary enactments. Therefore, in the event of a conflict between the *kadi* court and the civil court, the civil court's ruling prevails except where the case in question is exclusively within the jurisdiction of the *syariah* courts.

Civil courts may hear cases involving conflicts between Muslim and non-Muslim parties. Disputes related to trusts created or operated by Muslims may be heard by the civil courts. Islamic laws concerning financial transactions are administered by the civil courts.

Nevertheless, the position of Islamic judges in the *syariah* court has been generally improved and is respected. These judges have undergone formal training in the modern administration of Islamic law at the International Islamic University Malaysia. The year-long diploma programme is part of the long-term process of upgrading the status of the *syariah* courts. There is a serious effort to unify the administration of Islamic law in the country.

The Federal Territory *syariah* court in Kuala Lumpur. Islamic law has yet to be standardized in all states.

Salient features of Islamic personal law in Malaysia

MARRIAGE	Non-Muslims cannot marry Muslims without first converting to Islam; men may marry up to four wives although all states require the consent of the Islamic courts before polygamy can be practised, without which polygamy is a criminal offence. Most states allow the first wife to object to the proposed polygamy.
DIVORCE	Unilateral divorce is available to men; women may apply to the *syariah* court for a divorce if the husband breaks the state nuptial oath, if the marriage is annulled on certain grounds or if the husband agrees to divorce with monetary consideration.
CUSTODY OF CHILDREN	The wife is presumed to be the best qualified to get custody over minors (under nine years), although this is subject to *syariah* court provisions and the overall welfare of the children. Children over nine may decide for themselves.
PERSONAL CONDUCT	The Islamic law in some states prohibits Muslims from certain kinds of employment; Muslims guilty of *zina* (adultery) or consumption of alcohol are not punished according to *hudud* (the Islamic penal code) but according to limited punishments determined by the state.
ADOPTED CHILDREN	Adopted children have no rights to the wealth or titles of their adoptive parents, although these may be bestowed as gifts or through a will (up to a maximum of one-third of the estate).

Islamic education

With the introduction of the National Education Policy, religious education was incorporated in the national curriculum both at primary and secondary school level. This resulted in a remarkable reduction in the enrolment of religious schools. Islamic subjects were incorporated into the national school curriculum. The First World Conference on Muslim Education in 1977 had a great impact on Islamic education in the Muslim world as a whole, and on the Malaysian education system in particular. The philosophy of the International Islamic University Malaysia is in line with the recommendations of this conference.

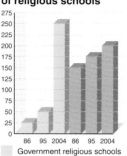
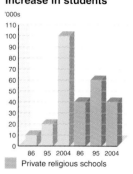

Increase in the number of religious schools

Increase in students '000s

☐ Government religious schools   ▨ Private religious schools

Source: Ministry of Education Malaysia, 2004

The graphs show the increase in religious schools between 1986 and 2004. Government religious schools have become increasingly popular. However, as seen on the above graph, the enrolment in private schools decreased when the Ministry of Education introduced a new policy in 2002 that meant private religious schools were no longer entitled to government funding.

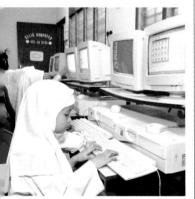

According to the Hadith (traditions) of Prophet Muhammad, education is compulsory for all Muslims.

Children in their school computer laboratory. The 1952 Education Ordinance eventually led to free, compulsory primary education for children of all races.

INSET: The earliest religious schools were called *pondok* (hut schools). This photograph shows the basic conditions they enjoyed.
BELOW: Modern religious schools have a curriculum similar to other schools, with an increased religious component.

Islamic education after Independence

With the introduction of the National Education Policy (1961) as recommended by the Razak Report in 1956, the Rahman Talib Report in 1960 and the Education Act 1961, all Islamic religious schools were placed within a new structure in the spirit of the National Education Policy (NEP), under which religious education was incorporated in the national curriculum both at primary and secondary school level. This new development adversely affected Islamic religious schools, resulting in a remarkable reduction in their enrolment. Aside from curriculum restructuring aimed at incorporating Islamic subjects into the national school curriculum, the policy of automatic promotion introduced by the NEP also contributed to the decline in the enrolment of Islamic religious schools.

Prior to this, Islamic religious schools had attracted a great number of pupils who had graduated from the Malay vernacular and English primary schools and who did not wish to pursue secondary school education for various reasons. Firstly, there were no Malay secondary schools. Secondly, pupils chose not to further their studies at the English secondary schools as these were usually located far from their homes, which caused transportation problems, and because of the financial burden such schooling posed.

In another development, some of the *madrasah*-type of religious schools in various states were ready to accept financial aid from the authorities due to financial problems, and this resulted in the acceptance of the new curriculum set by the state religious departments. For example, at primary level the new curriculum required the following subjects to be taught: *akidah* (faith), *ibadah* (rituals of worship), *akhlak* (ethics), *sirah al-nabawiy* (the life history of Prophet Muhammad), *qiraat al-Qur'an* (Qur'anic recitation) and *tulisan*

jawi (Jawi script). The curriculum excluded *balaghah* (rhetoric, eloquence), *mantiq* (logic), *tafsir* (exegesis) and *sarf* (grammar and syntax) which were part of the old curriculum.

At the secondary level, the curriculum was revised in accordance with the NEP. Malay replaced Arabic as the medium of instruction. Subjects such as English, Malay, mathematics, geography, history and general science were included in the curriculum in order to allow the students to sit for national examinations. Religious subjects and Arabic were maintained.

The upshot of the implementation of the NEP in the early 1960s resulted in the decline of Islamic religious schools because of reduced student enrolment. This trend continued for the subsequent two decades, until things took a new turn.

The impact of the Mecca Declaration

The Mecca Declaration on Islamic education in 1977, by a group of Muslim scholar-educationists at the First World Conference on Muslim Education, had a great impact on Islamic education across the Muslim World, and on the Malaysian education system in particular. The declaration stated that the greatest task confronting the *ummah* (Muslim community) in modern times was solving the problem of education, if there was to be a genuine revival of the *ummah*. The educational system had to be revamped and the division of Muslim education into an Islamic and a secular system had to be abolished. In order to function as an integrated part of Islamic ideology, the two systems had to be united. The emergent system needed to be infused with the spirit of Islam.

In response to this call, the Malaysian government took positive action in implementing the mission spelt out. Moreover, socio-political conditions during that time prompted the Malaysian government to reform the school curriculum. The Ministry of Education introduced a new integrated curriculum both at primary and secondary levels, known as Kurikulum Bersepadu Sekolah Rendah (Integrated Primary School Curriculum) (KBSR) and Kurikulum Bersepadu Sekolah Menengah (Integrated Secondary School Curriculum) (KBSM).

Islamic studies in Malaysian universities

Beside the Islamic courses and Islamic Studies programmes offered by the Department of Islamic Studies in University of Malaya and Islamic Faculty in Universiti Kebangsaan, public universities also offer Islamic courses.

In 1983 Islamic Civilization was introduced as a compulsory subject with the aim of providing students with a balanced exposure to Islamic civilization.

In 1995 the Ministry of Education introduced an amended form of the subject, Islamic Civilization and Asian Civilization. The implementation of it varies from university to university as seen below.

Implementation of the Islamic civilization course in universities

INSTITUTION	STATUS	INSTITUTION	STATUS
Universiti Kebangsaan Malaysia	Compulsory	Universiti Teknologi Mara	Compulsory
University of Malaya	Optional	Universiti Putra Malaysia	Compulsory
Universiti Sains Malaysia	Optional	Universiti Teknologi Malaysia	Optional

The religious component thus became part and parcel of the national school curriculum. A new concept was also introduced, the Sekolah Menengah Kebangsaan Agama (National Secondary Religious Schools) (SMKA).

With the increased awareness that surfaced amongst Malaysian Muslims towards Islamic education, there was greater demand for it.

The SMKA, the government religious schools, showed a 70 per cent increase in enrolment within ten years, accommodating over 25,000 pupils. The number of such schools increased by 90 per cent within the same period. The Sekolah Agama Rakyat (SAR) or private religious schools, also showed a significant increase: although in terms of schools, the increase was a mere 13 per cent; in terms of pupil population the increase was 48 per cent. This unprecedented new development prompted the government to take regulating the running of the system seriously. In 1984, LEPAI, an advisory body for Islamic religious education, was formed under the Conference of Rulers. Its task was to streamline the curriculum and to advise on the running of all private religious schools in the country.

The overwhelming demand for Islamic education from Muslim parents and the commitment from the authorities has given the system a new impetus. At least two historic events took place during this period. One was the establishment in Kuala Lumpur in 1983 of the International Islamic University Malaysia, an advocate of integrated system of education at tertiary level. The other was the promulgation of the National Education Philosophy (also emphasizing the importance of integrated development of education based on religious belief) adopted in 1987. These two events have undoubtedly become the cornerstone of Islamic education in Malaysia.

Education in the 21st century

A sincere and concerted effort has been made to streamline the Islamic education system in Malaysia so that it can be more accommodating, effective and competitive—on a par with national aspirations. A working committee has been set up at the national level to expedite the process of implementing a single, unified curriculum that caters for both the revealed knowledge and acquired knowledge components, as outlined in the concept of an integrated system.

The role of electronic media in education is not insignificant. Both government and non-governmental organizations and agencies are involved in providing educational programmes. The motivational programmes of Radio dan Televisyen Malaysia (RTM) and the Institute of Islamic Understanding Malaysia's (IKIM) radio programmes are provided by government agencies. Non-governmental agencies such as Saba Islamic Media produce videos and CDs of popular *nasyid* (Islamic songs), Muslim lectures from popular Muslim scholars and instructional discs on reciting the Qur'an, learning to pray and how to perform hajj.

Religious textbooks used in government schools.

The International Islamic University Malaysia

The International Islamic University Malaysia (IIUM) was founded in 1983 by the Malaysian Government. It is co-sponsored by the Organisation of the Islamic Conference (OIC) and several Muslim countries.

The university's board of governors includes representatives from sponsoring governments and organizations, including Malaysia as the host country, Bangladesh, the Maldives and Saudi Arabia.

The university is grounded upon an awareness of the perennial values of the teachings of the Qur'an and *sunnah*. It is committed to a rigorous, comprehensive approach to higher learning where knowledge is a trust from Allah to be utilized. The education provided at IIUM aims for the development of balanced integrated personalities. The uniqueness of the IIUM model, with its integrated curriculum, wide-ranging programmes and holistic system of higher education has earned the esteem of many renowned international scholars and leaders of the Muslim World.

The university philosophy was inspired partly by the recommendations of the First World Conference on Muslim Education in 1977. According to this philosophy knowledge shall be propagated in the spirit of *tauhid* (faith) and lead towards the recognition of Allah as the Absolute Creator and Master of mankind.

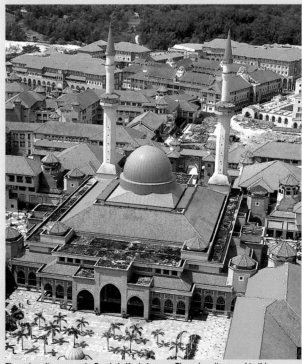

The university campus in Gombak, Kuala Lumpur. The university moved to this permanent site in 1996.

Rector of the International Islamic University Malaysia, Prof. Dr Mohd Kamal Hassan.

Students at the International Islamic University Malaysia come from all over the world.

Islamic financial institutions

Islamic financial institutions in Malaysia can be divided into traditional and modern. Traditional institutions were set up and supervised by the Islamic religious councils of each state and included bodies responsible for the collection of zakat *(poor tax),* wakaf *(donations) and* baitulmal *(public trust funds). Modern financial institutions include banks and development foundations. They have been established since the 1980s to cater to the increased demands for Islamic financial management and products. Islamic financial institutions are founded on the fundamental belief that interest-based lending is* haram *(prohibited).*

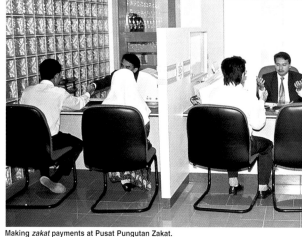

Making *zakat* payments at Pusat Pungutan Zakat.

Terms used in Islamic banking

Bai' Bithaman Ajil–Contract of exchange
A contract of exchange involving sale of goods on immediate delivery but against deferred payment settlement terms.

Ijarah–Leasing
A rental contract for goods or services. The rent and rental period must be pre-agreed between the parties.

Istisna'–Sale on order
A contract of exchange where the price is paid progressively in accordance with stages of delivery or completion. Commonly used for the purchase of new houses.

Murabahah–Cost plus sales
A contract of exchange where the profit margin on the sale is disclosed.

Musharakah–Joint venture
A joint venture contract where all parties contribute capital and management and share profits according to an agreed ratio. Losses are shared according to capital input.

Mudharabah–Trust financing
Agreement where one party provides 100 per cent of the capital and the other the management expertise. Profits are distributed according to pre-agreed proportions; losses are borne by the owner of the capital.

Ar-Rahnu–Borrowing
A borrowing arrangement where an asset is used as collateral.

Takaful–Islamic insurance
Islamic insurance involving a group of members who agree to jointly guarantee against any loss or damage suffered among them.

Wadiah–Safe custody
A safe custody contract for deposits of goods or valuables given to a custodian for safe-keeping.

Traditional Islamic financial institutions

The first Islamic Religious Council was set up in Kelantan in 1915, with the object of centralizing all administration of Islam under British rule.

Islamic religious councils have limited funds. This restricts their activities. Under these circumstances, traditional Islamic financial institutions have been unable to play a significant role in the Malaysian economy.

Over the years, the significance of *zakat* has increased through the privatization of its collection through the Pusat Pungutan Zakat (PPZ). The first initiative was taken by the Federal Territory of Kuala Lumpur, followed by the states of Penang, Selangor and Melaka. *Zakat* collection counters have also been set up in commercial banks.

Conventional banks, including well-known international names, also offer Islamic banking services, as can be seen from these leaflets offering credit card and home financing schemes.

Modern Islamic financial institutions

The Islamic resurgence in Malaysia in the late 1970s contributed significantly to the establishment of a number of Islamic financial institutions. These institutions provided an alternative mode of financial transaction for Muslims. Increasingly, non-Muslims are also using the services of such institutions.

The first modern Islamic financial institution set up in the country was the Lembaga Urusan Tabung Haji (Pilgrims Management and Fund Board). Established in 1962, its function is to mobilize the savings of Muslims intending to perform the hajj. These savings are invested in a manner deemed halal until individual savings accrue to an

amount sufficient to perform the hajj. As the hajj is one of the five pillars of Islam, Muslims in the past sold their assets in order to raise enough money for the pilgrimage. The Lembaga Urusan Tabung Haji has grown into a financial giant, with investments in real estate and various stocks. It also arranges flights to Saudi Arabia and oversees the welfare of pilgrims during the hajj.

The Islamic Economic Development Foundation of Malaysia (YPEIM) was initially set up by the government in 1976 as a trust that would collect voluntary contributions from the public for the advancement of Muslims. The institution was fairly inactive until its revamping in 1984, when it launched various new schemes. The investment activities of the foundation include real estate, stocks and equity participation in Islamic insurance.

The most significant contribution the foundation has made with respect to economic development has been in ameliorating the condition of the poor by providing interest-free loans. This lending scheme is

This branch of Maybank in Shah Alam caters solely for Islamic banking. Other banks also have special Islamic banking windows.

Islamic banking

Islamic banking is based on the principles of *syariah* (Islamic law) and the *sunnah* (traditions) of Prophet Muhammad which are applicable to financial, banking and business affairs. All banking transactions and investments must be in line with the requirements of the *syariah* and as such should not involve *riba* (interest). Therefore, Islamic banks do not offer loans in the sense of conventional banks; instead they offer *musharakah* (joint ventures) and *mudharabah* (trust financing). Unlike conventional banks, an Islamic bank must ensure that the project funded is not only feasible but also beneficial.

The idea of modern Islamic banking was introduced to the world at the Conference of Finance Ministers of Muslim countries in Jeddah in 1973. The Dubai Islamic Bank became the first ever Islamic bank to be launched in 1975. Subsequently, Islamic financial institutions were set up in other Muslim countries. The first Islamic bank in Malaysia was Bank Islam Malaysia Berhad, which was set up in 1983.

Islamic banks, like conventional banks, provide a variety of services, including electronic banking, consumer financing, trade financing and corporate financing. Bank Islam also offers its customers the convenience of an interest-free credit card.

In the 1980s Bank Islam was the first Malaysian bank to operate based on *syariah* principles.

Bank Muamalat was set up as a result of a bank merger exercise in the late 1990s using the assets and liabilities of the Islamic banking windows of three financial institutions.

administered under a trust called the Amanah Ikhtiar Malaysia (AIM), established in 1988.

Interest-free banking

Islamic banking was ushered into Malaysia by a report that proposed the setting up of a system that would be in sympathy with the principles of the *syariah* (Islamic law) and the prophetic *sunnah* (traditions). The first such bank, Bank Islam, was established in 1983 with an authorized capital of RM500 million, and a paid-up capital of RM80 million. Funds were contributed by the Islamic religious councils, the Lembaga Urusan Tabung Haji and the government. It grew rapidly. By 2004 it had more than 80 branches and a paid-up capital of RM563 million. It has become a model bank in the country, managing to compete successfully with

other financial institutions in terms of profits and services. The number of depositors exceeds 450,000, and includes non-Muslim Malaysians.

Bank Islam has created four wholly-owned subsidiaries: Unit Trust Management Bhd, BIMB Securities Bhd, Al-Ijarah Company (leasing) and the Al-Wakalah Nominees Company (portfolio management). Having achieved international recognition, Bank Islam has developed a complete portfolio of Islamic banking services.

The economic crisis in the late 1990s resulted in the merger of a number of smaller banks. As a result, the Islamic banking arms of Bank Bumiputra Malaysia Berhad, the Bank of Commerce and BBMB Kewangan Berhad were combined and a second Islamic bank, Bank Muamalat, was formed. Since March 1993, interest-free banking services have become available at conventional commercial banks throughout the country through 'Islamic windows'. This was seen as a positive step towards extending the scope of Islamic banking. The services provided are supervised by Bank Negara Malaysia, the Central Bank of Malaysia, to ensure that they do not contravene Islamic teachings.

Islamic insurance (takaful)

Syarikat Takaful Malaysia was the first Islamic insurance company in the country. It was set up in 1985 as a wholly-owned subsidiary of Bank Islam. This company provides a wide range of insurance services that include general and family insurance schemes. It proved to be so popular with Malaysians that towards the end of 1994, a second Islamic insurance company called Takaful Nasional, a subsidiary of the Malaysian National Insurance established in 1972, was set up. In 2004, a new Islamic insurance company called Takaful Ikhlas was established.

Other financial services

An Islamic unit trust was established in 1993 by the then Arab-Malaysian Bank. Later in the same year, the Asia Unit Trust company introduced an Islamic unit trust that enabled Muslims to participate actively in unit trusts in an Islamic way. A number of other unit trusts have since been set up to cater to the demands of religiously conscious Muslims.

By 2004 Takaful Nasional had opened offices throughout the country, catering to the needs of Malaysia's population, both Muslim and non-Muslim.

The headquarters of the Lembaga Urusan Tabung Haji (Pilgrims Management and Fund Board) in Kuala Lumpur.

A sample of a Takaful Nasional contract certificate.

Following the success of Islamic-based insurance, a second Islamic insurance company, Takaful Nasional, was set up in the mid-1990s. Islamic financial institutions in Malaysia have proven to be successful and stable.

Dakwah organizations

The term dakwah *denotes Islamic missionary activity and has only come into use in recent decades. In the past, the term* tabligh *(preaching) was used. Every Muslim is considered a* da'i *or missionary. Organized* dakwah *movements in Malaysia can be traced back to 1960 when Tunku Abdul Rahman Putra, the first prime minister, founded the Pertubuhan Kebajikan Islam Malaysia (PERKIM)—Muslim Welfare Organization Malaysia—which propagates Islam in non-coercive ways. Subsequently, several other* dakwah *organizations have been established.*

The first Prime Minister, Tunku Abdul Rahman Putra (centre), at PERKIM's Annual General Meeting in 1978. He was a founding father of the organization.

The PERKIM building in Jalan Ipoh, Kuala Lumpur. PERKIM was the first registered *dakwah* organization in the country.

The history of dakwah in Malaysia

Until comparatively recent times, *dakwah* (propagation) activities were simply carried out by religious leaders, Islamic scholars and teachers at Islamic schools. This was probably a continuation of the tradition of the early Arab and Indian-Muslim missionaries who introduced Islam to the local people through interaction with them. However, with the bureaucratization of Islam, *dakwah* became one of the functions of the state religious councils.

PERKIM

Following Independence in 1957, *dakwah* activities started gaining momentum, particularly with the setting up in 1960 of PERKIM, a nationwide organization which propagates Islam to interested non-Muslim Malaysians in non-coercive ways. The organization's

founder was Tunku Abdul Rahman Putra. Co-founders of this organization were prominent Malaysians including Tan Sri Mubin Sheppard, Haji Ibrahim Ma and Tan Sri S. O. K. Ubaidullah. The organization's multi-ethnic character was evident from the very beginning. Tunku Abdul Rahman Putra's emphasis on multi-ethnic cooperation and understanding created the desired impression that Islam was not a religion meant only for Malays.

To increase the understanding of Islam among new converts, PERKIM carries out several activities: providing Islamic education, arranging for accommodation and aiding new converts who face problems as a result of conversion. While some of its activities are supported by the government, most are financed by funds raised by the organization itself, through appeals for funds to corporations and individuals during the fasting month. More recently, the organization has been involved in the rehabilitation of Muslim refugees from Cambodia.

RISEAP

In 1980, PERKIM and the Muslim World League organized a conference on *dakwah* in Kuala Lumpur. This conference led to the formation of RISEAP (Regional Islamic Dakwah Council for Southeast Asia and the Pacific) in November 1980. The conference was attended by various Muslim organizations in the region: Australia, Brunei, Fiji, Hong Kong, Indonesia, Japan, Korea, Malaysia, Maldives, Myanmar, New Caledonia, New Zealand, Philippines, Singapore, Sri Lanka, Taiwan and Thailand. Many of these organizations have since joined RISEAP, which meets every two years.

RISEAP's first Chairman was the late Tunku Abdul Rahman, the first Prime Minister of Malaysia. The council's secretariat is in Kuala Lumpur.

RISEAP seeks to promote international Muslim unity in the sprit of brotherhood for the advancement of Islam. In particular, RISEAP aims to foster cooperation and closer relationships between Muslim organizations in the region and to coordinate efforts to create an efficient and unified Islamic movement. RISEAP promotes research into

---

PERKIM activities

In 1962, PERKIM set up the Institut Dakwah Islamiah PERKIM (IDIP) (PERKIM Institute for the Propagation of the Islamic Faith) with the aim of training converts and non-Malay Muslim youths as religious teachers and *da'i* (Muslim missionaries). PERKIM also organizes lectures and discourses about Islam for non-Muslims.

In 1975, PERKIM first set up a secretariat with the aim of providing assistance to refugees from Indochina. Since then, PERKIM has also assisted refugees from Bosnia-Herzegovina and other parts of the world.

One of its main activities is the propagation of the Islamic faith. To this end, PERKIM organizes religious education classes for converts. Apart from this, PERKIM also provides general welfare services for converts, and has set up a special fund for converts in need of financial aid.

A conversion ceremony organized by PERKIM, held at the house of the Saudi ambassador in the early 1980s.

Islam: *DAKWAH ORGANIZATIONS*

the problems affecting Southeast Asian Muslims with a view to taking appropriate corrective measures, and has established charitable trusts to collect, invest and distribute funds to support activities in the region. RISEAP has conducted many training courses in Malaysia for Muslim workers and youth leaders from Muslim minority communities in Southeast Asia and the Pacific islands.

YADIM

A major government-sponsored *dakwah* organization is YADIM (Yayasan Dakwah Islamiah Malaysia, the Islamic Dakwah Foundation of Malaysia). Founded in 1974, YADIM focuses on coordinating the *dakwah* activities of various organizations across the country. It also provides financial aid and other assistance to *dakwah* organizations in Malaysia.

YADIM's mission includes the creation of a positive image for Islam so that more people will appreciate Islam. It also seeks to involve young people in *dakwah* activities, and to produce skilled, knowledgable and wise propagators of the religion. To this end, YADIM organizes various programmes.

ABIM

The Muslim Youth Movement of Malaysia, better known by its Malay acronym, ABIM (Angkatan Belia Islam Malaysia) was founded in 1971 by student activists from Universiti Malaya. Its mission is to be a multi-dimensional non-political movement with the objective of realizing Islamic aspirations based on the principles of moderation and non-violence. It has established kindergartens and schools throughout Malaysia and has been active in social work and community service both in Malaysia and overseas. It also participates in inter-religious and inter-civilizational dialogues.

JIM

Jamaah Islah Malaysia (JIM) was officially registered as a society with the Registrar of Societies in 1990 with the aim of fulfilling the modern requirements of *dakwah*. The movement was born out of a conviction that the principles of Islam have been misconstrued by some people. JIM believes in promoting Islamic ideals and stresses on Islamic principles, professionalism and universalism.

The activities of Jamaah Islah Malaysia (JIM) focus on dispelling misconceptions about Islam within the Muslim community itself.

MACMA

The Malaysian Chinese Muslim Association (MACMA) was established in 1992 with branches and representatives in all states in Malaysia. MACMA's mission is to effectively cater to the welfare of Chinese Muslims both materially and spiritually, and to communicate with the predominantly non-Muslim Malaysian Chinese population. The association holds regular classes on Islam as well as discussions and gatherings to bring its members together, and publishes a bi-annual bulletin.

Persatuan Al-Hunafa

Persatuan Al-Hunafa (Al-Hunafa Association), located in Selangor, is another Chinese Muslim based organization which was registered in 1983. It represents the interests of its members, renders assistance to them in times of need and provides them with religious instruction and guidance including the provision and distribution of Islamic literature—all with the approval of the Jabatan Agama Islam (Islamic Religious Department).

HIKMAH

Harakah Islamiah (HIKMAH), formerly known as BINA (Angkatan Nahdatul Islam Bersatu), was registered in Sarawak in September 1993. It is a non-governmental organization that organizes programmes and activities for its members and Muslims in Sarawak. Together with PERKIM, HIKMAH organizes various programmes for newly converted Muslims, provides free medical check-ups to the community and operates child-care centres and pre-schools.

USIA

The United Sabah Islamic Association (USIA) was established in 1969 after a congress at which three Islamic associations in Sabah—Islamic Association of Putatan, Islamic Association of Tawau and Islamic Association of Sabah—agreed to merge into one. USIA was established to safeguard Muslim interests in Sabah, to improve the socio-economic status of Muslims in the state and to organize programmes for its members and others. In the 1970s, USIA participated in efforts to convert members of the indigenous communities of Sabah to Islam.

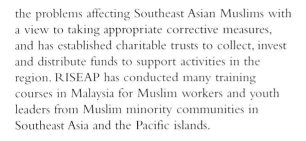
The Yayasan Dakwah Islamiah Malaysia building. Amongst other services, YADIM aims to benefit the *ummah* (Muslim society) by providing a number of information sources including books, journals, CDs and multimedia services.

Malaysian Chinese Muslim Association (MACMA) President Dato' Haji Mustapha Ma giving a talk at MACMA headquarters in Kuala Lumpur as part of the association's Programme for Women.

A community service project organized by BINA, the forerunner of HIKMAH: building a bus stop at Kampung Pinang, 40 kilometres from Kuching.

Prime Minister Dato' Seri Abdullah Ahmad Badawi with PERKIM President Pehin Sri Tan Sri Dr Haji Abdul Taib Mahmud (left) viewing photographs on display at the opening ceremony of the General Assembly of RISEAP held in Kuching, August 2004.

The headquarters of the United Sabah Islamic Association (USIA), Kota Kinabalu, Sabah.

Islamic organizations and the Muslim world

Regardless of the ethnic differences within it, the Muslim world is considered as one ummah (community), as emphasized in the Qur'an in Sura al-Anbiya verse 92, which states, 'Surely this ummah of yours is one community'. This verse clearly states that a single universal community is the basis of Islamic solidarity. The thoughts and actions of Muslims may differ according to time and place but the basis of Islamic solidarity still remains, as far as the concept of one ummah is concerned. Therefore, it is important for a Muslim nation to maintain ties with others through Islamic organizations.

The need for global Islamic organizations

No one can deny the internationally significant role of the Organisation of the Islamic Conference (OIC). However, the necessity or desirability of having a unified political entity for the *ummah* is a matter of debate in the Muslim world. It is important for Islamic organizations to forge meaningful relations and to help the Muslim world create a forum for Muslims to resolve conflicts and work for the formation of an Islamic bloc.

The Organisation of the Islamic Conference

The Organisation of the Islamic Conference is an inter-governmental organization established to pool all members' resources, combine their efforts and speak with one voice internationally to safeguard the interests and ensure the progress of Muslims the world over.

Structurally, the OIC is composed of three main bodies: the Conference of Heads of State and Government, the Conference of Foreign Ministers and the General Secretariat. The Conference of Heads of State and Government is the supreme authority that meets once every three years at the Islamic Summit to lay down the organization's policy. The Conference of Foreign Ministers meets once a year to examine the progress of the implementation of decisions taken at the Islamic Summit, while the General Secretariat is the main executive organ of the organization, responsible for implementing all decisions endorsed by the two higher bodies.

Malaysia has been strongly involved in the OIC since its inception, when the first Prime Minister of Malaysia, Tunku Abdul Rahman, was appointed as the first Secretary General (1971–73). In 2003, Malaysia played host to the organization's tenth summit. At that summit Malaysia was elected to chair the OIC for the next three years.

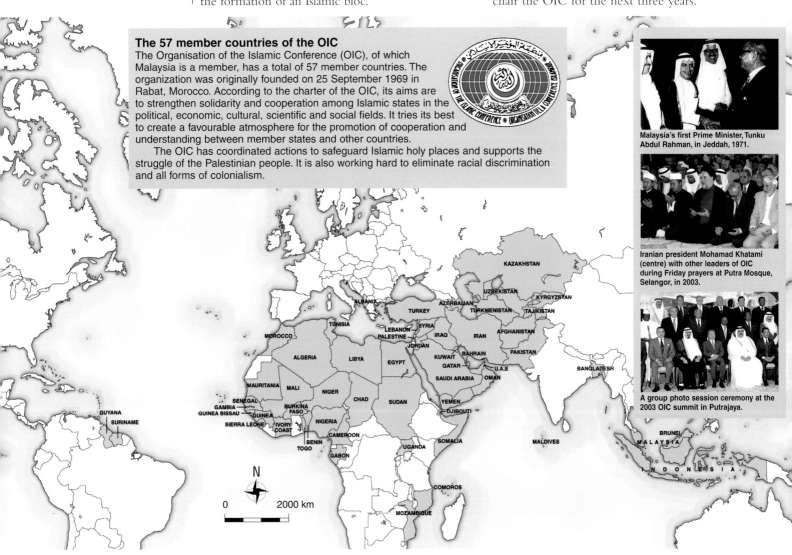

The 57 member countries of the OIC
The Organisation of the Islamic Conference (OIC), of which Malaysia is a member, has a total of 57 member countries. The organization was originally founded on 25 September 1969 in Rabat, Morocco. According to the charter of the OIC, its aims are to strengthen solidarity and cooperation among Islamic states in the political, economic, cultural, scientific and social fields. It tries its best to create a favourable atmosphere for the promotion of cooperation and understanding between member states and other countries.

The OIC has coordinated actions to safeguard Islamic holy places and supports the struggle of the Palestinian people. It is also working hard to eliminate racial discrimination and all forms of colonialism.

Malaysia's first Prime Minister, Tunku Abdul Rahman, in Jeddah, 1971.

Iranian president Mohamad Khatami (centre) with other leaders of OIC during Friday prayers at Putra Mosque, Selangor, in 2003.

A group photo session ceremony at the 2003 OIC summit in Putrajaya.

Prime Minister Dato' Seri Abdullah Ahmad Badawi with foreign delegates at the OIC Conference held at Putrajaya Convention Centre, Malaysia, 22 April 2004.

In Malaysia, matters related to the OIC are administered and supervised by the government while the Ministry of Foreign Affairs is responsible for implementing actions decided by the OIC.

Since the inception of the OIC, cooperation has been achieved in many areas. One such example is in information and communications, through the setting up of bodies that include the Standing Committee for Information and Cultural Affairs (COMIAC), the Islamic Conference of Information Ministers, the Islamic States Broadcasting Organization (ISBO) and the International Islamic News Agency (IINA).

The OIC has established institutions to cater for specific economic areas, among them the International Association of Islamic Banks (IAIB), the Islamic Development Bank (IDB), the Islamic Centre for the Development of Trade (ICDT), and the Islamic Chamber of Commerce and Industry. Legal instruments to help strengthen economic cooperation between OIC countries have also been adopted.

In the cultural and social fields, the OIC has been coordinating joint Islamic action among member states, such as preserving and promoting a common Islamic heritage.

This organization also strives to create a generation of Muslim youth who are conscious of Islamic values and the achievements of Islamic civilization.

The tenth OIC summit in Putrajaya

At the ninth OIC Summit, which was held in Doha, Qatar, in November 2000, Malaysia was chosen to host the tenth session.

The eight-day summit, which was held in Putrajaya in October 2003, was the largest gathering of Muslim leaders in three years, with the participation of the heads of state and governments from the 57 member countries of the OIC.

A special logo was designed for the summit, with a distinct pattern at its centre whose design is based on an arabesque, a pattern that is characteristic of Islamic art. It also represents the principal teachings of Islam which form the basis of the organization. The pattern is round to symbolize the global nature of the OIC.

The logo is predominantly blue, symbolizing truth, harmony, loyalty, sincerity and responsibility. It is complemented by green, a colour that suggests empathy and compassion.

The Institute of Islamic Understanding Malaysia (IKIM)

The Malaysian government established the Institute of Islamic Understanding Malaysia (IKIM) in 1992, a brainchild of the Prime Minister at that time, Dr Mahathir Mohamad. A founding member and current chairman Tan Sri Ahmad Sarji bin Abdul Hamid was appointed on 16 February 1992. IKIM is a research-based institute that strives to uplift the understanding of Islam amongst Muslims and non-Muslims by highlighting its universal values and all-encompassing principles. It was formed to correct the negative image of Islam. Among its aims are to explain that Islam is a religion that promotes peace and is based on tolerance and dynamism. It also assists in the development of a harmonious society, to provide a platform for Muslim and non-Muslim scholars to discuss or analyse issues of mutual benefit and to disseminate proper understanding of international issues that have a direct impact on Muslims.

The institute has published over 90 newsletters, journals, books and periodicals and has regular features in mainstream newspapers in Malay and English. IKIM has also organized various seminars and conferences, and provides research, training and consultancy services for the public.

IKIM aims to promote understanding of Islam globally. It has signed many memoranda of understanding with international and local bodies and collaborated with international organizations in organizing seminars, dialogues and conferences.

The Islamic Economic Development Foundation of Malaysia (YPEIM)

The Islamic Economic Development Foundation of Malaysia (Yayasan Pembangunan Ekonomi Islam Malaysia) (YPEIM) was set up in 1976.

It was later reorganized and relaunched by Tun Dr Mahathir Mohamad in July 1984. YPEIM has grown into an important Islamic institution, making an impact throughout Malaysia through its various socio-economic activities aimed at eradicating poverty within the Malay community.

To strengthen its fundamental economics, YPEIM ventures into opportunities and invests in strategic and profitable businesses sanctioned by its board of trustees and a special committee.

The activities of YPEIM include collection, receipt and administration of funds raised from among the Malaysian Muslim population and corporate bodies through various schemes, such as salary deduction, *amal jariah* (charitable work), national *wakaf* (donations) development scheme and corporate caring scheme. These funds are channelled either into core programmes or invested in strategic and profitable businesses. All profits made from these ventures are reinvested in other ventures, or used to fund the organization's core programmes.

The Institute of Islamic Understanding Malaysia (IKIM) is primarily concerned with research. It runs conferences on Islamic issues and produces publications.

IKIM's radio station, IKIM.fm, is the first of its kind in the country.

IKIM radio

IKIM has its own 24-hour radio station, IKIM.fm. Launched in 2001 to cater for the demands of the Islamic-oriented media, it was the first Islamic digital radio station in the country.

Programmes aired over this station usually have an overt religious message but are aimed at being educational and entertaining at the same time.

The YPEIM building in Kampung Attap, Kuala Lumpur.

Islamic influence on society

The influence of Islam on Malaysian society is evident in several ways, ranging from dakwah *activities in the 1970s to forms of attire and art. Islamic influence is evident in the media, school uniforms and in the provision of prayer rooms in offices and shopping complexes. The emphasis on halal principles in food preparation and consumption and the application of Islamic norms and practices in medical establishments, banks and* takaful *insurance also show Islam's influence on everyday life.*

Since the 1980s, a number of medical establishments that base their treatment methods on Islamic principles have been set up.

The establishment of the Islamic Arts Museum in Kuala Lumpur reflects the interest in Islamic culture among Malaysians.

The beginnings of Islamic influence

Since the coming of Islam to the Malay Archipelago, it has influenced many aspects of Malay life. The different times of the day are usually referred to in terms of prayer times; so, for example, a dinner invitation by a Muslim host would perhaps be 'after *maghrib*', meaning that the guests are expected to arrive after the evening prayer.

In modern times, Islam has influenced other spheres of Muslim life in Malaysia as well. In an effort to allow Muslim men to perform the Friday prayers, for example, offices have longer lunchtimes on Fridays. This was started after Independence. Similarly, states that were predominantly Malay opted to have their rest day on Friday instead of Sunday. Today, this is still the case in Terengganu, Kelantan and Kedah.

School uniforms—then and now

Islamic influence is also evident in school uniforms. Instead of pinafores and skirts, many Muslim and, to a lesser extent, non-Muslim schoolgirls wear the *baju kurung* (traditional Malay dress for women). An increasing number of Muslim schoolgirls also wear the *tudung* (headscarf) to cover their hair. Schoolboys often wear trousers instead of shorts. In some schools, Muslim schoolboys wear the *baju Melayu* (traditional Malay dress) and *songkok*, the traditional Malay velvet cap, on Fridays.

Above: Schoolgirls wearing pinafores in the 1980s. Even Muslim students commonly wore this uniform.

Below: It is now more common to see Muslim schoolgirls in *baju kurung* and *tudung* and Muslim schoolboys in long trousers.

Islam Hadhari

Prime Minister Dato' Seri Abdullah Ahmad Badawi formally launched a guidebook on Islam Hadhari in February 2005. Islam Hadhari is an approach that emphasizes the development of the *ummah* (Muslim community) consistent with the tenets of Islam. It incorporates 10 general principles:

- Faith and piety in Allah.
- A just and trustworthy government.
- A free and independent people.
- A vigorous pursuit and mastery of knowledge.
- A balanced and comprehensive economic development.
- A good quality of life for the people.
- Protection of the rights of minority groups and women.
- Cultural and moral integrity.
- Safeguarding of natural resources and the environment.
- Strong defence capabilities.

Since the 1970s, Islamic influence has become much more obvious in Malaysia. This can be seen from the broadcasting of the *azan* (call to prayer) on national television and radio to the presence of prayer rooms in public buildings. As a result of renewed Islamic awareness, more Muslim women in Malaysia now cover their hair with headscarves. Muslim girls are now prohibited from taking part in beauty contests because these are not in accordance with Islamic teachings.

Holistic conception of Islam

Beginning in the 1960s, the understanding of Islam among Malaysian Muslims underwent a subtle change. Previously, the emphasis had been on the ritualistic and personal aspects of the faith. Then emerged the consciousness of Islam as a complete way of life.

This new awareness led in the early 1980s, among other developments, to the establishment of the International Islamic University Malaysia, the establishment of interest-free banking and other financial services. Bank Islam Malaysia was the first bank to provide an alternative to the conventional banking system, while the *takaful* system provides an alternative system for insurance and related services; the *al-Rahnu* system, introduced later, provides an alternative to conventional pawn shops. These alternative systems have gained wide acceptance and have attracted Muslims and non-Muslims alike.

Dress

From the 1980s, the wearing of the *tudung* by Muslim women became increasingly popular. The availability of clothing in general suitable for Muslim women also increased. Islamic influence was seen in the trends in school uniforms. Today, few Muslim schoolgirls wear pinafores or skirts with short-sleeved blouses, as worn in the past. Even many non-Muslim schoolboys prefer to wear long trousers instead of shorts.

Since the 1990s, there have been a number of female presenters and performers on national television who wear the *tudung*. Even non-Muslim presenters wear the *baju kurung* on Fridays and Islamic festivals. This culture of wearing traditional

Malay dress on Fridays has even been adopted by non-Muslim women—some wear the *baju kurung* or *baju kebaya* to work.

Prayer rooms and kiblat indicators

Most hotels, shopping complexes, government offices and other public buildings have a prayer room (*surau*) where Muslims can perform their prayers. A *surau* or *wakaf* (small prayer room) are provided for the same purpose at rest areas along highways.

Hotel rooms often have indicators showing the *kiblat* (direction of prayer), while some private publishers have undertaken to provide hotels with copies of the Qur'an in its English translation. In most hotels, *sejadah* (prayer mats) are also available.

Medical establishments

Islamic influence is also evident in some clinics and medical centres. These often have Arabic or Malay names, suggesting an Islamic bias and they promote Islamic norms and practices. Female doctors, if possible, are present to attend to women patients, while the medications used should be halal. At births, some male doctors perform the recitation of the *azan* into the infant's ear on behalf of the father.

Halal restaurants and food

Since the 1980s, there has been an increased awareness regarding halal food (see 'Halal and haram'). Even international fast-food chains serve halal food at their outlets.

Most hotel restaurants also serve halal food, substituting pork with other types of meat. So, for example, a Western dish with bacon or ham is instead prepared using beef bacon or turkey ham.

The Prime Minister's Office in Putrajaya, with its domes, is Islamic in architecture.

Sausages and cold cuts are made using beef, chicken and turkey in place of pork.

Art and architecture

Islamic art forms avoid the representation of people and animals and focus on the glorification of Allah. Efforts have been made to create art that is in line with Islamic principles and is based on elements inspired from the calligraphy of the Qur'an and its related ornamentations (*al-zukhruf*). This interest in Islamic art is reflected in the establishment of the Islamic Arts Museum in Kuala Lumpur and the artistic efforts of such masters as Syed Ahmad Jamal.

An awareness of the need for alternatives in art and popular culture has led to the emergence of popular *nasyid* (devotional music) groups such as Raihan, Rabbani and others. Their songs show an unmistakable Arabic influence with local colouring. The messages in these songs indicate a return to the norms and values of Islam. *Nasyid* songs are even popular with some non-Muslims in Malaysia.

Islamic influence began to be seen in architecture from the 1980s. Examples include the design of the Dayabumi Complex in Kuala Lumpur, which was completed in the mid-1980s, the Institute of Islamic Understanding Malaysia (IKIM) complex, the International Institute of Islamic Thought and Civilization (ISTAC), the Kolej Perubatan Di Raja Perak (Royal College of Medicine Perak) and the architecture of the Prime Minister's Office in Putrajaya, the new administrative capital.

Islamic architecture is a major feature of: 1. The Mines Resort, Kuala Lumpur; 2. The International Institute of Islamic Thought and Civilization (ISTAC); and 3. Kolej Perubatan Di Raja Perak (Royal College of Medicine Perak).

Media and entertainment

The print media

Islamic influence is evident in newspapers and magazines. Newspapers publish articles dealing with various aspects of Islam on Fridays and Sundays, including questions and answers for guidance on a range of matters, and timetables which show the times of the five daily prayers.

Over the years, many magazines dealing with religious issues have been published in the Malay language. These range from magazines such as *Pengasuh* (Islamic Religious Council of Kelantan) published in the early decades of the 20th century to more recent publications such as *Dewan Agama dan Falsafah* (Forum on Religion and Philosophy).

Recently, a number of 'Islamic' Malay language fashion magazines have appeared. Such magazines, aimed at the large number of women who choose to wear Islamic styles of dress, are a fairly new phenomenon, although through the 1990s a number of religious magazines occasionally included Islamic fashion features. Even long-established Malay-language fashion magazines *Jelita* and *Wanita* have, over the same period, also occasionally featured Islamic attire, usually in conjunction with Islamic festivals such as Hari Raya Aidilfitri.

Islamic values on television

Since the 1980s there has been an increasing number of programmes with an Islamic content on national television. These programmes initially

This kind of headgear, a long shawl wrapped around the head, was popularized by the actress Wardina.

were mainly instructional. However, with an increased awareness of Islam as a civilization, a series of programmes on Islamic history and art have been broadcast.

One of the most popular programmes has been the *Jejak Rasul* (literally, 'In the Prophet's Footsteps') series on TV3. First screened in the mid-1990s, during the fasting month, this series traces the history of Islamic civilization and showcases historic Islamic sites, among them the holy cities in Saudi Arabia and the birthplaces of prophets, messengers and Islamic scholars. Later versions showed some sites that became important to Islamic civilization even after the death of Prophet Muhammad and his companions. Due to its success on television, the documentary series has also been successfully marketed on videotape.

Entertainment

Over the past decade, Malaysian celebrities have contributed to the popularity of Islamic-influenced clothing. The popular *nasyid* (devotional music) group Raihan was responsible for the popularity of a shirt modified from the traditional *baju* (tunic) of the *baju Melayu* that became known as '*baju Raihan*' while the actress Wardina Safiah Fadlullah is credited for popularizing the '*tudung Wardina*', a kind of scarf wrapped around the head in a style reminiscent of headgear worn by Middle Eastern women.

Members of Raihan wearing buttoned tunics, modelled on Malay traditional dress, which they have helped popularize.

Halal and haram

In Islam, activities and things can be classified in various ways. Activities may be obligatory (fardhu or wajib), desirable (mandub or sunat), permissible (mubah), undesirable (makruh) or prohibited (haram). Things are either permissible (halal) or prohibited (haram). As a result of the Islamic resurgence in the latter part of the 20th century, Muslims in Malaysia have become more sensitive to activities, foodstuffs and other substances that are not permissible in Islam. Where foodstuff is concerned, a rigorous process has been devised to ensure food certified as halal is genuinely so.

The concepts of halal and haram

There is some confusion among non-Muslims as to the concept of halal (permissible) and *haram* (prohibited) in Islam. Non-Muslims are often under the impression that these concepts refer exclusively to the classification of food items. In fact, these are classifications that can be applied to all human activities and items according to Islamic law. So, for example, under Islamic law, actions are classified as obligatory (*fardhu* and *wajib*), prohibited (*haram*), desirable (*mandub*), undesirable (*makruh*) or permissible (*mubah*).

Actions such as prayer, performing the hajj pilgrimage, giving *zakat* (poor tax) and fasting in Ramadhan are all obligatory once certain conditions have been met. The building of mosques and doing charitable work are considered desirable, while engaging in violence is prohibited. Smoking is an undesirable action, if not totally prohibited, while conducting business or trade is permissible.

Things, on the other hand, are only classified as either halal—permissible—or *haram*, in which case they are prohibited. There is one basic rule that can be applied for all things, which is that they are considered as halal unless there is evidence in the sources of Islamic law that forbids them. As an example, grapes are halal while wine is *haram*, because the Qur'an states that wine is *haram* and must not be consumed.

The National Fatwa Council

As all actions and items must be classified under Islamic law, there arose the need for a regulatory body for religious rulings or *fatwa*. The demand for a body of this nature was triggered by the Islamic resurgence in Malaysia which began in the 1970s. The result was the establishment in 1970, of a federal-level Fatwa Council of the Malaysian National Council for Islamic Affairs, which in turn comes under the Conference of Rulers. The function of the National Fatwa Council is to deliberate, decide on and deliver rulings with regard to issues affecting Islam and the Muslims.

Although its rulings are not binding for all the states of Malaysia, the National Fatwa Council has nevertheless managed to provide a commendable

Halal guides are useful for Muslims, especially those with more adventurous tastes.

guide for Malaysian Muslims to follow. As early as 1970, the council deliberated the issue of organ donation and transplantation. At the time, many Muslims were unclear as to whether these procedures were permissible or not under Islamic law. After considering the relevant judicial principles, the council then made the ruling that both procedures are permissible in Islam. Since this ruling was made, Muslims in Malaysia have donated or accepted organs such as kidneys and hearts with the understanding that organ donation and transplants are sanctioned by Islam. The underlying principle for this ruling was that such transplants are meant to save the lives of patients.

The National Fatwa Council is not only responsible for rulings regarding actions and procedures. It was the body responsible for the banning of an unregistered religious movement known as Darul Arqam, or Al-Arqam, in 1995. In this matter, the council decided that the movement was a deviant cult with teachings that contravened Islamic beliefs.

Halal Certification Process

Foodstuffs and medicines

The Islamic resurgence has brought about a much more overt concern about the dietary requirements of Muslims. It is not merely a question of avoiding pork, which is specifically prohibited in the Qur'an, or the slaughtering of animals in the manner prescribed by the religion. Rather, Malaysian Muslims have become aware of whether or not ingredients used in processed foods such as chocolates, biscuits and ice cream are permissible according to Islamic teachings.

In order to be classified as halal, food must not contain the meat or parts of animals forbidden by Islam, alcohol, or substances referred to as *najis* (filth) under Islamic law. For example pork, blood, carrion and intoxicants are substances that are considered as *najis*. Even the equipment used to prepare or process halal food must be free from items of non-halal animal origin or *najis*. In order to ensure a product remains halal, there must not be any mixing of halal and non-halal products during transportation, storage or display.

In the early 1980s, Malaysian Muslims were made aware that gelatine is of animal origin. Not only was it widely publicized that pig bones were often used in the making of gelatine, there also arose the question of whether other animals used for making this product had been slaughtered in the ritually correct manner. As a result, manufacturers of foods that contained gelatine switched to alternative substances. One of the most widely publicized uses was that of gelatine in ice cream. In many ice creams an alternative setting agent using plant-derived substances is now used. The advent of biotechnology has also called for the issuance of religious rulings on certain substances. For instance, with regard to genetically modified (GM) foods, the National Fatwa Council made a ruling in 1999 that GM foods that contain porcine-derived genes are not to be consumed by Muslims. This is in view of the availability of foods from non-porcine sources.

Yet another landmark consensus of the National Fatwa Council is the ruling on the use of vaccines against diseases including measles, tuberculosis, whooping cough, diphtheria, tetanus and polio. A ruling issued in 1989 made it permissible for Muslims to be given vaccines obtained from animal

sources but only if these are ritually 'pure'. Only if such vaccines are not available can vaccines from 'impure' sources be used. In 2002, a *fatwa* was issued stating that pilgrims wishing to perform the hajj should only be injected with bovine-derived meningococcal vaccine, not porcine-derived preparations.

With regard to medication, Muslims are becoming more aware of the use of permissible and non-permissible remedies. Capsules made from gelatine obtained from 'impure' sources are prohibited, as gelatine can be obtained from non-halal animals. Medication, too, should only contain permissible ingredients. The Ministry of Health has directed manufacturers to print the contents of pharmaceutical products and traditional medicine prominently on the packaging to enable Muslims to know whether or not these are permissible according to Islamic rule.

Halal and haram non-food items

The concept of halal or *haram* is not restricted to items that are meant to be taken internally. Ritual cleanliness is important to Muslims. As such, the use of any item that is derived from sources deemed ritually unclean or containing substances considered as *najis* is to be avoided. Shoe shops alert Muslim customers by labelling pigskin shoes as such and supermarkets indicate pig-bristle brushes as *tidak halal* (non-halal). In the 1990s, a protein remover and other products used for cleaning and maintaining contact lenses were found to use porcine-derived ingredients. These products are still on sale but are now clearly labelled they are not halal. As contact with pork requires ritual cleansing, pet food containing pork is usually clearly labelled. Some cosmetics companies assure Muslim customers that their products are ritually clean.

In the 1980s, a *fatwa* stated that perfumes with alcohol are permissible for use during prayer as the alcohol used in perfumes is not the same as that in alcoholic beverages.

Greater understanding of the halal concept has enhanced harmony among Muslims and non-Muslims in Malaysia. Eateries run by non-Muslims such as the above Chinese restaurant provide halal food.

Top: Items that have been certified halal can be consumed or used by Muslims without worry over ritual cleanliness.

Bottom: The non-halal section of a supermarket with a non-halal check-out counter, is often separate from other sections.

The certification process

Malaysia is a serious advocate of halal foods. A committee for the evaluation of food, drinks and goods used and consumed by Muslims was established under the then Islamic Affairs Division of the Prime Minister's Department in 1982. The committee was responsible for instilling awareness about the halal status of foodstuffs among producers, distributors and importers.

Items certified halal in Malaysia carry an official logo.

The government has made it mandatory for all meat imported into Malaysia to be halal. The Department of Islamic Development Malaysia (JAKIM) and Department of Veterinary Services Malaysia must certify the premises of origin of the product as halal. A team of two auditors visits the processing facility in the exporting country to consider the awarding of halal certification. In 1994, the Malaysian Government introduced voluntary halal certification of food products. This helps producers by enhancing consumers' confidence, providing an opportunity for export to the global halal market and promoting a competitive advantage over their competitors. The halal certification process begins with the sourcing of raw materials, and the inspection is carried out throughout the supply chain. Upon the awarding of the certificate, monitoring is done regularly by the Domestic Trade and Consumer Affairs Ministry and JAKIM to ensure compliance.

Modern methods of slaughter for mass consumption require different methods, yet the halal requirements must still be met.

More traditional slaughter at a market. Mass consumption and modern lifestyles make scenes such as this increasingly rare.

Restaurants and eateries have also begun displaying the halal logo to attract Muslim customers.

On 16 August 2004, Prime Minister Dato' Seri Abdullah Ahmad Badawi launched the Malaysian Standard General Guidelines (MS1500:2004) governing halal food production, preparation, handling and storage, the first such standard ever developed by a country at a national level. This development is in line with the government's aim to develop Malaysia as the regional hub for halal food products.

Islamic dress

When the Malays converted to Islam, there arose the need to define a manner of dress that adhered to the requirements of Islam. As a result, the clothing of both men and women was modified so that it covered the **aurat** *(the parts of the body that should not be exposed in public). Middle Eastern influences can be seen from the traditional* **kebaya** *to the popularity of the ankle-length Arab-style robe called* **jubah**. *In recent years, it has become a trend among Muslim women in Malaysia to wear a headscarf commonly called the* **tudung**.

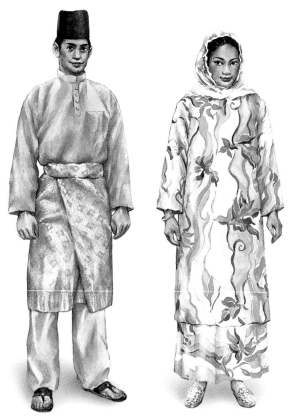

The Malays adapted their clothing to suit the requirements of Islam. The *baju Melayu* and *baju kurung* are meant to cover the *aurat*.

Malay wedding costumes

In Malaysia, the groom at a Muslim wedding is most often dressed in the traditional *baju Melayu* consisting of a pair of trousers and a tunic, complete with the *samping* (a cloth worn over the trousers) and *songkok* (the traditional velvet cap). The bride is most often dressed in a *baju kurung* or *baju kebaya*. Though strong colours are traditionally used for Malay costumes, shades of white are preferred nowadays; pastel colours are also popular.

Though considered a remnant of Hindu culture, the tradition of *bersanding*, or sitting-in-state, continues among Malays, with some modification, even after the Islamic resurgence of the 1970s as it is considered to be the highlight of the wedding. However, since then it has become common to find brides wearing the *tudung* (headscarf) under a veil of lace to cover their hair. The *bersanding* is considered so important that some brides who usually wear the *tudung* remove it just for this event in order that they may look their best in traditional Malay dress.

The wedding dress is often made of *songket*, the traditional woven cloth with gold thread. Satin and lace are also used. Even Muslim converts often wear variations of the traditional Malay dress and may also wear the *tudung*.

Very religious couples may opt for simpler costumes when getting married. Especially in the east coast states of Malaysia it is not unusual to find bridal couples wearing the *jubah* (Arab-style robe) for their wedding.

In Sabah and Sarawak, the bridegroom may wear a *jubah* (robe) and match it with a *songkok* wrapped with a piece of satin.

The Malay wedding ritual of the *bersanding* is still respected today though it is now common for brides to wear the *tudung*.

Islamic influence in traditional Malay dress

Malay clothing has retained some characteristics that can be traced to the days of the Melaka Sultanate. Islamic influence, shown in clothing that covers the *aurat*, is already mentioned in the Malay Annals. The *aurat* for men is the parts of the body between the navel and knee whereas the *aurat* for women, in the tradition of the Shafii School, is the whole body except the face and hands.

The Malay Annals attribute the invention of the *baju Melayu* to Temenggung Hassan. Sultan Muhammad Shah (reigned 1414–24 CE) of Melaka precisely outlined the *cara Melayu* or 'Malay style' of clothing and forbade Malays to wear what was known as the *cara Keling* (Kalingga style) or the Arab-Persian style known as *cara atas angin*. The latter was permitted only for prayers at the mosque, for those who had performed the hajj, for imams and *khatib* (the speaker who delivers the *khutbah* or sermon during the congregational Friday prayers). The 'Malay style', complete with the *tengkolok* or *destar* (headgear) and *baju* (tunic) that could not be opened all the way down at the front but was worn by slipping it over the head, is mentioned as having been worn by rulers when they went to the mosque to perform prayers. The *tengkolok*

was an integral part of the traditional Malay dress code. The complete outfit consisted of a *baju*, *samping* (a cloth worn over the trousers), *destar* and *ikat pinggang* (cummerbund).

When the Malays converted to Islam, they maintained their own style of dressing. The *serban* (turban) and *jubah* (Arab-style robe) were only worn at certain places and events, such as for the congregational prayers at the mosque, or were restricted to be worn by the imam or *kadi* (Islamic judge). These items of clothing were held in such high esteem that the sultan's *serban*, *jubah* and his prayer carpet were carried to the mosque in a ceremonial procession. The sultan dressed in the 'Malay style' when going from the palace to the mosque, where he would put on the *jubah* and *serban* before performing prayer.

Covering the aurat

Islamic influence in the clothing of Malay women can also be seen in that the clothing was meant to cover the *aurat*. The *Pustaka Selangor*, a historical text about the history of the state of Selangor, prescribed that Malay women should wear their sarongs long below the knees and that their *baju* should be long and wide at the bottom. In line with Islamic requirements, the material used should be thick so as not to show the shape of the body. Women at the time also used the *kain kelubung*, a piece of cloth that was worn to cover the hair and the upper part of the body. As for the men, their *baju* had to be long and a piece of cloth, the *kain samping*, was worn over the trousers to cover the lower parts of the body down to the knees. With regard to the dress code of women, in line with the requirements of the Shafii School, only clothing that covers the whole body, except for the face and the palms, is permissible. The *baju kurung* and *kebaya* are still popular among Malay women today, who wear it with a *tudung* (scarf) covering the head and chest but not the face. However, in search of a broader Muslim identity, many Malaysian Muslim women have adopted other styles of dress, including those influenced by clothing worn in other Muslim countries such as Iran and Turkey.

The jubah

The *jubah* is an ankle-length robe of Middle Eastern origin. In the Melaka empire, commoners were not permitted to wear this garment. Only the *ulamak* (religious scholar), imam and *kadi* (judge), or those who had performed the hajj were allowed to wear the *jubah*. The *jubah* worn by pilgrims who had performed the hajj was white, while the version worn by the *ulamak* and *imam* was black or grey in colour. It had a high collar and was buttoned down at the front, and was either worn with a *ketayap* (prayer cap) or a *serban*. Instead of wearing loose trousers under the *jubah*, as many Arabs do, Malay men usually wear their sarong. Initially, the *jubah* was a Middle Eastern import brought in from Mecca.

Many Malaysian women also wear the *jubah* over their *baju kurung*. This type of *jubah* is usually made of a dull-coloured plain cloth and was buttoned down in front and at the sleeves, so as not to expose

Muslim headgear

Selendang. Abandoning the heavy *kain kelubung*, which covered the head and the upper body, Malay women in the early 20th century opted for the thinner *selendang* to cover their hair. The *selendang* remains popular among Muslim women of the older generation.

Tudung. As Muslim women in Malaysia first became conscious of the Islamic requirements with regard to the female *aurat*, the *tudung* or scarf became increasingly popular. This kind of scarf, tied behind the head, is usually associated with 1970s fashion.

Tudung dakwah. This style of *tudung* was popular in the late 1970s and 1980s. It covers not only the hair but also the chest and consists of a square piece of cloth folded in half to form a triangle and then sewn to join the two sides together.

Tudung labuh. Also called the *mini-telekung*, this kind of headgear covers the entire upper body. This type of *tudung* is a part of the school uniform of some religious schools. Otherwise, it is often paired with a *jubah* (robe).

Tudung. In the late 1990s, a more relaxed style became popular. Muslim women opted for scarves of different colours and patterns. These were often flipped back over both shoulders or pinned down on one shoulder with a brooch.

Songkok. This velvet cap, said to have had its origins in the fez, is usually made of black velvet and is the most common headgear for Malay men.

Ketayap. Also called *kopiah,* it is of Middle Eastern origin and previously was mainly worn by pilgrims who had returned from the hajj.

Serban. This type of headgear actually consists of two separate pieces, a cap and a scarf, which is wrapped around the head.

More and more Muslim women in Malaysia are wearing the *tudung* (headscarf). *Tudung* styles have changed over the years.

As for men, wearing headgear has always been an integral part of the Malay dress code. The *baju Melayu* worn by Malay men would seem incomplete if not accompanied with the wearing of the songkok, a velvet cap said to be a version of the Turkish fez. Other types of headgear are also used such as the *ketayap* and the *serban*. The traditional *tengkolok* or *destar* is no longer commonly worn by Malay men except as part of wedding costumes or during traditional Malay martial arts or dance performances.

the arms. Nowadays, the *jubah* has become a popular garment among Muslims in Malaysia and is imported or made locally in many styles and colours. In the late 1990s, a type of garment known as the '*mini-jubah*' started to make an appearance. It consists of a pair of loose trousers worn under a knee-length or calf-length blouse instead of an ankle-length robe.

The sarong

In spite of all the new trends or innovations in Muslim dress, the traditional sarong, which is of Indian origin, is still widely used in Malay homes. Malay men normally use the sarong for the daily prayers, for informal dress at home and, together with the *baju Melayu*, for going to Friday prayers.

A Malay woman wearing a *jubah* and *tudung labuh*, while two of her daughters are wearing a kind of pantsuit commonly called a '*mini-jubah*'.

The *jubah* as worn by the iman pictured left, is a standard uniform for staff in a mosque. Many Muslims emulate them, mostly those returning from the hajj.

Indicators of development of the Muslim ummah in Malaysia

The level of development of a country is measured by using the conventional economic, social and human development indices. For Islamic countries, however, an additional index may be used to indicate the level of adherence to the basic tenets of Islam as well as the achievements which benefit the Muslim community (ummah). For Malaysia, an Islamic Development Index (IDI) achieves this objective.

The Five Pillars of Islam (rukun Islam)

Faith or belief in the Oneness of God and the finality of the prophethood of Muhammad

Establishment of the daily prayers	Concern for and almsgiving to the needy (*zakat*)	Self-purification through fasting	The pilgrimage to Mecca for those who are able

The observation of the Pillars of Islam

The application of the five pillars of Islam measures one's level of piety, which is highly subjective. Nonetheless, it is still possible to numerically measure relevant indicators that are directly related to the practice of three out of the five pillars, namely the obligation to perform five daily prayers, pay *zakat* and perform the pilgrimage by using relevant proxies.

Ummah Development Index

Essentially, the Islamic Development Index (IDI) represents an extension of the existing Development Composite Index (DCI) introduced by the government, comprising the Economic Development Index (EDI) and Social Development Index (SDI). Taken together, the DCI and IDI form an 'Ummah Development Index' (UDI) which provides a more comprehensive measurement on the level of progress achieved by Muslims in Malaysia. There are 11 indicators of the IDI that depict three major elements: the observation of the Islamic pillars, religious education and the development of Islamic finance and economics.

The development of Islamic economics

In terms of economic development, two sets of indicators are used. Firstly, information that denotes Muslim participation in the economy, and secondly data that points to the advancement of the Islamic financial system. For Muslims, it is crucially important to achieve a balance between worldly affairs and the preparation for the hereafter. In other words, Muslims must not only be able to perform their religious duties but must also be economically advanced and financially independent.

The participation of Muslims in the economy

The participation of Muslims in the economy can be measured in two ways, namely through their investments in Permodalan Nasional Berhad (PNB) and their involvement in the professional fields.

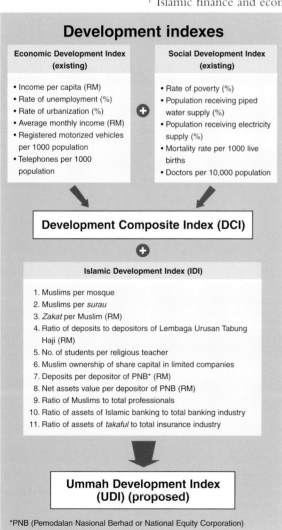

Development indexes

Economic Development Index (existing)
- Income per capita (RM)
- Rate of unemployment (%)
- Rate of urbanization (%)
- Average monthly income (RM)
- Registered motorized vehicles per 1000 population
- Telephones per 1000 population

Social Development Index (existing)
- Rate of poverty (%)
- Population receiving piped water supply (%)
- Population receiving electricity supply (%)
- Mortality rate per 1000 live births
- Doctors per 10,000 population

Development Composite Index (DCI)

Islamic Development Index (IDI)
1. Muslims per mosque
2. Muslims per *surau*
3. *Zakat* per Muslim (RM)
4. Ratio of deposits to depositors of Lembaga Urusan Tabung Haji (RM)
5. No. of students per religious teacher
6. Muslim ownership of share capital in limited companies
7. Deposits per depositor of PNB* (RM)
8. Net assets value per depositor of PNB (RM)
9. Ratio of Muslims to total professionals
10. Ratio of assets of Islamic banking to total banking industry
11. Ratio of assets of *takaful* to total insurance industry

Ummah Development Index (UDI) (proposed)

*PNB (Permodalan Nasional Berhad or National Equity Corporation)

The obligation to pay zakat

The payment of *zakat* signifies the economic and financial progress of Muslims. *Zakat* is the portion of a Muslim's earnings, profit or assets that is due to the less fortunate. The collection of *zakat* increases as the Muslims' economy improves. Nevertheless, it takes a strong conscience to perform *zakat* as, like the other pillars, it is self-regulatory in nature.

Since 1999 both the total *zakat* collected and *zakat* per Muslim have shown an average annual growth exceeding 10 per cent.

Beginning in 2005, the Government has agreed to extend a tax rebate of up to 2.5 per cent of total revenue of companies for *zakat*.

Collection of zakat in Malaysia

Zakat collection (RM million)

1998	1999	2000	2001	2002	2003	2004
198	191	255	302	312	408	473

Zakat per Muslim (RM)

1998	1999	2000	2001	2002	2003	2004
14.88	13.99	18.07	20.97	21.18	31.65	31.32

Source: Pusat Pungutan Zakat, 2004

The obligation to perform the pilgrimage

Muslims who are financially and physically capable are obliged to perform pilgrimage to Mecca. In this regard, deposits at Lembaga Urusan Tabung Haji (Pilgrims Management and Fund Board) are used as a proxy to indicate the ability of Muslims to perform the pilgrimage.

The total deposits have expanded relatively faster than the number of depositors. Average deposits, hence, rose to a record high of RM2392 in 2004 from RM1962 in 1998.

Measuring the ability of Malaysian Muslims to perform the pilgrimage

Year	No. of depositors	Total deposits (RM million)	Average deposit per depositor (RM)
1998	3,440,971	6753	1962
1999	3,708,283	7768	2094
2000	4,023,790	9128	2268
2001	4,328,942	9976	2304
2002	4,534,318	9525	2100
2003	4,718,888	11,287	2392
2004	4,906,917	12,085	2463

Source: Tabung Haji, 2004

RIGHT: Malaysian pilgrims make preparations at the Tabung Haji Complex in Kelana Jaya before their flight to Jeddah, January 2004.

Ownership of share capital of limited companies

In general, the economic success of Muslims (who form the majority of the Bumiputera community) is measured by their share ownership of limited companies. This has increased substantially from only 2 per cent in the early 1970s to a high of 20.6 per cent in 1995 before falling to 18.7 per cent in 2002 following the regional crises.

The adequacy of religious education in Malaysia

Religious education is particularly important for Muslims to support moral and spiritual development, something that is also crucial for the creation of a progressive *ummah* and nation.

Since 1998 the number of students and teachers have expanded steadily at between 5 and 9 per cent per annum, suggesting a greater tendency among parents to enrol their children at religious schools. An interesting point to note is the favourable student per teacher ratio for religious schools.

Number of religious schools, students and teachers in Malaysia

Year	No. of schools	No. of students	No. of teachers	Students per teachers
1998	249	99,368	5945	16.71
1999	250	105,642	6189	17.07
2000	227	129,560	7423	17.45
2001	231	128,566	7535	17.06
2002	327	123,494	7042	17.54

Source: JAKIM, 2002

The obligation to perform the daily prayers

Although it is non-obligatory for Muslims to perform prayers in mosques or *surau* (with the exception of Friday prayer), they are strongly encouraged to do so. The number of *surau* has grown faster than mosques, as *surau* are cheaper and easier to construct.

Places of worship in Malaysia and ratio of Muslims to places of worship

Year	No. of mosques	No. of surau	Muslims per mosques	Muslims per surau
1998	4443	13,629	2995.27	976.45
1999	4469	13,899	3049.27	980.44
2000	4476	14,748	3149.33	955.82
2001	4498	14,829	3203.16	971.60
2002	4594	15,518	3203.22	948.29
2003	5266	16,257	2636.06	854.52
2004	5492	17,113	2804.07	899.00

Source: IKIM, 2004

Investment in unit trusts

Bumiputera investment in Permodalan Nasional Berhad (PNB) represents a significant share of Muslims' participation in the economy.

Both the number of PNB investors as well as the net asset value (NAV) have expanded favourably by 2.4 per cent and 10.7 per cent respectively between 1998–2004. In 2004 it was also estimated that more than 50 per cent of Muslims in Malaysia had invested in unit trusts issued by PNB with NAV per investor exceeding RM5600.

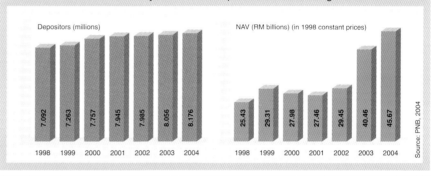

Source: PNB, 2004

The development of an Islamic financial system—Islamic banking and takaful (Islamic insurance)

The assets of Islamic banking and *takaful* both displayed phenomenal average growth of 23.7 per cent and 54 per cent respectively from 1998 until 2004. Within the period, the assets of the Islamic banking system and *takaful* accounted for 10.5 per cent and 5.6 per cent of the respective sectors' total assets.

These figures demonstrate that the Muslim community in Malaysia has achieved a high degree of progress.

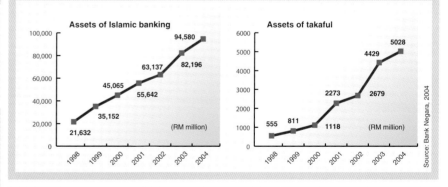

Source: Bank Negara, 2004

Muslim professionals

Muslim participation in professional areas such as law, accounting, architecture and medicine indirectly illustrates the level of education among Muslims as well as their standard of living. On average, the number of Muslim professionals increased by 9 per cent per annum between 1998 and 2002. In 2002 Muslims accounted for 37 per cent of the total number of professionals in the country.

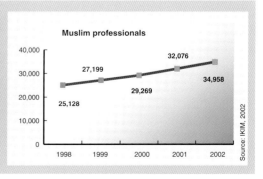

Source: IKIM, 2002

1. Kwan Yin Temple in Penang, which was built in the 19th century, acted as a focal point for the growing Chinese community, not only in Penang but also for Medan in Sumatra, southern Thailand and northern Malaya.

2. A child playing with a lantern on the street during the Chinese lantern festival. Lantern processions, often led by children, are a common sight during this festival which falls during the eighth lunar month each year.

3. The vigorous lion dance is usually performed during Chinese festivals to usher in good fortune and ward off evil spirits.

4. Buddhist devotees light oil lamps as a symbol of the light of wisdom defeating the darkness of ignorance.

5. Wesak Day celebrations, marking the birthday of Buddha, Melaka.

6. In Theravada Buddhism, Gautama Buddha is considered to be the 28th Buddha. The statues at the Mahindarama Temple in Penang represent the previous Buddhas.

BUDDHISM AND CHINESE RELIGIONS

Malaysia has a sizeable population of Buddhists from the Chinese, Sinhalese and Thai ethnic groups. Of these, the Chinese are by far the largest community. Small numbers of Chinese have lived in Malaysia for many centuries, but their communities swelled during the 19th century with immigration during the British colonial period. The Chinese were centred mainly in tin mining towns and other large settlements. Nowadays they are established all over Malaysia and have integrated with society at large.

Buddhism is usually seen as a gentle religion that does not actively seek converts. Devout Buddhists merely seek to enlighten those who already profess the religion and to guide them in leading a religious life. Both the main schools—Theravada and Mahayana—are followed in Malaysia. Each form has its own temples and associations. However, whenever there are important religious events or festivals, Buddhists of all traditions come together. A good example is the Joint Wesak Celebrations Committee where different Buddhist temples come together to organize the annual activity which celebrates the birth, enlightenment and passing away of Buddha.

'Pure' or fundamental Buddhists, Taoists and Confucianists are in the minority among the Chinese in Malaysia. Many may nominally be Buddhist or Taoist but they may recognize beliefs and practices across a range of Chinese religions and adopt aspects of a number of them in their religious life. Traditional Chinese values, many developed from the teachings of Confucius and Lao Zi, are widely accepted and influence daily life. In many temples, clan houses, guilds and dialect associations, which serve as local temples and focal points for various Chinese communities, statues related with Buddhism and Taoism are placed under the same roof. However, statistics from the 2000 Census indicate that around 20 per cent of the population, mainly Chinese, are Buddhist and a further 3 per cent follow Chinese religions including Confucianism and Taoism.

The practical, adaptable, generous and ancient character of Chinese religions has encouraged the emergence of new sects, such as I-Kuan Tao and De Jiao Hui (Moral Uplifting Society), which try to integrate the teachings of various religions. These sects, which do not appear in China anymore, still sustain their ministry in Malaysia. Rather than rejecting, many Chinese religious groups and worshippers honour the beliefs of other religions and declare 'all religions carry good deeds to people'. As a result, Chinese folk beliefs in Malaysia include beliefs in local guardian spirits which originated from traditional animism and mysticism, and the worship of sacred monks and spirits popular among the Thais. Chinese Malaysians have, historically, also elevated local heroes and leaders to patron saints and guardians.

Incense purifies the ritual space and is lit as an offering to the gods.

History of Buddhism in Malaysia

A large number of artefacts, such as terracotta seated Buddhas and Buddhist votive tablets, discovered in various parts of Peninsular Malaysia, particularly in the Bujang Valley of Kedah, point to the existence of Buddhism as early as the 5th century CE. Buddhist influence, however, declined in the 11th century with the waning influence of the Srivijaya kingdom. Buddhism also spread to the northern part of the Malay Peninsula from Thailand. Chinese and Sri Lankan immigrants, who came to Malaysia during British rule, brought Buddhism back to Malaysia in the 19th and 20th centuries.

The growth of Buddhism

→ Mahayana Buddhism
→ Theravada Buddhism

0   1000 km

Terracotta Buddhas have been found in many parts of Malaysia, especially in the Bujang Valley. This seated Buddha dates from the 10–11th centuries CE.

There had been a small number of Chinese traders in Malaysia for several centuries, but significant changes to the demographics occurred in the mid-19th century with the opening of tin mines. Bringing along their Mahayana Buddhist beliefs, many Chinese immigrants, such as this group of distinguished Chinese, found success in the agriculture and tin-mining sectors.

Srivijaya

There is evidence that Mahayana Buddhism had begun to spread in Malaysia by the 5th century CE and flourished until the 8th century. During this period much of the region was under the control of the Srivijaya kingdom—the first great Indonesian kingdom, which controlled the Strait of Melaka, the port kingdoms of both the Malay Peninsula and much of Sumatra. Srivijaya was the centre for Buddhist learning at this time, and was well known for its Sanskrit scholars. The writings of the Chinese monk Yiqing suggest that Kedah was a major religious satellite centre.

Anthropological analyses of customs and beliefs suggest that Buddhism did not influence the daily lives of the local people as much as Hinduism.

Although there is no evidence of any local ruler or sizeable population converting to Buddhism, artefacts found in riverbeds and disused tin mines in the northern part of the Peninsula show that Buddhist settlements were established. Kedah was an important port at the time. Indian traders would arrive at the northwest coast in their boats, cross the Peninsula by elephant, and continue their journey to China over the South China Sea. Gunung Jerai, the highest peak in Kedah, acted as a beacon for these traders. Historical evidence suggests that south of Gunung Jerai, together with Hindu sites, there were many early Buddhist ones. This is evidenced by statues and other artefacts dating from 6th to 8th centuries CE and some temple ruins.

Thai influence

Theravada Buddhism was introduced to Indochina in the 1st or 2nd century CE and has since played a dominant role in the spiritual and cultural life of its people. In the 10th century, Buddhism spilled across the border from Thailand into the regions of Kelantan and Terengganu. In addition to geographical proximity, it must be noted that Kelantan and Terengganu were both under Thai rule until the signing of the Anglo-Siamese Treaty in 1909, which transferred control of these two states to the British.

In the northern states of Kedah, Perlis, Perak, Penang and Kelantan, there are an estimated 500,000 Malaysians of Thai origin who practise Theravada Buddhism.

This four-armed bronze Avalokitesvara, one of the most important Bodhisattva (enlightened beings) of Buddhism, was found in 1908 in an opencast tin mine in Sungai Siput, Kinta Valley, Perak.

Chinese and Sri Lankan immigrants

When the power of the Srivijaya kingdom waned in the 11th century, Buddhist influence in the region gradually disappeared.

Immigration played an important part in re-introducing Buddhism to Malaysia. In the 19th century, particularly under British rule, there was an influx of Chinese traders and workers who came to work in the tin mines and brought with them their Mahayana Buddhist beliefs. In the early days of their immigration, they were mainly concerned with building clan or ancestral houses which acted as focal points for their communities. It was only later that monks from China established Buddhist temples in various parts of the country. One of the most outstanding of these is the Kek Lok Si Temple in Penang. Considered to be one of the largest Buddhist temples in Southeast Asia, it was built at the end of the 19th century adopting Thai, Burmese and Chinese stylistic influences.

Early Chinese Buddhist immigrants built clan and ancestral houses rather than temples. These served a dual purpose as community centres and places of worship. This 1828 engraving shows a clan house in Melaka.

Buddhist devotees praying during Wesak Day.

Sinhalese immigrants from Sri Lanka also came to seek work, particularly in the railway industry. They brought with them the Theravada form of Buddhism and built temples such as the Buddhist Maha Vihara in Brickfields, Kuala Lumpur, which was founded in 1894. Besides building temples, both these groups of immigrants established schools and hospitals to serve the needs of their communities.

Buddhism today

The majority of Buddhists in Malaysia are Chinese. The Mahayana School, which is the form of Buddhism practised in China, Korea and Japan, predominates. Buddhism, however, is characterized by pluralism which means that the Mahayana, Theravada and Vajrayana (Tantric) traditions are all practised in Malaysia, though the Vajrayana tradition is relatively new—centres have been established in Kuala Lumpur, Ipoh and Penang.

Over the years, Buddhism in Malaysia has developed its own distinct character. To a certain extent, the various Buddhist traditions have amalgamated. This is evident in the Wesak Day festivities, which are held to commemorate Buddha's birth, enlightenment and attainment of nirvana. Until the late 1950s, only Sinhalese Buddhists in Malaysia celebrated this festival on a large scale. However, Wesak Day is now celebrated grandly by all Buddhists. Often, processions are held. Such large-scale celebrations are a phenomenon unique to Malaysia and Singapore.

Kek Lok Si Temple Penang

The Kek Lok Si Temple houses a large statue of Kuan Yin (the Bodhisattva of compassion). Also known as the 'Temple of Supreme Bliss', Kek Lok Si is the largest in Southeast Asia. It was constructed in 1893, but new additions have been made over the years. These include the white Ban Po That Pagoda (Pagoda of Ten Thousand Buddhas) built in seven tiers and dedicated to Bodhisattva Tsi Tsuang Wang. The 30-m pagoda displays various regional architectural styles, reflecting the various religious traditions commonly practised by Malaysian Buddhists.

Buddhist beliefs and world-view

Both Mahayana and Theravada Buddhism are practised in Malaysia. Despite the minor variations in the different schools of Buddhism, there is no divergence in the fundamental beliefs. Like followers of the religion the world over, Buddhists in Malaysia believe in the Four Noble Truths relating to suffering, karma, rebirth, and nirvana. The path to salvation, that is, the end of suffering, is in each person's hands and can be reached by following the Eightfold Path. Buddhist doctrine strongly advocates the middle path of moderation in all things.

The lotus symbolizes purity or the state of enlightenment. It has come to symbolize the doctrine of Buddhism, with its roots in the mud and its flowers in the pure air.

The dharma or teachings of the Buddha

The Buddha taught that the avoidance of the two extremes of enslavement to sensual pleasures and self-mortification was the first step to attaining spiritual enlightenment. A Buddhist should live a life of simplicity and dignity, but at the same time avoid actions that torture the body and distract the mind. A good Buddhist is expected to live in moderation, to practise goodwill and show compassion towards all beings by acknowledging that everything that exists is bound inextricably to everything else.

Karma and rebirth

The Buddha's teachings are founded on the belief that ignorance is the common problem plaguing human existence. Attachment to the ego leads to the perpetuation of certain actions. In Buddhist doctrine, this is what causes humans to go through continual rebirths, known as *samsara*. The concept of being born into life forms relative to the merit earned in the previous life is known as karma. If there is no karma, then there is no further existence. Buddhists do not believe that the inequalities existing in society are determined by an all-powerful deity. Everything that happens is not the result of karma alone. This would make a person solely a victim of his past actions. Karma is just one of the determinants of the working of the universe. For the Buddhist, the aim of life is not to earn good karma, but to transcend karma and attain the supreme state of nirvana.

Paintings are often used to decorate Malaysian temples and as teaching aids. These depict scenes from Buddha's life. Pictured above is a scene of Prince Siddhartha encountering, for the first time, a dead body being taken to the burial ground.

Bodhisattvas

Two Bodhisattva commonly worshipped by Mahayana Buddhists in Malaysia are Amitabha and Avalokitesvara (Kuan Yin). Temples in Malaysia have separate halls dedicated to specific Bodhisattva.

LEFT: In the 5th century CE, a monk named Dharmakara attained enlightenment. As a Bodhisattva he is known as Amitabha.

RIGHT: Kuan Yin, the Bodhisattva of compassion, has her origins in the male Bodhisattva, Avalokitesvara. Kuan Yin is also depicted having 1000 arms and 1000 eyes. She is worshipped as the giver of children.

Theravada and Mahayana Buddhism

Buddhism is divided into two major schools, Theravada and Mahayana. The word Theravada means 'path of the elders', and refers to the teachings of the Buddha as preserved in the Pali canon (early sacred texts). Generally more orthodox, followers of Theravada tend to uphold all the rules and preserve the tenets of the original oral teachings of the Buddha. Its spiritual ideal is *arhat* (spiritual perfection)—one who is self-liberated from all forms of suffering. Theravada Buddhism is today found in Sri Lanka, Myanmar, Thailand, Cambodia and Laos.

Mahayana Buddhism developed about 600 years after Buddha passed away. The word Mahayana means 'greater vehicle' and its basic philosophy is to attain enlightenment for the benefit of others. Instead of self-liberation, Mahayana Buddhism encourages followers to work towards enlightenment by developing a compassionate heart to help all sentient beings. Beings worthy of attaining nirvana but who remain on the human plane assisting others to reach enlightenment are known as Bodhisattva.

The Mahayana tradition acts as an umbrella body for a great variety of schools. They include Tantric (Vajrayana) Buddhism found in Tibet and Mongolia, and the Pure Land (Amitabha) School and Ch'an (Zen) School, popular in China, Korea and Japan. Mahayana Buddhism is prevalent in China, Japan, Korea, Vietnam and Tibet.

Both the Mahayana and Theravada schools share the same fundamental teachings of the Buddha, especially the Four Noble Truths and the Eightfold Path, law of karma (moral retribution) and rebirth. All Buddhists also acknowledge Gautama Buddha as the founder and teacher of Buddhism.

However, the two traditions differ in the interpretation of the path of enlightenment and certain philosophical and psychological aspects of Buddhist doctrine. For instance, while meditation or mental development is found in all Buddhist traditions, the method varies. In Malaysia Buddhists from both traditions can be found. The majority of Malaysian Buddhists, who are predominantly Chinese, follow the Mahayana tradition. The smaller ethnic communities of Thais, Sri Lankans and Burmese in the country follow the Theravada tradition. However, due to the missionary efforts of English-speaking Sri Lankan monks since the 1950s, many Malaysian Chinese are now exposed to Theravada Buddhism. A more recent phenomenon is the introduction by visiting Tibetan monks of Vajrayana Buddhism which is being adopted by an increasing number of Malaysians.

The Mahayana School admits both men (monks) and women (nuns) into the *sangha* (monastic community). Their traditional Chinese robes are subdued in colour.

After spending 49 days under the Bodhi tree, Prince Siddhartha finally achieved nirvana and became the Buddha—the enlightened one.

The Buddha preaching to his disciples under a tree.

Depiction of the Buddha's final moments. He asked his followers not to grieve for him and to work towards attaining their nirvana.

This Buddha statue in the Buddhist Maha Vihara in Kuala Lumpur exhibits many symbolic characteristics including the Buddha's aura, elongated ear lobes, and the right hand extended in the gesture of bestowing blessings.

Nirvana

The result of following the Eightfold Path is the attainment of nirvana or the most perfect peace of enlightenment. Nirvana means 'the extinguishing of the flame of desire'. However, nirvana should not be misconstrued as nihilism. Instead, nirvana is the antithesis of ignorance and the most perfect bliss.

The life of the Buddha

The Buddha was born around 560 BCE as Siddhartha Gautama, the prince of the Shakya people in India, near the border with Nepal. His early years were spent sheltered in his father's palace. One day he left his father's palace and saw four things that changed his life completely. The first was an old man bent double with age, the second was a man ravaged by disease, the third was a dead body being taken to the cremation grounds and, finally, a holy man who seemed full of dignity and inner peace. The young Siddhartha decided that he wanted to discover the true meaning of life. He gave up his royal life, leaving behind his wife and son to become an ascetic. After many years of wandering and learning he still remained dissatisfied.

Eventually he went to Bodh Gaya (in northeast India) where he sat under the Bodhi tree and vowed not to leave until he had attained enlightenment. After 49 days of meditation he attained nirvana and from that time on he was known as the Buddha, which means 'the one who is fully awake'. For the next 45 years the Buddha travelled extensively in India, teaching and establishing monastic communities.

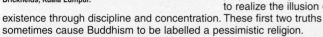

A Buddhist devotee praying at the Buddhist Maha Vihara in Brickfields, Kuala Lumpur.

The Four Noble Truths

The Four Noble Truths form the central foundation of Buddhism. The **first noble truth** states that there is *dukkha* (dissatisfaction and suffering) in life. Birth, old age, death, disease, hunger and thirst—from which no one is free—all constitute suffering. To be separated from loved ones, to be forced to mingle with those one dislikes, to experience anguish, to live in uncongenial surroundings, to experience unpleasant noises—these are all ways in which human beings suffer.

The **second noble truth** states that suffering in all forms is engendered by ignorance and craving. Buddhist teaching holds that the root of suffering is desire. Human beings suffer because they constantly desire gratification. The answer, as propounded by the Buddha, is to realize the illusion of existence through discipline and concentration. These first two truths sometimes cause Buddhism to be labelled a pessimistic religion.

The **third noble truth**, however, counters this argument. Buddhists argue that the Buddha was being realistic when he drew attention to the universality of dissatisfaction. He did not say, 'You must suffer.' Rather, he said, 'There is suffering.' And, like a good doctor, he prescribed the cure, 'I show you on the one hand suffering, and on the other hand, the way out of suffering.' This is the third noble truth. Once the mind is awakened to the causes of suffering, it is easy to find a cure.

The **fourth noble truth**, the Eightfold Path, describes the way to spiritual liberation, or nirvana, and is the backbone of Buddhist practice.

The Eightfold Path

The Noble Eightfold Path comprises right understanding, right thought, right speech, right action, right livelihood, right effort, right mindfulness and right concentration.

1. Right understanding entails perceiving the world as it really is, from moment to moment, without any preconceptions or false imagining.

2. Right thought concerns the focusing of one's attention: whatever one spends a lot of time thinking about, positive or negative, gains more power. As such, good thoughts are always necessary.

3. Right speech—knowing the correct thing to say and eschewing violent or obnoxious words as well as knowing when to be silent—is considered of vital importance in the Eightfold Path.

4. Right action has five precepts as guidelines (see 'Buddhist worship and practice').

5. Right livelihood means that one should engage in work conducive to peace, understanding and harmony, and not work that causes suffering to others.

6. Right effort involves applying oneself sincerely to achieving one's goal by overcoming habits, resistances and negative thoughts.

7. Right mindfulness concerns being fully aware of one's actions, thoughts and feelings.

8. Right concentration involves the application of one's attention on an object without being distracted.

The Wheel of Law symbolizes the Buddha's teachings (*dharma*).

Buddhist worship and practice

The Buddha image is one of the objects of worship for Buddhists as it represents the spiritual ideal they aim for—enlightenment. In practising the Five Precepts, Buddhists take their first step towards enlightenment. Buddhist worship also involves religious symbols to aid spiritual practice, including prayers and meditation. Offerings, in the form of incense, flowers and candles are also an important part of daily worship.

The Triple Gem

The object of worship in Buddhism is known as the 'Triple Gem', which refers to Buddha, his teachings (*dharma*) and his community of enlightened disciples

By praying at an altar, where there is an image of Buddha and reciting from Buddhist scriptures, a devotee seeks refuge in the Triple Gem.

(*sangha*). Buddhists look to the Triple Gem because it is the ideal spiritual guide. Buddha is regarded as the First Gem.

The ritual for seeking refuge begins with a salutation to Buddha in the Pali language, '*Namo Tassa Bhagavato Arahato Samma-sambudhassa*' ('Homage to the Blessed One, Accomplished One and Fully Enlightened One'). Following this opening, devotees recite stanzas from Buddhist scriptures to seek refuge in the Triple Gem. These stanzas are usually said in front of a Buddha image, either at home or in the temple. Each stanza is repeated three times. This is done because Buddhists believe that the mind can be distracted and so words or chants may not be said with full conviction. Repeating a chant three times is common in many Buddhist ceremonies, for this ensures that the mind concentrates during at least the final repetition.

Symbols of worship

Bells are used by Buddhists in religious services.

A painting of 'The Wheel of Life'. Such wheels are often found as wall paintings outside Buddhist temples. The wheel is turned by the wrathful Yama, Lord of Death. At the centre of the wheel are three symbols of the cardinal faults of humans: hatred (the snake), greed (the pig) and desire (the cock). The inner wheel shows the six spheres of existence into which beings are born depending on their bad or good karma built up during life. The outer circle of the wheel shows the 12 karma formations through which rebirth and death take place.

The Reclining Buddha statue in Wat Phothivihan Thai Buddhist Temple in Kelantan is the longest in Malaysia at 40 metres.

Beads
Buddhists practise meditation in place of prayers. There are two basic types of meditation, tranquillity meditation (*samatha*) and insight meditation (*vipassana*). Most Buddhists practise both types of meditation. The former leads to concentration, while the latter leads to attainment of insight or enlightenment. In Malaysia, insight meditation is a popular practice among many Buddhists.

In the Mahayana Buddhist tradition, beads are commonly used by devotees during meditation and chanting. Beads are a symbol of unity and harmony. Each bead on the string represents an individual who is not isolated and independent but is connected with others making up a whole. This represents the Buddhist view of the inter-dependent nature of the universe.

Beads are used in many religions as meditation aids.

Gongs and bells
In the Mahayana tradition, gongs and bells are commonly used during worship and other ceremonies. Traditionally, they are used for three basic reasons.

Firstly, the monk or the person leading the religious service uses the bell to signify the various stages of the service, from beginning to end. Secondly, they are used to set the tempo or the speed of the chanting. Thirdly, bells are used to aid devotees during meditation as the ringing of the bell clears the mind.

The Buddha image
Buddhists do not actually worship the image of Buddha itself but what it represents, that is, the highest ideal of a fully perfected and supremely enlightened being. They do not pray to obtain worldly gain or even to be rewarded with rebirth in heaven. The Buddha image represents the concept of enlightenment. His image is a symbol of compassion and perfect wisdom. When it is worshipped at an altar, it is also present in the hearts and minds of the devotees.

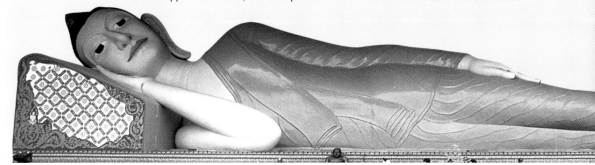

The sangha

Sangha literally means 'congregation'. In Buddhism, it refers to the community of Buddhist monks and nuns and, indeed, to all enlightened followers of Buddha. It is revered by all Buddhists because it is a part of the Triple Gem. Buddhists usually distinguish between the 'conventional' *sangha* (*bhikku sangha*) comprising only ordained disciples, and the 'spiritual' *sangha* (*ariya sangha*), which consists of all enlightened disciples.

There is no compulsion in Buddhist teachings for a Buddhist to become a monk, though the advantages of monkhood are mentioned often in the scriptures. Becoming a monk is a personal decision and there is no specific time of the year considered to be especially auspicious for becoming a monk.

Theravada sangha

In the Theravada *sangha*, all males above the age of 20 who are healthy, not in debt and who have not committed a crime are eligible to become monks. First they have to learn the teachings of Buddha and then make a request to a senior monk to be accepted into the *sangha*. Once permission is granted, they go through a ceremony

Lighting oil lamps signifies the light of wisdom over the darkness of ignorance. The ritual reminds devotees to continuously seek knowledge.

where they shave their heads, don saffron robes and observe the Ten Precepts as novice monks (*samanera*). These Ten Precepts are similar to the Five Precepts of lay Buddhists and an additional five precepts specific to monks. In the Theravada Buddhist tradition, one can leave monkhood whenever one wishes as the vows are not life-long.

Mahayana sangha

In the Mahayana *sangha*, the variations are cultural rather than doctrinal. Women are admitted to the *sangha* as nuns. Monks and nuns observe rules similar to the monastic rules of the Theravada monks. Mahayana monks and nuns usually take life-long vows and are strict vegetarians.

In order to encourage Malaysian Buddhists to experience monkhood, several Buddhist groups hold novitiate programmes for their devotees. The Buddhist Missionary Society of Malaysia organizes an annual novitiate programme at the Buddhist Temple in Brickfields, Kuala Lumpur. During the two weeks, the novice learns about the scriptures, the need to practise discipline and humility towards others, sound morality, and the virtues of a simple life.

A Thai Buddhist altar depicting Buddha in various poses. The Buddha on the upper platform is in a pose which symbolizes meditation. The lower Buddha, in the pose known as 'calling the earth to witness', indicates Buddha's victory over Mara (the personification of evil in Buddhism).

Offerings

Flowers
In Buddhist temples, flowers symbolize impermanence. Buddha taught that all things in this world are in constant change and that nothing is permanent. Flowers are beautiful in the morning but wither in the heat of the day. Thus, they represent the transience of the world.

Flowers represent the constant change in the world.

An offering of flowers floating in holy water.

Incense
Incense comes in many different colours and shapes. It is lit as an offering to Buddha and as an act of dedication to him. When a person burns incense, the sweet fragrance purifies the air and represents kindness and compassion. With these qualities within, the devotee will be ever-ready to help those in need.

Candles
Candles symbolize wisdom. In the physical world, light allows us to see things. Without the sun or other forms of light, the world would be dark and we could not see anything. In the spiritual world, physical light does not help one to see. One can only see through the light of wisdom and understand the true nature of life.

LEFT: A Mahayana monk offering candles to Buddha as a symbol of devotion.

RIGHT: Three joss sticks are presented when paying homage to the Lord Buddha. The first represents his wisdom, the second, his purity, and the third, his kindness.

Wesak Day celebrations

Wesak Day is celebrated on a large scale in Malaysia.

Processions are held on the roads leading from major temples. The celebrations begin at dawn when devotees gather at the temples to meditate, and end with candlelit processions.

Wesak Day is the most important date in the Buddhist calendar as it marks the birth, enlightenment and death of Buddha. In Malaysia, Wesak Day falls in May and is a public holiday. Processions, with beautifully decorated floats, are often held. Devotees also light joss sticks, candles and oil lamps as offerings to Lord Buddha. It is customary to make donations and provide food for the needy on this day.

Buddhist organizations and movements

Apart from numerous temples, there are more than 700 registered Buddhist organizations in Malaysia. They provide religious education for Buddhists and are actively engaged in social and welfare work. There is also an active Buddhist youth movement headed by the Young Buddhist Association of Malaysia. Buddhist societies are also found in some universities, colleges and schools.

Seminars and events on Buddhism are regularly held by the Taiping Buddhist Association (Perak) for the Buddhist community in Taiping.

Temples

Apart from serving as places of worship, Buddhist temples also play an important role in religious education and social welfare activities. The Kwan Im Teng in Petaling Jaya (Selangor), for instance, is well known for its charitable work such as granting scholarships to underprivileged students, and providing financial aid to the poor and sick. Many other temples, including the Penang Free Clinic, also provide free medical services and carry out other charitable activities.

There are around 1000 monks and nuns living in temples in Malaysia. They are often looked upon by the Buddhist community at large as religious leaders, teachers and counsellors. They command great influence over the Buddhist community and have played a crucial role in the development of the religion in the country. Among the outstanding ones are Venerable (Ven.) Dr K. Sri Dhammananda and the late Ven. Chuk Mor, who are well known for their written works and lectures. Ven. Chuk Mor was also a distinguished calligrapher. The late Ven.

The swastika is used as a symbol on logos of many Buddhist associations and also at temples. In Buddhism, the word 'swastika' means 'to be well'.

Kian An was active in social welfare work and the late Ven. Kim Beng was renowned for his writings and lectures.

Buddhist organizations

Buddhist organizations, unlike temples, are generally managed by laymen, with monks and nuns as advisors. They are devoted to the study and practice of Buddhism. Chanting sessions and services are held regularly within the premises of these organizations. From time to time, lectures on Buddhism are organized. Apart from these, Buddhist organizations are also actively engaged in social and welfare activities, such as blood donation drives, free medical services and charity for the elderly and underprivileged members of society.

Many of these organizations are based in residential homes or modest commercial premises though some, among them the Taiping Buddhist Association, the Klang and Coast Buddhist Association and the Sandakan Buddhist Association, own large premises. Some of these buildings resemble temples and are often regarded as such.

There are three Buddhist schools in Malaysia, the Siang Lim Primary School in Melaka, the Phor Tay Primary School and the Phor Tay Secondary School in Penang. Buddhist children, however, have ample opportunity to learn and study Buddhism as most associations hold weekend *dharma* (teachings of Buddha) classes.

The Cheng Huah Kindergarten in Penang was set up by the Malaysian Buddhist Association. The association encourages other Buddhist organizations to set up *dharma* (teachings of Buddha) classes for children and adults.

Prominent figures in Buddhism

Ven. Dr K. Sri Dhammananda (1919–) was born in Sri Lanka. He arrived in Malaysia in 1952 as a young monk at the invitation of the Sasana Abdhiwurdhi Wardhana Society and has been instrumental in the development and growth of Buddhism in Malaysia. His greatest achievement is the establishment of the Buddhist Missionary Society in 1962, based in the Buddhist Maha Vihara, Kuala Lumpur, which now has more than 10,000 members. He assisted in setting up the Consultative Council of Buddhism, Christianity, Hinduism and Sikhism. Ven. Dr K. Sri Dhammananda is also a prolific writer.

Ven. Kim Beng (1913–99) served as the chairman of the Malaysian Buddhist Association for many years before he retired and was a very highly respected Mahayana monk. He was one of the pioneer Buddhist monks in the country and played an important role in getting the Malaysian government to declare Wesak Day a public holiday for the whole country. Ven. Kim Beng contributed greatly to Buddhism through his writings.

Ven. Chuk Mor (1913–2002) who was the chief abbot of the Triple Wisdom Hall in Penang was born in China in 1913 and was fully ordained as a monk in 1928. He settled in Malaya in 1953 and was the first chairman of the Malaysian Buddhist Association. He also founded the Malaysian Buddhist Institute in Penang. Besides being a prolific writer, he was well-known internationally as an artist and calligrapher.

Buddhist organizations in Malaysia

The Malaysian Buddhist Association
The Malaysian Buddhist Association (MBA) was formed in 1959, two years after Independence. Its membership is open to Buddhist societies and temples, as well as to organizations and individuals. Its objective is to promote unity, friendship and social welfare among Malaysian Buddhists. This association became the umbrella body of Buddhist organizations in Malaysia and its membership currently stands at around 30,000. However, organizations which do not adopt Mandarin as a medium of communication or are not Mahayana are not affiliated with it.

The establishment of the Malaysian Buddhist Institute in Penang in 1970 is a major achievement of the MBA. This institute provides courses in Buddhism at all levels and has since its inception produced more than 1000 graduates, with more than 50 of them becoming monks or nuns.

The Malaysian Buddhist Association runs a Sunday kindergarten and a Malaysian Buddhist Institute which promotes Buddhist education and trains monks and nuns.

The Buddhist Maha Vihara
The Buddhist Maha Vihara in Brickfields, Kuala Lumpur, was founded in 1894 as the Brickfields Buddhist Temple. It is managed by the Sasana Abdhiwurdhi Wardhana Society (established in 1895) and is an important centre for Buddhist learning. Operating within this temple is the Buddhist Institute Sunday Dharma School, which conducts weekly religious classes for children and adults. The temple also serves as a training centre for Buddhist students in institutions of higher learning. They often congregate here to study the *dharma* and to take part in leadership and personal development programmes. An annual training programme for novice monks is also conducted at this temple.

The Buddhist Maha Vihara Brickfields houses several Buddhist societies, a Buddhist monk training centre and the Buddhist Institute Sunday Dharma School. There is also a library and bookshop.

The Buddhist Missionary Society (BMS) also operates within the premises of the Buddhist Maha Vihara. This society is recognized for its publications, such as the *Voice of Buddhism* and numerous booklets. It is one of the very few English-medium Buddhist organizations in Malaysia. Most other Buddhist organizations use Mandarin as the medium of education and communication.

The Young Buddhist Association of Malaysia
The Buddhist youth movement began with the formation of the Penang Buddhist Association Youth Circle by Ven. Dr Sumangalo, an American Buddhist monk, in 1955. By 1958, there were seven youth circles in the

Trainees participate in an activity during the Young Buddhist Association of Malaysia's 18th National Council Induction Training Programme, August 2004. The association aims to develop a society of wisdom, compassion and gratitude and unite the Buddhist youth.

Malay Peninsula, and the Federation of Malaya Buddhist Youth Fellowship (FMBYF) was formed. By 1965, the FMBYF had a membership of 11 affiliates, about half of the existing youth bodies.

At the first National Buddhist Youth Seminar held on 29 July 1970, the delegates resolved to dissolve the FMBYF. In its place, a new national youth organization, the Young Buddhist Association of Malaysia (YBAM) was formed.

Today, the YBAM has a total membership of 234 organizations representing about 100,000 individuals. It is recognized by the Ministry of Youth and Sports as the sole representative of Buddhist youth in Malaysia and is represented on the Malaysian Youth Consultative Council. It is also affiliated with the Malaysian Youth Council.

In 1980, the YBAM initiated the formation of the Young Buddhists Foundation. This foundation, unlike other Buddhist organizations, is registered with the Registrar of Companies as a non-profit organization. Its membership is open to all Buddhists regardless of age. Its main objective is to unite the Buddhist youth and to inspire them in cultivating wisdom, compassion and gratitude through four main service areas: *dharma* propagation, education, culture, and welfare. Some of its successful projects are the formation of the Malaysian Buddhist Sangha Fund, which sponsors Buddhist monks and nuns in their studies, the establishment of around 50 personal charity funds or memorial funds which offer scholarships and grants to underprivileged students, and the managing of the Buddhist audio-visual library and bookshop. The YBAM is well known for its journal *Eastern Horizon* which is published three times a year and has a worldwide readership.

The Malaysian Buddhist Sangha Council
Historically, the Malaysian Buddhist community has been dependent on the immigrant *sangha* from Sri Lanka, Myanmar, Thailand and China to administer their religious and spiritual needs. Lately, more Malaysians have become Buddhist monks, thereby helping to create an indigenous Buddhist *sangha*. In Malaysia, all members of the *sangha*, be they Theravada or Mahayana Buddhists, belong to the Malaysian Buddhist Sangha Council, which was formed in April 1995.

More and more Malaysians are becoming monks, therefore contributing to a home-grown *sangha*. This 1954 picture shows newly ordained young novices on the way to the temple to make offerings. A few of these young novices have gone on to become full-time *sangha* members.

History of Chinese religions in Malaysia

The Chinese have been coming to the Malay Peninsula and Borneo for many centuries. The earliest recorded community is a small settlement established in Melaka by Hokkien traders (from Fujian province, China) in the 15th century. Confucianism, Taoism and Buddhism are the three main faiths. The influence of these can be seen in Chinese culture and everyday life in Malaysia—calligraphy, Taoism, worship of Tien Guan (the Heavenly Duke), rituals of filial piety and ancestor worship.

Chinese temple at Kota, Taiping, 1899.

Temple doors at Cheng Hoon Teng Temple, Melaka, depicting the Gods of Entrance. There usually are two gods at entrances—one on each door. These gods protect the temple from evil spirits.

A talisman such as this amulet of the star spirits *Luh-ting* was used by members of secret societies to protect their lives in battle.

A membership certificate of the Cantonese Ghee Hin Society. The largest of the Chinese secret societies in the 19th century, its members were involved in the Larut wars of the 1860s and 1870s over control of the tin mining industry.

History of Chinese religions

The interaction and integration of teachings and practices of Confucianism, Taoism and Buddhism with foreign and local religions have resulted in distinct Chinese religious identities in Malaysia. There is a plethora of sects, especially in Taoism. Chinese Buddhists have inherited some Mahayana (Greater Vehicle) sects which are now lost in India. They also founded many new sects, such as Zen and Tiantai which later spread to Korea and Japan.

Inter-faith relations between Confucianists and other faiths have created two main philosophical schools—Li Xue (the school of rationalism) and Xin Xue (the school of the mind). Since the Yuan Dynasty (1260–1368), Quan Zhen, which is the main orthodox stream of Taoism in northern China, has emphasized harmony between the three main faiths by encouraging the cross-learning of the *Diamond Sutra* (Buddhism), *Lao Zi Tao te Ching* (Taoism) and the *Doctrine of Filial Piety* (Confucianism). Some of the new religions and neo-Taoist sects tried to form a new theology by integrating the three faiths during the Ming (1368–1644) and Qing dynasties (1644–1911), but were oppressed and labelled as cults. Although most of these cults disappeared in China, their temples and organizations can be found in Malaysia.

The theology or social philosophy of the three main faiths and other Chinese religious groups share similar basic tenets. One must follow Confucius's teachings in the secular world by undertaking daily charitable activities and by looking after the needs and dignity of others. Of particular importance is respect for elders, teachers and leaders. Confucianism may not be an institutionalized religion, but its influence on all Chinese religious practices is strong.

However, it should not be forgotten that these three main faiths only became well established in China during the Han Dynasty (206 BCE–220 CE). Before then China's primitive and folk beliefs, such as ancestor worship, animism, totem worship, shamanism and heavenly will, were widely adopted and manifested in a host of traditional beliefs, practices and legends. These are still important today among various groups. Many non-Chinese religions, including Catholicism and Islam, have also played a role in the interfaith process of Chinese religions.

One of the most interesting phenomena to show Chinese religious philosophy is the attitude towards other religions. Some non-believers of Chinese traditional religions, for example community leaders who are followers of different religions, are worshipped by the Chinese. The Chinese have shown their respect to these leaders by building shrines to them. An example of this is the worship of the spirit of deceased native leaders.

Arrival of the Chinese

Chinese sea merchants settled in the Malay Peninsula long before the 19th century, when mass migration of Chinese to Malaya occurred. These early merchants set up trading settlements along the Strait of Melaka, intermarried and many eventually became known as the Straits Chinese. They built shrines dedicated to their native deities as well as cemeteries for those who died. The shrines served as an important link to their home towns. The settlements remained relatively insignificant until the mid-19th century, when tin and gold mining in Peninsular Malaysia, Sarawak and North Borneo (Sabah) attracted many Chinese to the burgeoning mining and agricultural settlements. The Chinese population boomed as a result of the high demand for labour, and a large immigrant Chinese community developed. With the growth of communities came a need for temples in which to

Tua Pek Kong, Sarawak's oldest temple, is a prominent landmark in Kuching. Estimated to be built in 1770, the first recorded renovation of the temple was in 1856.

Local Chinese deities

Liu Shan Bang
When the Sarawak Hakka gold miners launched an 'anti-colonial' uprising in 1857, Liu was their leader. He died fighting. After Independence, Sarawak's state government declared him a hero and placed a statue of him in front of the state museum in 1984. The Chinese declared him 'Dai Pak Gong' for establishing Kuching as the capital of Sarawak and worship Liu and other martyrs of the 1857 uprising in temples in the city.

'Datuk' Siak
A native whom the Chinese held in respect in the Beroga tin mining area, on the border of Selangor and Negeri Sembilan, was 'Datuk' Siak. He was in charge of local community relations. His tomb is worshipped by the Chinese as they regard him as a protecting spirit. A large temple dedicated to him built in the early 20th century in Negeri Sembilan is now a tourist attraction.

The entrance to Datuk Siak's cave temple. It is believed that Datuk Siak lived in this cave and that his spirit still dwells there.

Statue of Zhong Wan at the temple of Zhong Wan in Jalan Pasar, Kuala Lumpur.

Zhong Wan
Zhong Wan was a Taoist priest from the Lushan sect of Tian Shi Tao, based in Hui Zhou and Jia Ying Zhou, both Hakka counties in Guangdong Province, China. This region was one of the main places of origin of Chinese Malayan immigrant workers. According to oral history, Zhong Wan was the master of the Hakka and Cantonese priests who spread Taoism teachings to Malaya. He was one of the earliest priests to come to Malaya to provide medical and spiritual services to the people. Two memorial temples, one in China and another in Kuala Lumpur, were built in the late 19th century after he was 'immortalized'. Many Taoist temples display his tablet for devotees to worship.

Zhang Li
Zhang Li was leader of the Chinese settlements in Penang in the 18th century. With two of his associates, he came to Penang before the British established a settlement there and founded the first Chinese settlement. At the beginning of the 20th century Zhang Li was credited by his followers as the 'real' founder of Penang. A temple was built beside his tomb in Tanjung Tokong, Penang and branches of this temple are located in George Town, and Alor Star, Kedah. The Chinese regard him and his associates as the protectors and patron saints of northern Malaysia and honour them with a Hakka nickname 'Tua Pek Gong' or 'Dai Pak Gong' which means 'Great Eldest Uncle'. His role is to maintain the prosperity of Chinese in their founding settlement.

Zhang Li's Temple in Tanjung Tokong, Penang. His tomb is next to the temple.

Saw Ah Chong
Saw Ah Chong or Panglima (Commander) Ah Chong was the leader of the Ghee Hin secret society which founded more than 16 tin mining settlements in Perak. The municipal government of Taiping has named a road after him as a memorial to his contribution to Malaysia's tin mining economy. He fought in the Larut wars (strife between Chinese tin miners belonging to different secret societies), but was

This urn, dated 1895, is believed to hold the remains of Saw Ah Chong.

captured and sentenced to death by the Malay chief of Matang, Perak. He set a condition to his captors that the majority of his followers must be released and allowed to retreat to Penang. This heroic deed is re-enacted in the Malay *bangsawan* (Malay opera) in Perak. Chinese worship him as a guardian spirit. As a patron saint of the settlements, Saw's main temple was built at the mouth of the Matang River, the earliest port in Perak in the 19th century. Several branches of the temple have been built along the coast of Perak.

In a twist to local traditional worship and offerings, devotees can worship Saw by placing offerings of pork. As Saw was a nationalist hero offerings must be in line with Asian norms—certain fruits and products such as beer and wines are strictly prohibited as worship offerings.

practise their religious rituals. Most immigrants were illiterate or poorly educated peasants and coolies, so Buddhist and Taoist monks were brought in from China to run the temples and look after the spiritual needs of the immigrant communities.

Role of social organizations
Social organizations in Malaya and Borneo were an important means of providing assistance and guidance to the new immigrant society. Membership is based on common surnames, locality, dialect or trade. A common patron saint is essential as the spirit of every organization. The organizations cater to the economic, social and recreational well-being of the members, as well as their spiritual needs. They organize ancestor worship, oversee burials, maintain the upkeep of cemeteries, settle disputes and take care of schools.

The four main dialect group associations were the Guangdong (Cantonese), Fujian (Hokkien), Chao Zhou (Teochew) and Kejia (Hakka). Alongside the united front of several dialect groups were the highly organized secret societies such as the Ghee Hin and Hai San societies which played an important role in controlling the Chinese immigrant workers from the 17th to early 20th centuries. Leaders of these societies were acknowledged as the community leaders and Malay chiefs called them 'Kapitan China'. Some of these leaders are now considered patron saints by various Chinese communities.

Chinese religions in Malaysia have evolved, and today are an amalgamation of Chinese and local values and beliefs, as illustrated by the locally created deities.

Confucianism and Taoism in Malaysia

Both Confucianism and Taoism have a strong influence on the Chinese communities in Malaysia. The social ethics and moral teachings of Confucius are blended with Taoist beliefs. While many Taoist beliefs were brought over from China, some local developments have taken place amongst the various dialect groups—in Penang, the Tian Heng Shan sect (originally from Hainan) evolved and spread throughout Malaysia.

Confucius's tablet in front of his image at the altar in the temple of the Chung Hwa School in Penang.

Confucianism

Confucianism was founded by Kong Fu Tze (Romanized to Confucius by early Jesuit missionaries) who was born in 551 BCE in Lu state (modern day Shandong province). Confucianism believes in 'treat others as we wish others to treat us'. Confucius strongly advocated the importance of proper conduct, filial piety and ancestor worship. Confucianist ethics and teachings influence all the various religions of the Chinese.

Chinese people of various origins who came to Malaysia brought their own beliefs and patron saints and integrated them harmoniously within the individual community temples. The continually changing order of importance among Chinese deities reflects the power politics and changing of relations between the dialect groups. One of the main deities still popularly worshipped widely today is Confucius.

The *Yin-Yang* symbol represents the two opposing forces of nature in which Taoists believe. *Yin* is dark, female, passive and soft, and *Yang* is light, male, active, and hard. These forces are interdependent and each contains the essence of the other.

Worship practices in Guangdong Province (from where many immigrants came) have influenced the Malaysian Chinese. They worship Confucius by offering bean curd, celery, garlic and shallots. Bean curd is a symbol of a 'soft brain' (flexible and adaptable). Celery is the symbol of humility. In the Chinese dialects of Guangdong Province, pronunciations of garlic, celery and shallot are *chong*, *suan* and *kan*, which sound the same as the words 'clever', 'logical thinking' and 'hardworking'.

According to the records of the Catholic Church going back to the 1850s, the French priests in Balik Pulau and Bukit Mertajam in Penang organized classes to teach Confucian classics in their churches. Students in Chinese private classes actually set up tablets to worship Confucius, a deviation from traditional practices.

In 1898, the Qing Dynasty government encouraged Chinese overseas to set up modern schools to promote the values of Confucianism. In Penang, the Chung Hwa School, which was founded in 1904 as the first modern Chinese school in the Malay Peninsula was a pioneer project of this policy. The school regulations encouraged the directors, teachers, staff and students to collectively practise

Favourite gods

Malaysian Chinese have several gods whom they worship. The favourite ones are Guan Gong, Tian Guan and Sun Wu Kung.

Guan Gong

Guan Gong is a symbol of social stability. He was a historical figure who fought side by side with two brothers-in-arms in a war of unification after the collapse of the Han Dynasty early in the 3rd century CE. His exploits feature in the classic epic, *The Romance of the Three Kingdoms*. He has long been held as the most righteous person in history and deified in popular belief. He is widely worshipped by families, businesses and organizations of every Chinese dialect group in Malaysia.

Tian Guan

Tian Guan (Heavenly Duke) is worshipped as part of Taoist teachings and has become popular in daily worship in Malaysia. According to legend, Heavenly Duke is the chief representative of Heavenly Will whose role is to examine the conduct of individuals. He has full authority to review their merit and protect the aged. He has a strong sense of righteousness and will punish those who are sinful. Fire is considered a gift from heaven. Tian Guan likes to see lights lit in every house. The Hokkien, therefore, hang a red lantern in front of the main door to show their respect to Tian Guan. Almost every household, whether Buddhist or

Guan Gong is a warrior deity found in Chinese and Mahayana Buddhist temples.

Altar hung with a tablet which reads 'Luck from the Heavenly Duke' on a pillar in front of a house.

Taoist, features a tablet with the words 'Tian Guan Shi Fu', meaning luck from the Heavenly Duke, written on it outside their house, near the main door.

Sun Wu Kong (Monkey God)

Sun Wu Kong is considered to have attained enlightenment and become a protector of Buddhism. He is worshipped universally by the Chinese throughout Malaysia.

This deity is featured in the famous classical Chinese folk tale, *Journey to the West*. In the tale, the Monkey God was born from a piece of stone. After witnessing the death of another monkey, he wanted to attain immortality. In his quest he gained supernatural powers, taught to him by a Taoist priest. With these powers he declared himself invincible and fought the Jade Emperor in heaven.

The Jade Emperor asked for Buddha's help. Buddha imprisoned the Monkey for 500 years until the Master Tang San Zang of the Tang Dynasty, who was on his journey to the Western Heaven to gain the holy scriptures from Buddha and bring them back to China, agreed to have him as his disciple. The monkey helped his master and in the process obtained his retribution and was made the 'Buddha of Victory through Strife'.

Some Malaysian Chinese worship Sun Wu Kong by putting a pump in a bottle filled with water beside his statue. When the pump makes a popping sound they consider that the Monkey God is visiting the house.

A statue depicting the Monkey God.

Taoist sects in Malaysia

Since its origins, Taoism has branched out into many sects. Among the Taoist sects that are present in Malaysia are Guigen Tao, Hun Yuan, Xiangshui Fayuan, Tian Shi Tao, Tian Heng Mountain sect, Quan Zhen School and Jin Ying School.

Guigen Tao (Back to the Root) is practised by the Temples of Mother Earth found across Peninsular Malaysia. It incorporates both Taoist and Confucianist beliefs, where Wuji, the Sacred Mother, and Kuan Yin are the two major goddesses worshipped. In this sect, girls are brought up as vegetarians.

Hun Yuan (Original Chaos) is a male-oriented sect which is a branch of the White Lotus sect, founded early in the Ming Dynasty (1368–1644).

Xiangshui Fayuan is a branch of the Huizhou Buddhists (Fragrant Water Dharma School). Activities are initiated by monks for laymen. Altars are set up for worship using Buddhist scriptures and Taoist rites. However, unlike a Buddhist monk, the Master of Xiangshui Fayuan does not comply with monastic disciplines and may marry and consume meat. There are only five or six members, who are based in Petaling Street, Kuala Lumpur.

After the 11th century CE, **Tian Shi Tao** was officially accepted as the highest authority of all the Taoist organizations in southern China. This school comprises three larger well-known sects: Hezhaoshan, Maoshan and Longhushan. In Malaysia, most of the Taoist priests are related to the Lushan sect, a branch of Longhushan developed in Zhangzhou and Quanzhou.

A branch of the Lushan sect, known as Santanjiao, was developed by the Hakka in China and also Malaysia. This sect incorporates elements of Confucianism, Taoism and Buddhism.

Priests from the Chi Wei branch of the Lushan sect in Penang keep many 17th-century handwritten doctrines, some which are not preserved in China, in the Seng Ong Temple, Penang.

The **Quan Zhen School** was founded in the 12th century by Wang Chong Yang who became the official leader of Taoism in northern China. Branches spread widely in Hakka settlements in southern China. In the 19th century, a Hakka priest, Zhong Shan Kun, came to Malaya, where he founded the Hai Yun sect (Sea-Cloud branch) and formed more than six Taoist monastic temples in Malaya.

The **Jin Ying School,** although lost in China, is probably the largest Taoist sect in Malaysia and is widely spread throughout Southeast Asia. Several failed rebellions in Guangdong prompted members of this sect to retreat to Southeast Asia. In Malaysia, the disciples of Jin Ying were involved in anti-colonial actions. In their recruiting rituals for new members, Jin Ying priests would stand on tables and hold umbrellas, symbolizing their refusal to look at the sky of the Qing Dynasty and their refusal to stand on the land of foreigners, pointedly referring to Malaya's colonial status.

Rare Taoist handwritten texts brought from China still survive in Malaysia. These manuscripts held at the Seng Ong Temple in Penang, some of them over 100 years old, are only aired and on view once a year.

kneeling three times and kowtowing nine times. This ritual was practised facing the tablet of Confucius, especially on the opening or closing date of school and the 1st and 15th day of each lunar month. Confucius's birthday was declared a sacred holiday for the school.

Today, the only Confucius temple in Malaysia is part of the Chung Hwa Primary School in Penang. The temple is now run by a Confucius association which was founded by a group of mainly English-educated Chinese in the early 20th century. Currently, the association still serves as the main donor to the school. Many Chinese schools in Malaysia still use the words from Confucian doctrine in their school names and mottos.

Taoism (belief in Dao)

The founder of Taoism, Lao Zi, was born in 604 BCE in Hunan, China. Taoism is based on many concepts and over time evolved into a religious culture. It is an indigenous traditional religion of China and is based on the ancient religious beliefs and practices of the Chinese, the worship of heaven and ancestors, as well as Taoist theories and beliefs regarding immortality together with some Confucian ideas. The core of Taoism is the principle of Tao which means 'learn from the natural way'. Lao Zi believed that people should live in harmony with nature. It is said that Tao explains the origin of the universe as the basis of all existing things and the law governing their development and change.

Since the 19th century, many worshippers and promoters of various Taoist sects have come to Malaysia. The local Chinese communities created gods by deifying elders and leaders who had contributed greatly to their community. They also were influenced by local

Lao Zi (604–521 BCE)

practices in Malaysia. For example, the Hakka, whose livelihood depended on mining and logging, adopted the local belief in guardian spirits (animism) and integrated it with Chinese folk worship. Nowadays, the guardian spirit beliefs manifest themselves as beliefs in the spirit of, for example, a household or a construction site. The Hakka Chinese also created gods by declaring their local heroes and martyrs as protectors of certain areas. An example is Sin Ming Lee, the slain *kapitan* (leader) of Lukut, Negeri Sembilan, who was declared patron saint of Kuala Lumpur and other mining towns by his disciple Yap Ah Loy (another *kapitan*).

The Chinese also brought other deities from their native lands such as the Teochews' Sanshan Guowang, the Cantonese Chongyang Zhushi (founder of the School of Quan Zhen Tao), the Huizhou's Taoist Tangong Ye and the Kayinzhou's Shupotai. Most of these Chinese beliefs have their roots in Taoism.

A number of Taoist sects now lost in China have survived in Southeast Asia and spread to Europe and America. These include Donghua Shan, Jin Ying, Zhenyi Tian Shi Tao, Lushan, Santanjiao and Xiangshui Fayuan. Apart from these, there are also folk belief sects that are influenced by Taoism, including Tongshan Tang and Wuji Da Dao, and the locally developed Tian Heng Shan. This sect evolved when a local, Tok Aruan, introduced witchcraft and incantations into Taoist practices. Taoist masters such as Huang Jinping of Penang and Zhong Shan Kun in Seremban then spread the teachings of the Tian Heng Shan and Hai Yun sects to other parts of Southeast Asia. In particular, the latter was responsible for building most Malaysian Chinese Taoist temples in the 19th century.

A Taoist devotee lighting joss sticks.

Chinese beliefs and world-view

Chinese beliefs are predominantly expressions of cultural characteristics, ethics and philosophy that have been widely observed by the Chinese over many generations. The guiding principles and theological dimensions of Confucianism and Taoism have long been the mainstay of Chinese culture. These beliefs focus on filial piety, ancestor worship and good behaviour. The Chinese believe that all virtuous actions will guide one to the path decided by Heavenly Will.

An altar cloth showing the Eight Immortals, local Chinese heroes, from different regions and times in China. From left to right: Zhongli Quan, Lu Dongbin, Zhang Guolao, Cao Guojiu, Tieguai Li, Han Xiangzi, Lu Caihe and He Xiangu. They symbolize good wishes and good luck and are regarded as models for achieving immortality through self-refinement.

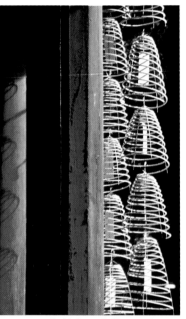

Taoists burn spiral incense when worshipping heavenly deities.

Transmission of responsibilities

The Chinese, influenced by Confucianism, which teaches filial piety and ancestor rites, and Taoism, which is the belief in the principle of Tao (see 'Confucianism and Taoism in Malaysia'), believe in the transmission of responsibilities to ancestors. Thus, the good or bad deeds of a person will affect his ancestors, offspring and subsequent generations. This belief instils in the Chinese a fear that their misdeeds may incur harm to their loved ones and encourages them to be responsible in their conduct. The Chinese also believe that unity in a family or clan is a way of uniting and pooling limited resources, therefore creating a system of survival; especially true for migrant communities.

Immortality

The Chinese emphasize that people must be optimistic about their lives and regard helping others as a pleasure. Many Chinese idioms and Taoist teachings as well as Chinese medical texts dwell on the prospects of everlasting life. As a result, the ideas of living forever without getting old, great fortune and longevity have become the content of blessings for many Chinese. Longevity is a much-prized ideal among the Chinese and those who live to a great age are revered and deemed to have followed the principle of Tao—'the way of heaven and earth'—in their earthly life.

Belief in Beidou (Northern Dou)

The constellation Europeans call the Big Dipper is known to the Chinese as Beidou. In 4000 BCE, the Chinese decided that this constellation comprised nine stars, compared with the seven perceived by Europeans. Only Taoism, which originates from ancient Chinese beliefs, emphasizes praying to Beidou. The belief in Beidou came from the observations of Huang Di (Yellow Emperor), a legendary figure regarded as the common ancestor by the Chinese. Huang Di is said to have contributed greatly towards the development of Chinese civilization and the worship of Beidou, which was important in the Original Oneness School or Tian Shi Tao. This sect is said to have been founded by the celestial master Zhang Daoling (Tian Shi) during the Han Dynasty and was the first institutionalized Taoist movement.

The Chinese believe that when Beidou rotates, it has a great effect on the stars, the weather and time. The Chinese use Beidou to identify the pole star, ascertain directions, create compasses and to demarcate the seasons.

Achieving sainthood

The Chinese believe that through self-refinement, a person can get rid of the limitations of his/her present life and enter the stage of immortality, sainthood or even deification. According to the Confucian classic *Record of Rite: the Legitimacy of Praying*, those who succeed in living by the following rules, 'Use good policy to benefit people; make sacrifices for the nation; work hard for people until death; deter severe misfortune and calamity; protect people from illness', can become deities. Those who cultivate these habits to accumulate merit can achieve immortality. It is not only human beings who can become deities or saints; creatures can also attain the same status—an expression of the belief in the equality of all forms of life.

Talismans

Charms or talismans are pieces of paper, wood or cloth with characters or symbols printed on them. Some talismans are enhanced by sacred seals or flower words (these words are meaningless, but they help a priest concentrate when he is transmitting mystical energy to the talisman). Talismans are viewed as messages or orders from gods, given by priests or mediums for use in the secular world. Talismans are used for curing diseases, preventing evil spirits from disturbing humans, alleviating negative forces hampering a person's life or simply to bring good luck.

In many instances talismans are used to mystify and ritualize objects of daily use and give them sacred meaning. For example, a mirror with flower words hung over a doorway will reflect the negative energy of evil spirits. Believers use a talisman as a form of protection. Some believers wear a talisman as a pendant, a waist belt or just keep it in a pocket. Each talisman is unique in its function.

There are many different types of talisman. Apart from those worn, some can be stuck on doors or buried underground, others can be hung in vehicles as guardians. In the performing arts, an artist sticks a talisman on his weapons, containers or sculptures to prevent evil spirits from possessing them. Talismans can either be black and white, or yellow and green with Chinese characters written in Chinese ink, red mercury or blood.

Talismans are also used during lion dance performances—a sacred activity purifying the area where they are conducted. The talisman is usually stuck on the lion's back and is meant to prevent evil spirits from entering. Secret societies in Malaysia use talismans not only for protection but also as a secret sign of membership.

A 'Five Thunder's General' talisman inscribed with sacred words and the name of a deity protects the household from bad luck and evil spirits.

Praying to heaven, earth and parents

Chinese civilization originated from small farming societies along the banks of the Huang He (Yellow River) which flows across China. The community focused on skills, which were acquired and handed down from one generation to the next, and strong ties to sustain itself. New generations built upon the foundations of previous ones, and a feeling of gratitude to parents and ancestors for the life given by them developed. For sustaining life, the earth and the sky were also honoured. In China, only Taoism and Confucianism believe that the greatness of heaven and earth cannot, however, overshadow the great esteem with which parents are held. Taoism emphasizes praying to ancestors and believes that the souls of ancestors are a mystical presence surrounding descendants and taking care of them.

Three souls and seven vigours

Chinese believe a person's spirit comprises three souls and seven vigours. After death, the three souls go in different directions: one back to earth in peace; another for rebirth (it is said that it will go to Beidou where the death is recorded); and the third to reside at a small wooden tablet as an ancestor to be worshipped by the family and protect the descendants.

The vigours, which are considered to be uncontrollable, harmful energy will gradually disappear after the decay of a corpse. The ritual to avoid the vigours from transferring themselves onto the family members and to enlighten the soul takes 49 days. Family members of the deceased have to pay respects to the dead every seventh day. At the first and seventh intervals, the vigours will jump on the one he or she likes most, adversely affecting the health of that mourner. To avoid this happening, all mourners must be dressed in black to blur the vision of the vigours.

Heavenly Will to help the weak

Lao Zi (the founder of Taoism) taught that the intention of heaven is to reward a person for his kindness and to penalize him for his wickedness. This belief has helped those who are unfortunate or unfairly treated to remain hopeful. Heavenly Will, known in Chinese as *tian yi* or *tian tao*, is still today a popular theme in television series, movies and literature.

Three Treasures

Taoism's key text is *Dao De Jing* (Classic of the Way and its Virtues), written by Lao Zi. Its central message is that Tao is the constant force in the universe and that following the 'way of Tao' is the secret of life. In chapter 67, Lao Zi states, 'I have three treasures. Uphold and protect them. First, benevolence; second, simple living; and last but not least, dare not be the first'. Benevolence means to show kindness and love. Simple living means to be thrifty and content with a simple life of few needs and desires. Dare not be the first means to be humble and politely give way—people should not compete to marginalize others. Taoism, upon inheriting these principles, has developed them into guidelines for self-refinement.

Convex mirrors above doors absorb and deflect negative energy.

Feng shui

Feng shui is a 4000-year-old Chinese system developed to help people live in harmony with their surroundings and channel the environment's energy forces appropriately. It combines geography, mystical beliefs, astrology, folklore and common sense. The words *feng shui* mean 'atmosphere and circulation' and derive from the natural environment of land and rivers. While the feng shui school of environment (Luan Tou) emphasizes the physical effect on the human senses, the school of metaphysical calculations (Li Qi) is concerned with capitalizing on positive energy lines (*chi*) and avoiding negative ones. The integration and practice of both feng shui schools have gained great popularity throughout the world recently, but its principles have been respected by Chinese Malaysians for many centuries. Whilst not really religious in nature, these beliefs are widely practised in Malaysia and incorporated into the daily life and decisions of many Chinese, particularly in building construction, interior design and the building of cemeteries and tombs.

Many old temples in Malaysia clearly demonstrate feng shui principles, such as being situated half-way up a hill overlooking water (the sea or a lake). All five elements of fire, earth, wood, water and metal are placed in prescribed positions in the temple to ensure auspiciousness. Such practices demonstrate that the temple is in unity with the natural forces surrounding it. With the protection of a hill behind and clear vision over a lake in front, the position of such a temple is often likened to a mother holding a baby safely in her arms.

The Di Zang Temple at the Nilai Memorial Park, Negeri Sembilan, one of the most prominent memorial parks in Malaysia, is one of the few new temples built according to feng shui principles. The hill behind protects it from negative energy.

Chinese festivals

Chinese festivals take place according to the lunar calendar and mark a variety of events from the changing of the seasons to the worship of specific deities, spirits and ancestors, and the commemoration of historical personalities and events. In Malaysia, festivals are celebrated with family members and also the ancestors, who are remembered through offerings made at their shrines. Chinese New Year is celebrated universally, while other festivals vary in importance between the various dialect groups found throughout the country.

Red is the favourite colour at Chinese New Year. The yellow markers indicate donations made to the temple.

Chinese calendar (Yin-Yang almanac)

The Chinese calendar, which has been used since the Xia Dynasty (c. 2100 BCE), combines the solar (*yang*) calendar and the lunar (*yin*) calendar. The Chinese divide the 365 days in the solar calendar into 24 seasons according to the position of the sun (on its ecliptic route) and by the natural phenomena of each season. The lunar calendar calculates dates based on the changing shape of the moon. Each year of the Chinese lunar calendar is divided into 12 months; the months can have either 29 or 30 days and the total number in a year can be 354 or 355. To

A procession in Bau, Sarawak. In the Chinese tradition people are said to possess the characteristics of the animal year in which they are born.

resolve the contradictions between the two calendars, the Chinese introduced the concept of an intercalary month into their lunar calendar. Usually each month of the lunar calendar falls at the transition of two solar seasons; however, every three years one of the lunar months will fall on a solar season and that particular month will be the intercalary month. The Chinese calendar divides the 12 months of the year into 12 branches of the

Major Chinese festivals celebrated in Malaysia

Chinese New Year

The Chinese Lunar New Year, as its name suggests, marks the first day of the first moon in the Chinese lunar calendar and is the most important festival for the Chinese community in Malaysia. The main event is the family reunion dinner which is held on New Year's Eve. The festival is celebrated for 15 days and a common practice throughout this period is the giving of *ang pow* (red packets) containing cash by married Chinese to single people, especially youngsters. It is a two-day public holiday in Malaysia. Throughout the period of the festival there is much visiting and special street stalls and decorations are set up in districts with a large Chinese population.

Ang pow (red packets) usually have new year greetings written on them. It is customary for them to be given by family members and also employers. The money given must always be an even number.

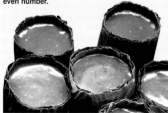

The *nian gou* (New Year cake) is a circular brown cake made from rice flour and sugar. Its stickiness symbolizes standing by one another, while its sweet taste promises the consumer a good and prosperous life.

A very popular dish at Chinese Lunar New Year is *yee sang* (an exotic raw fish salad), which is tossed by everyone seated at the table. This communal tossing of the salad signifies a wish for all to have good fortune in the coming year. *Yee sang* is also eaten on All Humans' Birthday.

Birthday of the Jade Emperor

The Birthday of the Jade Emperor falls on the ninth day of the first moon in the Chinese lunar calendar. The Jade Emperor is considered one of the great beings—ruler of the created universe—in Taoism. The Hokkien Chinese commonly call this day Thih Kong Ser and consider it to be even more important than Chinese New Year. Brought by the early immigrants to Malaysia, this custom has become a part of local religious culture. On the eighth day of the first moon, the Hokkien community enjoy great celebrations. They offer sugar cane, which signifies the sweetness of life, and its sections represent the different stages of life. They set up an altar to pray and make offerings to the Jade Emperor between 11 pm and 1 am. The celebration starts on the eve of Jade Emperor's birthday. All night long, crowds throng the Thnee Kong Thnua (temple) at the foot of Penang Hill to pay homage. Cities such as Penang and Johor Bahru, which are predominantly Hokkien, celebrate this festival with great spirit.

Yuan Xiao (Lantern Festival)

The Yuan Xiao or Lantern Festival is known locally as Chap Goh Meh (Hokkien for '15th night'). As its name suggests, it is celebrated on the 15th day of the Chinese New Year, which is the first full moon of the year and marks the end of New Year. On this day there are great celebrations. Traditionally, it symbolizes the start of spring and lanterns are decorated by many households. These lanterns show the Heavenly Duke, who is thought to come to earth at this time, that all is well and that he

Statue of the Jade Emperor.

Traditional style red Chinese lanterns strung out across a street on Penang Island during the Yuan Xiao festival.

earth which are symbolized by 12 animals, as are individual years in a cycle of 12. The animal signs are rat, ox, tiger, hare, dragon, snake, horse, sheep, monkey, rooster, dog and boar. For feng shui and fortune telling, the traditional almanac calculations are mainly based on the solar calendar, not the lunar.

Oranges, a traditional Chinese festival gift.

Chinese festivals

In Malaysia, a wide variety of Chinese festivals are celebrated, reflecting the many different immigrant communities. Over time, some characteristics, such as offerings and worship rituals and the emphasis given to specific festivals, have evolved in the Malaysian context. The fruits used as offerings, for example, are mainly tropical; different from those used in China.

Usually, the festivals that are widely accepted and repeatedly celebrated have multiple objectives and cultural meanings. Many have connections with farming seasons as well as religious practices. Chinese festivals in Malaysia can also indicate differences between dialect communities. For example, the Penang Hokkien consider the birthday of the Jade Emperor as important as Chinese New Year and celebrate it on a much grander scale than other Chinese dialect groups.

Popular Chinese festivals in Malaysia

FESTIVAL/CELEBRATION	MONTH
Li Chun (Beginning of Spring)	Usually on 4 or 5 February of the Gregorian calendar
Yuan Dan (New Year's Day)	1st day of the 1st moon in the Chinese lunar calendar
Song Qiong Ri (Day of Farewell to Poverty)	3rd day of the 1st moon in the Chinese lunar calendar
Ren Ri /Lao Sheng (All Humans' Birthday)	7th day of the 1st moon in the Chinese lunar calendar
Birthday of the Jade Emperor	9th day of the 1st moon in the Chinese lunar calendar
Yuan Xiao (Lantern Festival)	15th day of the 1st moon in the Chinese lunar calendar
She Ri (Community Day)	2nd day of the 2nd moon in the Chinese lunar calendar
Jing Zhe (Day of Awakening)	Around 6th March of the Gregorian calendar
Taoist Day/Birthday of the Supreme Elderly Master	15th day of the 2nd moon in the Chinese lunar calendar
Qing Ming (Tomb Sweeping Day)	5 or 6 April of the Gregorian calendar
Wesak Day	15th day of the 4th moon in the Chinese lunar calendar
Duan Wu (Dragon Boat Festival)	5th day of the 5th moon in the Chinese lunar calendar
Birthday of Kuan Yin	19th day of 2nd, 6th and 9th moon in Chinese lunar calendar
Qi Xi (Festival Double Seven/Chinese Lovers' Day)	7th day of the 7th moon in the Chinese lunar calendar
Zhong Yuan (Hungry Ghost Festival)	15th day of the 7th moon in the Chinese lunar calendar
Zhong Qiu (Mid-Autumn/Mooncake Festival)	15th day of the 8th moon in the Chinese lunar calendar
Nine Emperor Gods Festival	1st to 9th Day of 9th moon in the Chinese lunar calendar
Chong Yang (Double Nine Festival)	9th day of the 9th moon in the Chinese lunar calendar
Dong Zhi (Winter Solstice)	22 or 23 December in the Gregorian calendar
Wei Ya (Year End Feast)	6th day of the 12th moon in the Chinese lunar calendar
Song Zao Ri/Sao Chen Jie (Day of Farewell to Kitchen God/Dust Sweeping Day)	24th day of the 12th moon in the Chinese lunar calendar
Chu Xi (New Year's Eve)	Last day of the 12th moon in the Chinese lunar calendar

Coloured buns (turtles symbolize longevity) are given at festivals.

By burning Photor Kong, the King of the Hungry Ghosts (the incarnation of the Goddess of Mercy), devotees send him off to the spirit world.

can bestow prosperity on his followers. This festival is especially popular among immigrant Chinese communities. Traditionally, on this well-lit night, women were allowed out of their homes after winter. It was a night associated with looking for marriage partners, when women would toss oranges into the sea and wish for good husbands.

Zhong Yuan (Hungry Ghost Festival)

The Hungry Ghost Festival begins on the 15th day of the 7th moon in the Chinese lunar calendar and lasts for a whole month. According to Taoist legend, the gates of hell are opened once a year to allow spirits to wander among the living. To pacify these demanding ghosts, the Chinese offer joss sticks, food, paper gifts and hell notes. This festival is a time to forgive and repent any sins. It is also a time for doing acts of charity. Traditionally, during this festival Chinese opera troupes would visit local communities.

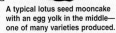

A typical lotus seed mooncake with an egg yolk in the middle—one of many varieties produced.

Zhong Qiu (Mooncake Festival)

Zhong Qiu or the Mooncake Festival is a mid-autumn festival that is celebrated on the 15th day of the 8th moon. It is a historical festival that marks the successful Chinese rebellion against Mongol rule in 14th-century China. The Chinese forces were successful against the Mongols by hiding secret messages inside pastry cakes—mooncakes. Mooncakes of many types are widely distributed and consumed at this time. The Mooncake festival initially started out as an important family event, but nowadays has become an outdoor event where lantern processions are held on the streets.

Nine Emperor Gods Festival

The Nine Emperor Gods Festival is celebrated by a large number of devotees from the first to the ninth day of the ninth moon in the Chinese lunar calendar to commemorate the birthdays of the Nine Emperor Gods.

These nine gods represent the constellation Beidou. During this festival, the Chinese perform prayers at temples dedicated to the Nine Emperor Gods and consume only vegetarian food. The first few days of the ninth month are also the birthdays of other deities who, during the celebrations, are thought to come to temples to join in the festivities. It is believed that they convey messages through devotees in a state of trance. These nine days have become a period for rituals such as walking on fire and thrusting hands into boiling oil. The festival culminates on the ninth day when the Nine Emperor Gods in the company of other deities are carried in procession around the community. By the authority of the Nine Emperor Gods the spirits of bad luck of the community are given a ceremonial send-off by setting adrift a decorated boat.

During the Nine Emperor Gods Festival devotees perform acts of penance, such as walking over hot coals.

Other festivals

The Chinese also celebrate a number of other important festivals such as Qing Ming (Tomb Sweeping Day), Duan Wu, Kuan Yin's Festival and Dong Zhi. The latter is a major festival, during which Chinese pray to their ancestors and prepare balls of coloured glutinous rice. The dragon boat race, part of Duan Wu, has found its own life in modern times as a sporting event.

The Day of Farewell to the Kitchen God is a domestic festival at the end of the year. The Kitchen God reports to heaven on everyone's deeds. He will have his mouth symbolically gummed up by offering honey to his tablet to sweeten his report or prevent him from speaking at all.

During Qing Ming ancestors' graves are cleaned—dirt is swept away, any undergrowth is pulled, and offerings of food and spirit money are made.

Buddhist and Chinese temples

The word 'temple' is used somewhat ambiguously in Malaysia to refer to a wide variety of Chinese places of worship. Temples vary from the unpretentious structures comprising tiny shrines to complex buildings consisting of grand halls separated by spacious courtyards. Whilst 'pure' Buddhist temples are few in number in Malaysia, many temples house both Buddhist and non-Buddhist deities.

Offerings in temples represent the combination and interaction of the five elements in the world—water, wood, fire, metal and earth.

Symbolism in Chinese and Buddhist temples

A dragon with a fish's body (*au yue*) is depicted on this temple roof.

Guardian lion at the entrance to a temple.

Chinese and Buddhist temples have certain distinctive features especially on the façade and roof, which is usually decorated with dragons and other auspicious animals. Lions are common, sacred guardians. There usually are two lions, a male and a female. The male holds a ball on his left paw and the female carries a child. Some temples also have a dragon with a fish head to hide all joining parts (pillar and roof) as a symbol against fire. Sharp or triangular shapes are considered harmful and are covered with lucky symbols.

Temples in Malaysia

In temple architecture, particular importance is given to the belief that all aspects of life are closely related to nature. This belief is expressed symbolically; the roofs of temples may resemble the shape of waves or the tails of swallows and fish. The colour red is also given prominence as it represents joy, prosperity and the sun. Temple layouts usually depend on the community the temple serves, which can be any one of the four major Chinese groups in Malaysia: Hakka, Hokkien, Cantonese or Teochew. However, the differences are very slight and stylistic rather then structural. For example, Hokkien temples have prominent, elaborate, steeply curved roofs whereas Teochew temples have flat roofs and Hakka temples have curved roofs not as elaborate as those of Hokkien style.

All temples maintain regularity and symmetry in their structure. Most temples have a hall or series of halls where the deities are housed. Larger temples have several halls, starting with the prayer pavilion where worshippers offer prayers before moving on to the main hall where the shrine of the most venerated deity is kept together with the temple bell and drum. Although Chinese temples are often dedicated to one particular deity, a temple usually houses images of several belonging to both the Buddhist and the Taoist pantheon. A temple is considered to be Buddhist if the patron deity is a Buddhist deity and it is considered syncretic or 'mixed' if both Buddhist and Taoist deities are displayed in addition to housing the numerous ancestral tablets. However, a Taoist temple houses only Taoist deities.

Buddhist temples

When immigrant Chinese, Thai, Burmese and Sinhalese came to Malaysia, they established Buddhist temples and associations throughout the country. The Chinese, being the largest group of Buddhist immigrants, have built the most temples. The majority of Chinese Buddhist temples in Malaysia belong to the Mahayana tradition. Although there is no clear boundary between Chinese Buddhism and other Chinese religions,

especially for everyday worshippers who take part in both systems, the separate identity of Chinese Mahayana Buddhism may be discerned from an examination of temples which are purely Buddhist as compared with those which include elements of both Buddhism and Chinese religions.

In pure Mahayana Buddhist temples, only Buddhas and Bodhisattva, such as Amitabha, Avalokitesvara (Kuan Yin) and Mahasthamaprapta are worshipped. Comparatively more numerous are *si* (Buddhist) temples in Malaysia that house many non-Buddhist deities in addition to the patron deity of Buddhist origin. For example, the Cheng Hoon Teng Temple in Melaka, the oldest Chinese temple in the country (built in the late 16th century), is not a Buddhist temple although it houses resident Buddhist monks who perform daily rituals.

Main altar   Incinerator

Dialect association/community temple

At its initial stage of establishment (1889), the Kwong Siew Association, Kuala Lumpur, a dialect association, doubled as a place of worship for its members. Later, it opened to the public for worshipping deities but still retained its status as a dialect association (as it still does). Such community temples are dedicated to patron saints, home town deities and ancestors.

In Malaysia, 'Chinese Buddhism' hardly exists as an independent system of religion and its distinctiveness can probably only be found in a few Chinese Buddhist temples and associations. The few 'pure' Mahayana Buddhist temples are largely in the Pure Land tradition, meaning that worshippers must not offer meat dishes on the temple premises.

Role of Buddhist temples

Historically, Buddhist temples have been centres of religious education and cultural activities. Temples were often the seat of education for the masses before the rise of secular schools and colleges.

For lay Buddhists, the temple is the place they come to worship and make offerings. In Theravada temples, devotees are present every day as they come to make food offerings to the monks. Buddhists believe that they gain merit when they offer food to monks. Occasionally, devotees invite monks to their homes for food offerings, although this is usually a temple activity.

Temples are also used to conduct Buddhism classes and meditation. Religious talks are usually held on Sunday mornings after the usual chanting and meditation classes. In some temples, 'Sunday Dharma Schools' have been set up for children.

Many Buddhist temples carry out social and welfare projects, including schools, orphanages, clinics and homes for the elderly. The first Buddhist orphanage, for example, was established by the Phor Tay Temple in Penang in 1936.

Temples of the Chinese religions

It is estimated that there are more than 1000 Chinese temples throughout the country. Ancestor worship, Confucianism and Taoism all find expression in a typical Chinese temple in Malaysia.

In most rural Chinese communities, there is usually at least one community temple managed by a temple committee. These are generally the largest and most ostentatious buildings in the neighbourhood. As well as centres of religious worship they are places of social and cultural activity. The Guangfu Gong in Penang, for example, is an important community temple whose congregation embraces the whole Chinese community of the state of Penang.

In contrast to the community temples, privately owned temples are smaller in scale and are more commonly referred to as *tan* (shrines). Temples of this category usually provide divination services, for example by spirit mediums who may be the shrine owners. If a shrine gains a reputation for its efficacy, it may be turned into a large temple within a short period as sponsorship of a temple is believed to be an expression of appreciation of the deity.

Chinese and Buddhist temples
Some of the major Chinese temples are found in Penang, Perak, Selangor, and Melaka where there are large Chinese communities.

The Cheng Hoon Teng Temple in Melaka, the oldest temple in the country, was built in 1645. The main hall (above) was completed in 1704.

Sam Poh Tong Cave Temple in Ipoh was built by Chinese monks who arrived there with the wave of Chinese immigrants around the beginning of the 20th century.

The lavishly and ornately decorated Puu Jih Syi Buddhist temple was built on the hilltop above Tanah Merah, south of Sandakan in 1987.

Nikkhodharam Temple in Alor Star, Kedah.

Thai Buddhist Temple in Tumpat, Kelantan.

Thai Buddhist temples can also be found elsewhere in Malaysia, including well-known ones such as Wat Chayamangkalaram in Penang, (which houses a 33-metre-long reclining Buddha statue), the Chetawan Temple in Petaling Jaya and the Nikkhodharam Temple in Alor Star.

Guardian dragons
The pearl symbolizes the life force of the dragon.

Subsidiary shrine

Guardian lion

A privately owned temple may also develop into a community temple. In this case, its sphere of divine protection will widen to include the community as a whole, and a temple committee will be set up to run day-to-day matters.

Chinese rites of passage

Birth, marriage and death are considered major events by all cultures. Adherents to Chinese religions are no exception and have their own ways of marking these major events in life. In modern times, however, many rituals have been discarded or shortened and adapted to fit in with today's society and lifestyles.

A couple receiving blessings from the deities on their wedding day, Cheng Hoon Teng Temple, Melaka.

Birth

The family is the primary unit in Chinese society. Children are of paramount importance in ensuring family continuity. Traditionally, it was the son who was expected to show filial piety by practising ancestor worship when his parents passed away. Without the birth of an heir to inherit the family surname, a family's 'incense fire' will be extinguished—there will be no one to venerate the ancestors. The birth of a baby boy is, therefore, considered an especially happy event.

During the full month celebration of the birth of a child friends and relatives are given red hard-boiled eggs, cakes and sweetmeats.

News of a pregnancy brings much excitement into a family. The expectant mother is expected to follow certain observances before the birth such as following a special diet, which includes soups made from Chinese herbs, to ensure that the foetus is carefully nurtured and protected. She is also discouraged from attending funerals, and sometimes weddings, for fear of affecting the 'harmonious' balance of the foetus.

An expectant mother usually prays to Kuan Yin (the Goddess of Mercy)—considered the patron saint of mothers. Amongst Theravada Buddhists, expectant mothers listen to Buddhist chants, believed to facilitate a safe, easy delivery.

After the birth, both mother and child undergo a month of 'confinement'. During this time the mother does not leave the house and she adheres to a special diet.

In some Chinese families, the custom of bathing the new-born baby before the Goddess of Children on the third day is still practised. This deity, called the 'Mother', is believed to watch over the child.

Naming the baby is also a matter of great concern to some families who believe that the composition of the name should refer to the five elements: metal, wood, water, fire and earth. This results from the belief that the choice of name will determine the destiny of the baby.

The most important event for the newborn baby is the first full month celebration. At this point the baby's head is shaved and ancestors and patron deities in the baby's home are offered incense and food as tokens of thanksgiving. Friends and relatives are given a package of special dishes by the parents. This package typically contains hard-boiled eggs, which are dyed red to symbolize the renewal of life. Their round shape also suggests harmony and unity to followers of Chinese religions. Other items that are typically included in the package are *ang koo* (red coloured buns) and *nasi kunyit* (turmeric rice).

Marriage

The Chinese believe that marriage is an integral part of life and thus great pains are taken to ensure a good match and bountiful posterity. Marriage is considered to be the rite of passage through which one attains adulthood.

The custom of matching the horoscopes of the couple before the match is confirmed persists among Chinese families in Malaysia who adhere to traditional practices. The prospective bride's horoscope is placed under the incense burner in front of the ancestral tablet for three days. The match is considered favourable if no inauspicious omens

A couple performing the tea ceremony which is the most important part of wedding rituals for the Chinese.

The tea ceremony

The tea ceremony usually begins by offering tea to the patron deities and family ancestors at the family altar in the bride's home. This is done to pay respects to the elders and to obtain their blessing. More important, however, is the serving of tea to parents and elderly relatives. The tea ceremony is repeated in the groom's home. The tea ceremony is, thus, an expression of acceptance into the groom's family. During the ceremony the bride and groom acknowledge the elders according to their 'rank'. In return the elders normally present *ang pow* (red packets containing money) or jewellery to the bride. Malaysian Chinese, regardless of their religious beliefs, continue to perform this ceremony as a part of their wedding day rituals.

Most Chinese weddings end with a dinner celebration at a hotel or restaurant.

occur within this time, such as quarrelling, death of livestock or the breaking of cooking utensils. Traditionally, at the end of the three days, an elderly relative of the prospective groom will be sent to the bride's parents to ask for her hand in marriage. Nowadays, the groom usually speaks directly to his prospective parents-in-law.

Agreement has to be reached on questions such as betrothal gifts to confirm the union, the exchange of gifts and the wedding date, as well as the customary rites to be observed on the wedding day. In the past, it was not uncommon for a marriage to be broken off due to disagreement over the betrothal.

Wedding ceremony

On the eve of the wedding the bride and groom undergo a 'hairdressing ceremony' in their respective homes. This is performed by a person with 'good destiny', someone with a living spouse, many children and grandchildren. Along with the 'hairdressing ceremony', auspicious words are uttered, wishing the couple a large number of offspring and eternal matrimonial harmony.

On the wedding day, the groom and his best man pick up the bride from her home. The groom is greeted by the bride's younger brother or a young male relation, who opens the bridal car door for the groom. He is rewarded with an *ang pow*. At this stage, the bride is fully dressed in her wedding gown. Her father will place the wedding veil on her head, symbolizing her attainment of adulthood. Before leaving, the couple will perform the tea ceremony. They will then drive to the groom's home.

Once there, the couple will repeat the tea ceremony for the groom's family. After this ceremony some couples go to the temple to receive blessings from priests and monks. The wedding day traditionally concludes with a dinner for relatives and friends. Traditionally, only the groom's relatives and friends were invited. Today, however, the bride's family and their guests usually attend. The guests present the couple with monetary gifts in *ang pow*.

Death

Malaysian Chinese observe various taboos and perform certain rites during the pre-burial mourning period. At the moment of death, family members burst into loud wailing and crying. The living room is cleared of all furniture and household items. A white banner is placed over the door of the home to announce that the family is in mourning. Close relatives and friends are notified of the death and an obituary notice is also placed in newspapers.

Family members of the deceased will then put on mourning garments. In the past, there were five

Burial and cremation

On the morning of the funeral family members and visitors pay their last respects to the deceased. Then, the coffin is placed on a hearse. Traditionally, close relatives and friends accompanied the deceased by walking all the way to the cemetery. Today relatives and friends will walk a short distance and then proceed to the cemetery in motor vehicles. The funeral procession may be headed by a traditional Chinese musical troupe or a brass band.

At the cemetery, the coffin is carefully lowered into the ground in accordance with geomantic calculations. A simple offering is made for the deceased. Family members and close friends turn their backs at this point to show that the separation from their loved one is too much for them—the grave is then closed by the grave-diggers. On arrival at home, a simple purifying ritual is conducted by the monk or Taoist priest, denoting the conclusion of pre-burial mourning.

In recent years, cremation has gained popularity. Cremation is different from burial only at the final stage of the funeral. On arrival at the crematorium, the coffin is pushed into an enclosed burner after a simple rite performed by a Buddhist monk or Taoist priest. Family members return the next day to collect the ashes, which are then put into an urn and placed in a columbarium. An incense urn and a photo of the deceased, carried by the eldest son and eldest grandson, respectively, are then placed on the ancestral altar at the family home.

The type of the cloth covering the head shows the relationship to the deceased. In this case the mourners are from the immediate family as they are wearing hemp.

A wife does not follow the procession; she remains at home, symbolizing that she will not abandon her husband.

grades of mourning, depending on the relationship of the mourner to the deceased. Mourners were differentiated by the types of mourning garments they wore. For example, the children of the deceased were considered the first grade and were required to wear hemp until after the funeral. Nowadays, it is more common for mourners to wear everyday clothes in white or black.

Traditionally, for one to seven days after the death friends and relatives are invited to come and pay their respects. A dinner of rice porridge is served. For the first 49 days after the death a paper ancestor tablet is placed on the home shrine and prayed to. After this it is burnt and replaced with a wooden one.

Rituals for the repose of the dead

The Chinese who are influenced by Buddhism believe that the soul of the deceased must make its way to the 'Western Pure Land'. Many rituals are conducted to assist the deceased's soul on this journey. Although there are many regional differences, certain standardized rituals include the ritual washing and clothing of the deceased, the encoffining and the offering of food, flowers, incense and the burning of an array of paper goods believed to be of use to the departed in the next world.

During the funeral period of normally one to seven days, Buddhist monks or nuns or a Taoist priest, depending on the faith of the deceased, are engaged to conduct the funeral rites to lead the soul to the next world.

Lanterns are hung in Chinese homes during funerals. The lantern has the age plus three years to show the age in lunar months of the deceased person, usually written in blue. However, if the age is written in red it indicates the deceased was over 100.

For the third anniversary of a relative's death a large paper house is built for the ancestor to reside in. It is then burnt to send it off to the next world.

Ancestor worship and spirits

In Malaysia, ancestor worship and consultation of spirit mediums are widely practised by devotees of Chinese religions. The practice of ancestor worship is rooted in the Confucian concept of honouring one's ancestors, which serves to reinforce the ethnic principle of filial piety. Spirit cults involve spirit mediums, where spirits of deities are believed to descend into the body of a person and speak to worshippers through that person.

A spirit possession in progress. When the spirit takes possession, its every whim and fancy will be entertained with the aid of charms and rituals.

Spirit mediums

Spirit mediums in Malaysia can be divided into two broad categories: spirit mediums who act as a mediator between the gods and the worshippers, and those who use planchette divination (spirit-writing). Well-known spirit medium temples and shrines provide consultation and divine healing services to devotees through spirit mediums. Spirit mediums are either associated with a temple or act privately. Besides these, religious groups conduct planchette divinations in addition to usual worship sessions. One of the functions of the mediums is similar with that of the fate-tellers or priests: they explain and resolve the problems faced by devotees in their daily lives. Their advice can be on illnesses suffered by devotees or any other obstacles faced due to unseen reasons such as bad karma, bad luck, incompatibility of partners, relatives or competitors and sometimes they even advise on bad human–spirit relations. In such cases the devotee has to appease the spirit based on the advice given by the medium.

They appease the offended spirit by making offerings at a particular time and venue, which can be a riverbank, roadside or any piece of vacant land specified by the medium.

In other instances, the solutions may include earning good merit by doing charity work, chanting mantras of various Chinese beliefs, lighting lamps and making offerings to certain deities. Devotees also purify themselves with flower water prepared by a medium or priest and thus considered sacred. Some Chinese offer food and burn hell notes (money created for use in the afterlife) in their backyards or the back lane of their house on the 1st and 15th day of every lunar month. They believe that this shows respect to all the spirits passing their homes.

Spirit mediums, Penang.

A worship tablet to the Heavenly Duke hung outside the main entrance of a house in Melaka. This deity is only worshipped in Malaysia and Singapore. He assesses individuals' merit and awards prosperity accordingly.

Main deities of spirit mediums

Spirit cults in Malaysia practise seances in which deities such as the Monkey God, the Third Prince, Kuan Yin (the Goddess of Mercy) and Guan Gong are believed to possess mediums. It is believed that high-ranking deities such as the Jade Emperor and Sakyamuni Buddha are above such possession and therefore rarely make an appearance.

Spirit cults in Malaysia also include indigenous traditions, such as the worship of 'Datuk' Kong, the Malaysian earth god. No pork is allowed in the offerings. Instead, shredded tobacco, areca nut flakes and betel leaves with lime paste and fruit are common offerings. This spirit portrays himself as an old holy man. When possessed by this spirit, the medium speaks gently in Malay and addresses devotees as *cucu* (grandchildren).

Kuan Yin, the Goddess of Mercy.

Datuk Kong shrines are commonly found along roads in Chinese communities.

Planchette divination

Planchette divination, or spirit-writing, is another form of spirit mediation, believed to date back to the Song Dynasty (960–1279). Spirit-writing is practised by religious groups in Malaysia such as the I-Kuan Tao, World Red Swastika Society, the Moral Uplifting Society (also known as De Jiao Hui) and several other temples and sectarian groups.

While divination by a spirit medium in trance is taken to be a shamanistic and superstitious form of divination, planchette divination is considered to be more rational and intellectual in nature. This is probably because divine messages in planchette divination are revealed in the form of classical Chinese poems or prose.

In the De Jiao Hui Association, planchette divination is done using a willow branch. Two planchette mediums hold the stick, each grasping one of the ends with one hand. Deities are invoked by chanting prayers. The mediums use the stick to write messages in the sand in a specially designed wooden tray. An assistant then records the messages, while another person reads out each character aloud. Another assistant levels the sand after each character has been read out. At the end of each message, the name of the deity who has delivered the message is announced.

Spirit possession

Spirit possession can either be involuntary or deliberate. The distinction between spirit medium and spirit possession is believed to be that while in both cases the entranced person is possessed by a spirit, with spirit mediums the spirit speaks to devotees through the medium. In spirit possession, the individual who is possessed may not function as an intermediary for communicating with worshippers but rather as a 'deity' who purifies and reunites the spiritual and secular worlds on his/her journey to the other world by performing symbolic rituals. In the past, spirit possession was a way of purifying the surroundings; temples would hold spirit possessions to augment their importance among devotees.

Lords of the Land Used

According to Chinese folk beliefs, the tangible and intangible effects of the living environment are partly monitored by the Lords of the Land Used (Di Zhu). Every building or space used has its interior Lords of the Land Used and outdoor Lords of the Land Used. The former are normally worshipped as a tablet on top of a piece of tile or brick under the altar in the hall of the building. The latter are worshipped without tablets or statues at the side of a gate or door post or at the corner of an outdoor pillar. Many Chinese in Malaysia have integrated their beliefs in the Lords of the Land Used from Hakka beliefs in southern China.

The left-hand side of the tablet is inscribed with the interior Lords of the Land Used, depicted as five directions. The Five Earth Dragon god is considered to be the personified feng shui energy of the four corners and the middle point of the building space. This god appears as a powerful dragon. On the right-hand side of the tablet Chinese or local spirits for wealth are found.

Some Chinese pray to the Lords of the Land Used by offering five bottles of the soft drink Fanta. This is a recent development; the pronunciation of the name is almost the same as the word *fada* which means wealth in Hakka and Cantonese dialects. Some Chinese do not make offerings to the outdoor Lords of the Land Used as they think that by doing so they would invite other spirits who could bring along negative energy and create bad human–spirit relations.

Making offerings to the outdoor Lords of the Land Used.

Ancestor worship

Ancestor worship is an important network of beliefs and practices in Chinese religions. It is historically the oldest and most basic aspect of Chinese religions. Archaeological finds have shown that ancestral rituals played an important part in Chinese religious life as early as the Shang and Yin dynasties, before 1000 BCE. In addition to associating ancestor worship with filial piety, most Chinese in Malaysia believe that the spirits of deceased ancestors should always be appeased in return for their blessings and a harmonious and prosperous life. In Malaysia, there are various forms of ancestor worship which can be divided into two broad categories: household worship and communal worship.

Household worship

Most Malaysian Chinese homes have an altar in the living room with offerings for the various deities.

Household worship takes two forms in Malaysia. In the first type, ancestral tablets which are placed to the right of the family altar, with the image of the patron deities on the left, are worshipped. Deities are always placed higher than ancestor tablets. The altar is normally placed facing the entrance of the house. Sometimes, ancestors are represented together on one collective tablet, consisting of a glass-framed sheet of red paper with the birth and death dates of the ancestors written on it. An incense pot is placed in front of the tablet.

The daily household ritual involves simply placing an odd number of joss sticks in the incense pot of the deities and an even number of joss sticks in the incense pot of the ancestors.

On the 1st and 15th day of each month of the Chinese calendar, a pair of red candles is lit and some fruit may be offered as well. Rich offerings will only be made on festival days, on joyful occasions or on the anniversary of the ancestor's death. At the end of the ceremony, joss paper is burned to augment the ancestor's life in the underworld.

A second type of worship, the practice of 'inviting the ancestors' has become increasingly popular. In this practice, no ancestral tablet is kept in the house but sometimes it is housed in a temple. Instead, a temporary altar is set up in the living room one day before a festival or on a joyful occasion. Incense is burned to invite the souls of the ancestors to return and participate in the family celebration. At the end of the festivities, the ancestors will be sent off, with joss paper burned for them.

This system of 'inviting the ancestors' is especially popular with the younger generation who live in urban areas and may not own a house. Many are unable to perform the daily ritual of burning incense for the ancestors. Some fear that if they keep an ancestral tablet they may offend the ancestors if they do not worship them regularly.

Communal worship

In Malaysia, many clan associations and ancestral temples have the tablets of the founding ancestors of a lineage, recent ancestors who have rendered meritorious service to the clan association and deceased members of the association on their shrine.

The shrine is divided into several sections. Topmost, in the central position, in the most superior position of the shrine, are the tablets of the founding ancestors of the clan.

Ancestral tablets usually contain the dates of birth and death of the ancestor.

Rituals for the ancestors are conducted two or three times a year: for the spring memorial (Chun Ji), the autumn memorial (Chew Ji) and the winter memorial (Dong Ji). The spring memorial usually coincides with Qing Ming. The autumn memorial, less commonly observed, coincides with the Hungry Ghost Festival, which falls on the 15th day of the 7th lunar month.

Families visiting the graves of their ancestors on Qing Ming. As space for traditional grave sites is becoming more and more restricted, cremation is becoming increasingly popular among Malaysian Chinese.

Qing Ming

Qing Ming is the Chinese All Souls' Day. This festival is said to be one of the oldest Chinese customs. It falls on the 106th day after the winter solstice, in the third month of the Chinese lunar year.

The practice of visiting the graves of the ancestors remains important during Qing Ming (also known as Cheng Beng) to many Chinese in Malaysia. Family members trim and clean the grave site and bring offerings of food and flowers. As cremation becomes more widespread, visiting the cemetery is being replaced by visits to the columbarium where the ashes of the departed ancestors are honoured in the same way.

1. Most Hindu temples in Malaysia have a *gopuram* built in tiers in South Indian style. Each tier has a symbolic meaning. The five tiers of this *gopuram* reflect the five senses.

2. During Thaipusam, devotees pierce their bodies as a sign of faith.

3. Women preparing a pot of rice during the Thai-Ponggal festivities.

4. These Shiva worshippers, distinguished by the white mark on their foreheads, are bringing pots of milk as offerings. The milk is used to bathe the deity.

5. Oil lamps are lit and offerings made by priests at most temple and domestic festivals and celebrations.

6. Devout Hindus often shave their hair and make an offering of it after making a vow to God. Here a devotee is making his offering and setting it afloat at Batu Caves, near Kuala Lumpur, as part of the rites and rituals conducted at a major festival.

HINDUISM

In the Hindu religion, the elephant-headed god Ganesha is believed to remove all obstacles. Thus, he brings joy and happiness to the family. There are many temples dedicated to him in Malaysia. To Malaysia's mostly Tamil population he is known more commonly as Vinayagar.

Although archaeological evidence shows that Hinduism existed in Malaysia long before the coming of Islam, the evolution and nature of Hinduism in Malaysia as it exists today is directly related to the process of migration of Indians, which began on a large scale during the second half of the 19th century as a result of the establishment of British administration and plantation agriculture. Malaysian Hindus now form about six per cent of the population and have integrated with the society at large while maintaining most aspects of their distinct culture.

The majority of Indians, mainly Tamils, Telugus and Malayalees, came to Malaysia to work as labourers and settled in plantations or were employed as manual labourers by the government. Some Sri Lankan Tamils and Malayalees were employed as clerks, supervisors and technicians. Other South Indians came from the commercial class and engaged in textile and retail businesses, and also in moneylending. All these diverse sub-ethnic groups brought with them their particular Hindu philosophical and religious traditions. The Tamils of South India and Sri Lanka, for example, adhere to the non-dualistic tradition (*Suddhadvaita*) which emphasizes Saivism (belief in Shiva), while the Telugus, Malayalees and many North Indians follow the tradition of qualified monism (*Visistadvaita*) in which Vaishnavism (belief in Vishnu) is emphasized. The North Indian and South Indian brahmins, on the other hand, follow the monistic tradition (*advaita*) of Sankara, which is the concept of God as the Supreme Being referred to as 'Brahman' in the Vedantic scriptures and 'Kadavul' in the Siddhantic texts.

Gods and goddesses in the Hindu belief system fulfil a devotee's need for guardian deities (*kaval*), personal deities (*istha*) and family deities (*kula*) whose assistance is sought when confronted with disease, calamities or personal predicaments, and for protection against evil spirits. Worship of these deities is normally carried out in temples as well as at home. It is possible to have worship conducted at home as most of the worshippers use the religious texts in their own languages. The system also allows for the worship of inanimate objects such as the *tulasi* (basil) plant and animate objects including the cow and the cobra. The *tulasi* plant is sacred to Vishnu and Shiva, and the cobra is associated with nearly every important deity (Shiva, Vishnu, Shakti, Ganesha, Murugan, etc.). Apart from its symbolism as a mother figure, the cow is sacred because of the belief that various deities reside in different parts of the cow, thus the taboo against eating beef. However, Hinduism accords greater significance to the worship of deities, who are usually regarded as manifestations of the Supreme Being.

Oil lamps are lit during major festivals. The peacock is the vehicle of the god Murugan. Each oil lamp has five points for wicks; these represent the five faces of Shiva to be worshipped and the five senses lit with the knowledge of God.

History of Hinduism in Malaysia

Hinduism, as one of the world's great religions, has evolved over a vast period of time—at least 5000 years. Several of its basic elements such as belief in God as the supreme Lord of all beings, popular worship of the Mother Goddess as a great manifestation of divinity, ritual bathing and use of iconographic symbols signifying various aspects of divinity can be seen in artefacts from the archaeological sites of Harappa and Mohenjo Daro. These sites in the Indus Valley (today in Pakistan) represent the earliest Hindu civilizations and date from 2500–1500 BCE.

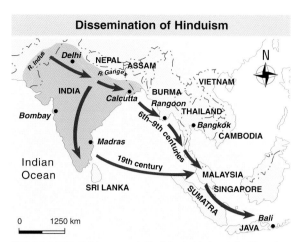

Dissemination of Hinduism

Hinduism is believed to have come to the Malay Archipelago in the 6th century through the trade route of Indian merchants. While on the island of Bali Hinduism is still the prevailing religion, much of the rest of the archipelago converted to Islam. With the Islamic resurgence of the 1970s, Hindu practices that were subsumed under the region's brand of Islam were filtered out. Much of present-day Hinduism in Malaysia is an import from India through the agency of the Indian migrants to the country and retains a strong resemblance to Hinduism in India.

The early development of Hinduism

In the period 1500–500 BCE, known as the Vedic period, Hinduism was enriched by the sacred revealed scriptures collectively known as the Vedas, philosophical treatises called the Upanishads, and the great epics of the *Ramayana* and the *Mahabharata* (which includes the *Bhagavad-Gita*) in Sanskrit.

Though the post-Vedic period saw the rise of several new systems of belief, such as Buddhism and Jainism, these did not undermine the fundamentals of Hinduism because of developments such as the Bhakti (devotional) movement in the medieval period (6th–15th centuries CE). During this time, Hindu scriptures in the form of devotional songs in praise of God were composed by scholarly saints in the many regional languages of India. During the Bhakti period numerous Hindu temples were built under the patronage of rulers who also promoted the development of Hindu fine arts such as music, dance, sculpture and painting.

Modern era

The renaissance of Hinduism occurred in the modern period (from the 18th century) under the leadership of eminent reformers, saints and scholars (e.g. Ram Mohan Roy, Sri Ramakrishna Paramahamsa, Swami Vivekananda, Rabindranath Tagore and Mahatma Gandhi). This came in response first to the Mughal conquest of northern India in the 16th century and, later, to the onslaught of modern European culture brought in the wake of colonization. The spread of English and Western education in India put an end to its intellectual isolation and brought it into contact with Western science and literature. In the light of the new knowledge, Hindu reformers were successful in purging Hindu society of many social evils and undesirable accretions and in helping the innate vitality of Hinduism to re-assert itself.

Though Hinduism has not been a proselytizing faith, its teachings have always attracted the attention of a vast number of people not only in the Indian subcontinent but also in many other parts of the world, including Malaysia.

Hinduism takes root in Malaysia

Hindu cultural relations with Malaysia date back at least 1500 years when the first Indian merchants began to frequent the Southeast Asian kingdoms for

Malaysia's oldest Hindu communities—Melaka and Penang

The Chitties of Melaka

Hindu influence continued to be diffused in the kingdom of Melaka in the 15th and 16th centuries CE, through Indian merchants from the Coromandel coast who founded a Hindu settlement in the city. The members of that community and their descendants intermarried with the local Malay population, adopting the Malay language, food and dress customs and came to be known as Ceti Melaka (Chitty). However, they retained their Hindu religious traditions and forms of worship. In the 18th century, the then Dutch colonial government granted them a piece of land to build a temple—the oldest working Hindu temple in Malaysia—the Sri Poyyatha Vinayagar Moorthi Temple on Jalan Hang Jebat, which was built in 1781. Sacred to both the Chettiar (traditional Hindu moneylenders) and the Chitty (Peranakan Indian-Malay) communities, the temple is dedicated to the deity Vinayagar (Ganesha), represented by an elephant's head made of black stone imported from India. At the annual Masi Magam festival, a sacred statue of Lord Subramaniam is conveyed on a silver chariot to the Nagarathar Temple at Cheng, about 10 km from Melaka town. The Chitty community was shifted to their own village (Kampung Gajah Berang) on the outskirts of Melaka during the British period.

A Chitty couple praying at their home altar, Melaka.

Penang's Chettiar community

With the founding of Penang as a major trading port by the British East India Company's Captain Francis Light in 1786 large numbers of people came from South India to settle. These included the Chettiars (a clan from Tamil Nadu) who were moneylenders and traders. This movement coincided with the beginnings of the Indian labour migration to Malaysia in the 18th and 19th centuries, which was encouraged by the British colonial power. Indian traders were also attracted to the growing port of Penang at this time. The growth of the Hindu population in Penang during the 19th century can be seen in the building of temples, for example the Sri Mahamariamman Temple in Queen Street, which was constructed in 1833, and the Nattukkottai Chettiar Temple, which is dedicated to Lord Murugan and caters to the Chettiar community.

Chettiar moneylenders in Penang Street, George Town, Penang.

The Bujang Valley, the oldest and richest historical site in Malaysia, is situated in Kedah. There are traces of 150 temple ruins which were left behind by early Hindu settlements. The above is the remains of a temple in Batu Pahat, Kedah.

trade. Hindu Brahmanical priests and scholars were invited by the local rulers to perform important religious and educational functions.

In Malaysia, the region of Kedah (known as Kataha in classical Sanskrit literature and as Kadaram or Kalakam in classical Tamil literature) is known to have been a great commercial centre by the 1st or 2nd century CE. The close relationship between Kedah (which was part of the great Southeast Asian kingdom of Srivijaya) and the Chola kingdom of South India is well attested to in Tamil sources of the medieval period as well. Religious monuments, such as Candi Bukit Batu Pahat in the Bujang Valley, Kedah and religious statuary dating to the 7th century CE have been discovered through archaeological excavations. Such finds provide ample evidence of the interaction between the local people and Hinduism from ancient times.

Hindu influences today

In the course of such interaction several elements of Hindu culture and civilization were adopted by the people of the Malay Peninsula and assimilated with political, religious, literary and linguistic aspects of their own culture and civilization. Thus, the institution of kingship was influenced by Hindu concepts, and the paraphernalia of the royal court ritual and ceremony was adopted. Some of these elements are known to have survived to this day (e.g. the royal installation ceremonies and the royal titles such as Duli Yang Maha Mulia Sri Paduka Baginda). Popular or folk Hindu beliefs also have mingled with indigenous folk beliefs and produced a pattern of beliefs which still persists (e.g. the rituals accompanying the *wayang kulit* or shadow play). The Sanskrit language, introduced by Brahmanical scholars officiating at the ancient royal courts, has left a marked impact on the vocabulary of the Malay language, enriching it with many new words and concepts. Malay contains many words of Sanskrit origin. The epic stories of the *Ramayana* and the

Mahabharata, disseminated largely through the medium of *wayang kulit*, have become part of traditional Malay literature and culture.

Historically, around 80 per cent of Indian immigrants were Hindu and this remains the proportion of the present Malaysian Indian population. Hindu plantation workers had temples built for them in the estates, which was in accordance with the Tamil adage which exhorts adherents not to live in a village or town where there is no temple.

The persistence of the Hindu religion in the Malaysian Indian tradition can be attributed to Hindu shrines and temples erected in both rural and urban areas. It is estimated that there are 2000 Hindu temples in Malaysia, including modest shrines as well as large temples. A significant feature of Hindu temples in Malaysia is that most of them are dedicated to the worship of the Mother Goddess (identified as Mariamman or Durga) while a substantial number are also dedicated to Lord Murugan or Lord Subramaniam. These are the two most popular Hindu deities worshipped in Malaysia. Another popular deity is Ganesha (Vinayagar or Pillaiyar in Tamil). As the remover of obstacles, Ganesha is found in nearly all temples, meriting offerings and puja (prayer).

As the vast majority of Hindus in Malaysia are of South Indian descent, it is the Hindu customs and practices of southern India that predominate. The main emphasis is on the Saivite faith (relating to the worship of Lord Shiva as the Supreme God), though there are also devotees of Lord Vishnu (known as the Vaishnavites), among those of northern Indian, Malayalee and Telegu descent. The *Bhagavad-Gita* is their most popular text, though Tamil-speaking Vaishnavites also recite verses from the collection of hymns known as the *Thivyappirapantham* composed from the 6th to the 9th centuries. The Saiva Siddhanta School of southern Indian Hinduism is also popular with those of Tamil origin.

A *wayang kulit* puppet portraying the Hindu god Rama. The *Ramayana* epic (life of Rama) is a popular theme in *wayang kulit* performances.

Hindu deity, the elephant-headed Ganesha, son of Shiva.

Sri Sithi Vinayagar Temple in Kuantan, Pahang, is one of the oldest in Malaysia. It is dedicated to the god Ganesha—known as Vinayagar in Tamil.

Hindu beliefs and world-view

Hinduism comprises many sects but the common denominator is their acceptance of the Veda (sacred texts dating back to 1500–500 BCE). However, the Upanishad (sacred philosophical books from 400–200 BCE), the Bhagavad-Gita (from the Mahabharata) and the Vedanta Sutras are said to be the foundation of Vedanta (one of Hinduism's major schools of philosophy) and the monism it expounds. In common worship a vast pantheon of distinct gods is one of the most striking features of Hinduism. Ultimately, they are all manifestations of God.

The *vimana* is the dome over the most sacred place in the temple, the *garbha-grham*, where the deity is kept.

'Om' is the most sacred sound for the Hindus, and is the beginning of all Hindu prayers. This Tamil Om symbol can be found in most Saivite temples in Malaysia. The 'Om' sound consists of three component sounds, 'A' (ah), 'U' (ooh), and 'M' (mm). Said together the individual sounds signify the trinity of the gods of creation, preservation and destruction. Om is the sound of infinity; the primordial sound. In Hindu cosmology sound was created first, not light, as in most other religions.

God

God the Almighty is the supreme eternal, impersonal, absolute reality without gender, form, name or attribute. He transcends all, including time and space. Yet eight attributes are ascribed to this state. He is said to be omnipotent, omnipresent, omniscient, all-perfect, independent, conscious, immanent and the embodiment of grace. He is in each being but is not tainted by the imperfections of matter. This impersonal God, out of his boundless compassion, assumes various forms and attributes, manifested in the Hindu pantheon, for the benefit of ordinary souls.

The Trinity

The Trinity (*trimurti*) consists of Brahma, Vishnu and Shiva. As Brahma, God creates the world for all souls by giving them a body and an abode in accordance with their previous actions (karma). As Vishnu, the Almighty sustains the universe and maintains order and justice. When the stipulated time for each body or world is over, He, as Shiva Rudra the destroyer, annihilates them. Thus creation, protection and destruction continue in an unending cycle. In Malaysia most Hindus are Saivites (followers of Shiva), though Vaishnavites (followers of Vishnu) also make up part of the Hindu population. There are, however, no followers of Brahma and thus no temple dedicated to him.

The trident, in Hindu iconography, symbolizes the unity of three primal forces: creation, destruction and preservation.

The stages of life—varnaashrama

Made up of two words, *varna* (caste) and *ashrama* (stage in life), this term is used to denote one's duties and obligations throughout life, according to one's place in society and stage of life.

Traditionally, four castes—brahmin (priests), *kshatriya* (warriors), *vaishya* (traders and agriculturists) and *shudra* (menial workers) are delineated. But in reality, the caste system takes account of many occupational divisions. However, among Hindus who migrated to Malaysia, the caste system is of little consequence in the modern economy and society.

A man's life was traditionally divided into four stages: *brahmacarya*, *grihastha*, *vanaprastha* and *sannyasa*. During the first stage, a person received an all-round education teaching him a skill for his secular life as well as the art of living a virtuous life. This was a period of celibacy. Then he married a suitable young woman and set up a home. Thus, he became a *grihastha* (householder). This stage is not for mere

The basic beliefs of Hinduism

The basic beliefs of Hindus may be summed up in five words—God, soul, karma, rebirth (*samsara*) and salvation (*moksha*).

Soul

The soul is immortal. Birth simply provides the soul with a new body, environment and experiences. Death is its departure from that body. The body, intellect and experiences in life are given to the soul according to its deeds in its past lives. As long as it is ignorant of its nature and capabilities and is enamoured of the world, it will undergo repeated births. But it can attain enlightenment through virtuous living and belief in God and His Supreme Grace. Once enlightened the soul is liberated from repeated births.

Karma and samsara

The thoughts, words and deeds of a person (or soul) in each birth constitute his karma, which determines his experience in future births. There is no direct correlation between one's condition and the previous life. The total karma of past births forms a whole and only a part of it is

Hindus move their hands over the sacred flame and to their foreheads in a sign of devotion.

meted out, to be experienced in each birth. The soul carries its burden through numerous births and keeps adding to it as a result of ignorance and carelessness. Therefore, it takes countless births before a soul can shed its karma. This journey through repeated births is called *samsara*. Belief in karma has been criticized as encouraging fatalism. But a true understanding of this concept should make a person take control of his deeds and remove his karma with God's grace.

Salvation

Salvation (*moksha*) is the state of freedom from further births and union with the Almighty. This union with God is interpreted variously. According to the Vedanta system of philosophy it is total union in which the soul loses its identity while in Saiva Siddhanta philosophy it is a state of union which is non-dual in nature. It is a positive state of eternal bliss.

The *Bhagavad-Gita* speaks of four paths (*marga*) to salvation. They are knowledge (*jnana*) of God or God-realization, meditation (*yoga* or *dhyana*), action (karma), meaning carrying out one's duties according to one's situation in life. This has to be done with a sense of dedication to one's own duties and to God. The fourth is *bhakti*—intense love for God. While *jnana* is considered the most difficult, *bhakti* is possible for all.

physical gratification but to raise a worthy family and perform social obligations including prayers for ancestors, worship and charity. Once family obligations are fulfilled, the couple withdraw from active social life and devote themselves to religious and spiritual search (*vanaprastha*). Finally, they renounce all desires and worldly belongings, becoming ascetics (*sannyasa*).

Purushartha

Purushartha relates to the purpose of man's life. According to Hindu ideals, a human being has four goals in life, namely virtue or appropriate behaviour, the pursuit of wealth and worldly success based on worthy principles (*artha*), the pursuit of pleasure including love, physical gratification and other domestic joys within the framework of his home (*kama*) and salvation (*moksha*). This concept of a complete life makes the *brahmacarya* stage very important for it teaches a person social norms and values to be practised throughout life.

Creation stories

In Hinduism, creation relates not merely to this earth but to the whole universe (*prapanca*). Many stories are available in regard to creation. According to Saivites, Shakti (the goddess or the active power of God in all the junctions of creation, preservation and destruction), who conjoins Lord Paramasina, stirs *maya* (matter) from which evolves *jagath* (the universe).

Vaishnavites believe that during the deluge and destruction of the universe, Narayana/Vishnu alone remains in *yoganitthirai* (sleep or meditation in which He is aware of everything) on a *banayan* leaf and Brahma (God of Creation) would appear from Vishnu's navel and start creating the universe. From the Vedic point of view, when Brahman (the Ultimate Principle) creates a golden egg (*hiranya garbha*) and enters the latter, Brahma would appear and start creating the universe.

World-view

The term *loka* means a part of the universe. Besides the earth and the other planets there are other worlds too, including heaven, hell and the world of *deva* (enlightened beings), all with inhabitants. These are souls sent to experience the joyous or painful effects of karma.

There is only one supreme spirit, though it is worshipped in many different names and forms. All religions and religious sects are ways of reaching that supreme spirit, who is within each soul. All living beings from plants to humans have a soul. Therefore, all living beings have to be loved and respected. The voice of conscience is believed to be the voice of God within one's soul.

The soul cannot carry anything with it when it leaves the body except for the karma based on acts virtuous or otherwise from previous lives. Thus a certain degree of detachment from worldly joys or possessions is implied, encouraging followers to be rid of anger, greed, cruelty and other negative qualities. Thus, Hindus do not believe that they pass through this world only once but many times on the journey to spiritual salvation.

Some important deities

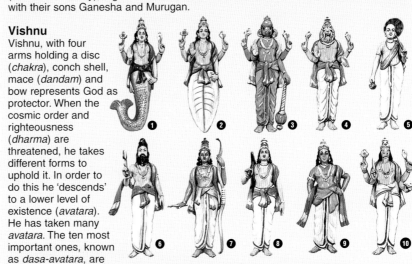

Shiva and Parvathi.

Shiva

Shiva has many forms. The *lingam* (a representation of cosmic energy) is his formless form, worshipped as the main deity in nearly every Shiva temple. He is also pictured as being absorbed in meditation (*yogi*), as the Supreme Teacher facing the south (Dakshinamoorthy), together with his consort, Parvathi, and sometimes both of them with their sons Ganesha and Murugan.

Vishnu

Vishnu, with four arms holding a disc (*chakra*), conch shell, mace (*dandam*) and bow represents God as protector. When the cosmic order and righteousness (*dharma*) are threatened, he takes different forms to uphold it. In order to do this he 'descends' to a lower level of existence (*avatara*). He has taken many *avatara*. The ten most important ones, known as *dasa-avatara*, are as a (**1**) fish (*matsya*), (**2**) a turtle (*kurma*), (**3**) a boar (*varaha*), (**4**) a man-lion (*narasimha*), (**5**) a midget (*vamana*), (**6**) Parashurama, (**7**) Rama, (**8**) Krishna, (**9**) Balarama or Buddha and (**10**) Khalki who is yet to come. His devotees, known as Vaishnavites, however, usually worship him as Vishnu, Rama, Krishna or Thirumal.

Statue of Durga at the Sri Nageswary temple, Bangsar.

Shakti

Shakti, meaning power or energy, is considered the female aspect of the Absolute and is worshipped either as the consorts of the Trinity—Brahma's consort is Sarasvathi, Vishnu's is Lakshmi and Shiva's is Parvathi, Kali or Durga—or in the form of a Mother Goddess. Sarasvathi (the goddess of learning and arts), Lakshmi (the goddess of wealth) and Parvathi (the goddess of success) and the various forms attributed to the Mother Goddess such as Mariamman, Durga, Kali and Rajarajeswary are also worshipped. Mariamman temples have found a place in most areas in Malaysia with a Hindu population from southern India.

Ganesha

Ganesha is also known as Vinayagar (without a superior), Pillaiyar (respected child of Shiva and Parvathi) and Ganapathy. He symbolizes wisdom and the ability to remove obstacles. As such, homage is paid to this deity with an elephant's head. Though he is regarded as a confirmed bachelor, Siddhi (success) and Buddhi (wisdom) are said to be his consorts. However, this form is rarely depicted in temples. He is a form of Shiva but in the Purana (stories of the creation and the gods written between 700 and 300 BCE) he is presented as the son of Shiva.

Murugan

Murugan is another son of Shiva and represents God's everlasting youth, beauty and heroism. Valli and Devayanai are his consorts. Together with his weapon, the spear (*vel*), they represent the three aspects of God's grace—desire (*icchai*), action (*kiriyai*) and knowledge (*jnana*)—which remove the karma and ignorance of souls and grant them salvation. He is also worshipped as a young boy of exquisite beauty (Balamurukan), a six-faced deity (Arumukan, Shanmuka) with 12 hands holding a bell, flag and various weapons including a spear which has given him the names Velan and Velayuthan.

Decorative temple figures—Ganesha and Murugan stand on either side of Shiva and Parvathi.

Hindu worship and practice

Worship or puja is an essential aspect of Hindu daily life. Though congregational worship is common, worship is a personal experience. God, in his many forms, is worshipped, but devotees usually have a personal attachment to a particular divine form. Rituals in worship may differ but the aims are usually the same. Hindus conduct their worship at various places and in various ways. The two main places are the home or temple, either in groups or individually. Conducting puja is the main form of communicating with God.

Brahmin priests chanting Vedic mantras in front of the holy fire during a special occasion.

Worship

The main aim in worship is to calm the mind and raise it to God so as to pave the way for the ultimate union with him. However, devotees also ask for specific favours such as good health, success in their undertakings, a good spouse, progeny and general welfare. Hindus also worship for the welfare of people dear to them, a departed soul or as thanksgiving for favours received. True devotees worship for the sheer joy of a personal relationship with God. Prayer calms the heart and mind, helps to develop the power of concentration and turns the worshipper towards God.

Dyana (meditation) and *japa* (repetition of a specific mantra) are also incorporated in domestic, individual and group worship. Care is taken to pronounce mantras correctly. When done quietly, it is called *manasika puja* (worship in the mind).

The most common form of worship is done with a likeness (image or picture) of the deity. Purification and decoration of the image, offering of water, flowers and vegetarian sweets or milk, singing the Lord's praises and prostration before him form the main parts of the puja. Worship is sometimes 'classified' according to the place, purpose and manner in which it is performed.

On festival days deities are carried through the temple grounds or towns to allow people to pay homage to them.

Temple worship

Worship in a temple is the most elaborate. It is usually performed three times a day —morning, noon and sunset. The two main parts of the worship are the ritual bathing of the deity (*abhishekam*), with milk, honey, lime and coconut juice and sandalwood paste, after which dressing and decoration of the deity are done behind a curtain. The other is puja proper where camphor and oil lamps are lit, food and flowers are offered, mantras are recited by the priest and religious hymns are sung. Puja bells are also rung during the bathing of the deity. Devotees are passive participants.

Domestic worship

Worship at home is very simple and often pictures of the chosen deity/deities are used, though some prefer statues in stone or bronze like temple images. At home, as in the temple, these images or pictures are cleaned on a regular basis (weekly/monthly and during fasts and festivals). Prayers are held in the morning and evening, though some people also say

Conducting puja

Puja allows the worshipper to commune directly with God. There are many variations to a puja session, but the various stages can be likened to receiving an honoured guest. Before undertaking puja it is important to have bathed or at least washed one's face, hands and feet and be wearing clean clothes. Shoes are always removed before entering a Hindu temple or place of prayer.

First stage – purification by driving out negative vibrations and invoking *deva* (enlightened beings) or good vibrations. This is done by ringing a bell and chanting a mantra by the person conducting the puja.

Second stage – meditation on God by chanting prayers and contemplating the Eternal One by chanting Vedic hymns or verses praising the Lord. These prayers are called *dhyaana* mantras.

Third stage – 16 phases of offering to the invoked god, as represented by a temple statue or image. The 16 offerings are made in five steps involving

chants to call the god or goddess to reside in the image, to allow the spiritual force to flow through the idol and into the assembled worshippers. *Pradakshina* (circumambulation) and *namaskara* (prostration) are performed.

Fourth stage – *visarjana* (sending the god or goddess back) is performed by chanting mantras. At the end of the puja, mantras are chanted and the entire puja is dedicated to the Supreme Lord.

The priest showing *arathi* (camphor fire) to the deity at a temple in Kuala Lumpur.

The priest in the inner sanctum where the main deity is kept. On either side are the *dvarapalkas* (guardians of entrance).

their prayers before retiring to bed. Water and flowers form the main offerings, while sweet rice, milk and other simple foods are offered on special occasions when the whole family participates in the worship. Due to modern lifestyles and time constraints, individuals often pray on their own.

Group or congregational worship

Homes and halls are used for congregational worship, usually for a particular purpose such as memorial prayers. It is, however, common for certain sects that are not temple based. Some groups have their own buildings where a section is designated as the prayer hall. Members get together, set up an altar and conduct the usual prayers as at home. Importance is

The six-faced Murugan (God of Heroism) seated on a peacock (his vehicle) with his consorts.

placed on the singing of hymns (*bhajan*) in which the deity's many names are repeated to music.

Food

The food offered to the deities and at religious functions is always vegetarian. Temples do not allow non-vegetarian food to be served. Apart from the fact that such food is ritually impure, it goes against the principle of *ahimsa* (non-violence).

Devotees are encouraged to observe vegetarianism at least on certain days of the week considered holy for the deity they worship as well as during festivals and fasts. Generally, Friday is commonly accepted as such a day.

Fasting

Fasting is not mandatory in Hinduism, but is encouraged as a means of attaining self-control and spiritual strength. Certain fasts are believed to bring about specific benefits, such as health and success, to those who observe them. There are also guidelines, including times for breaking fasts, for the observance

of most fasts. However, Hinduism recognizes individual strengths and weaknesses and, hence, there is a certain amount of flexibility. Heartfelt worship and virtuous living remain the most important aspects of religious observance.

Kavadi

Carrying of a *kavadi* is usually performed as a fulfilment of a vow made or favours received from God. This is a practice closely associated with the god Murugan. The *kavadi* consists of a cross-bar from which young coconuts or pots of milk, honey, sandalwood paste and rose-water are hung and taken to the deity as offerings. Sometimes it is attached to the body by fine metal rods representing the spears (*vel*) of Murugan used in his defeat of the evil Asura. This latter practice is no longer carried out in India and is today found only in Southeast Asia. Thaipusam day (see 'Hindu festivals') is the most common day on which this occurs. A devotee who wishes to undertake this feat has to fast for 42 days, abstaining from non-vegetarian food, liquor and physical gratification. He sleeps on a mat until the vow is fulfilled on the day of the festival. Some *kavadi* carriers also pierce their bodies with the sharp blades of small spears. This piercing of the flesh causes little pain or bleeding, thought to be due to the trance-like state devotees attain.

Guru

In Hinduism this word refers to a spiritual teacher. Literally it means 'a person who removes the darkness of ignorance and egotism'. He need not be a man of great education or even old and wise. But it is necessary that he has attained God-realization. Only such a person can help another to attain the same spiritual level. To the spiritual aspirant, the guru is the embodiment of God who gives him a 'new birth'. Hence the saying, 'Mother, Father and Guru are divine (God)'. A true guru can gauge the spiritual maturity of the aspirant before blessing him/her with God-realization. While spiritually immature people yearn for a guru, gurus also look for the mature soul who can be saved from repeated births.

Malaysia has its own share of gurus who have their own followers and organizations. One such was Swami Satyananda who founded the Pure Life Society in 1949. This society is based on the tenets of Hinduism but embraces the spiritual principles of all religions. It runs an orphanage where emphasis is given to interfaith spiritual fellowship.

The symbolism of offerings

Offerings are a devotee's expression of his/her love for the divine and a humble dedication of what God has provided. However, true devotion is the best offering.

Coconuts
The breaking of a coconut before God represents the destruction of the devotee's ego.

Camphor lamps
Lighting a lamp symbolizes the flame of truth which extinguishes the ego, allowing true union with God. In the evening, around 6 pm, many Hindus light a lamp, either at the temple or in their homes. This is called *arathi*. The lighting of lamps is also important in all Hindu festivals and at important events such as marriage.

Flowers and fruit
A wide array of flowers, fruits and leaves are given as offerings and show that even the simplest elements of nature please God.

Ghee lamps
These lamps are used for the festival of lights (Deepavali). In temples they are used as offerings of light to the deity.

Water
Water sustains life and sanctified water washes away impurities and sin.

Swami Satyananda (1909–61) was born in Ipoh and originally worked in the Malayan postal service. Before founding the Pure Life Society in 1949 he established an orphanage in Batu Gajah, Perak.

Hindu temples

The temple is an important institution in Hinduism—an essential component of the Hindu practice of worship. Not only is it looked upon as a sacred place where God resides, manifesting himself in the forms worshipped there, but also as a venue for religious observance and celebrations. The name of each temple is based on the divine form or symbol of the deity revered there. In Malaysia, where the majority of the Hindu population traces its origins back to southern India, the style of temples reflect this fact and are distinguished particularly by their carved gopuram *(towered gateway entrances).*

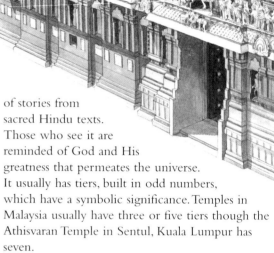

What a temple represents

Hindus regard the temple as the House of God (*deva grham*). Since God is the king of all, words like *prasadam* and *kovil*, which mean a royal mansion, are also used. Another very symbolic name is *aalayam* in which '*aa*' refers to the soul and '*layam*' means total absorption; hence, the temple is a place where the soul concentrates or is totally absorbed in thoughts of God. Another variation of this term is *devalayam*. Temples are places of beauty which remind devotees of God and help subdue their restless hearts and minds.

One of the corridors of the Nagarathar (Chettiar) Temple in Penang supported by teak pillars. This corridor seats hundreds of worshippers during meals served on banana leaves at festival times.

Temple structure and symbolism

Gopuram

A temple built in the Shaiva agamic tradition—according to *agama* (ancient traditional texts codified as Hindu architectural treatise c. 10th century CE, which give rules for the construction of temples) must be surrounded by walls and have a tall, imposing structure above the main entrance. This entrance is the *gopuram*. On it can be found statues and reliefs of gods and living beings, and depictions of stories from sacred Hindu texts. Those who see it are reminded of God and His greatness that permeates the universe. It usually has tiers, built in odd numbers, which have a symbolic significance. Temples in Malaysia usually have three or five tiers though the Athisvaran Temple in Sentul, Kuala Lumpur has seven.

- Three tiers represent the soul in three states, i.e. waking, dreaming and deep sleep;
- Five tiers relate to the five senses;
- Seven tiers symbolize the five senses together with the mind and the intelligence; and
- Nine tiers refer to the above seven plus the will and the ego.

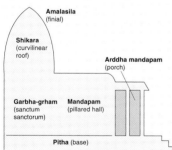

A simple temple built to serve the spiritual needs of employees on a plantation.

Veethi

Large temples are built in concentric circles with the main shrine in the centre. These circles are called *veethi* (or *piraharam*), situated one within the other. Malaysian temples usually only have one *veethi*.
One *veethi*—the human body;
Three *veethi*—the physical, spiritual and astral (soul) bodies;
Five *veethi*—the five different 'sheaths' or bodies that encase the soul and God who resides in the soul. These bodies are made up of food, air and breath, the mind, knowledge and bliss.

Inner structure

The structure of a temple, according to the agamic texts, can be of two types—one resembles the heart and the other the body. The latter, however, is more

North Indian style temples

A cross-section of a North Indian temple, distinct in style from the South Indian architecture.

The Lakshmi Narayan Temple in Sentul is the only North Indian temple in Kuala Lumpur.

North Indian temple style, called *nagara*, is distinguished by curvilinear towers called *shikara*, unlike the South Indian style which is characterized by *gopuram* (pyramidal gateways). There are few North Indian temples in Malaysia, perhaps the best known among them being the Lakshmi Narayan Temple in Kuala Lumpur. The idols in North Indian temples, such as Radha and Krishna, are made entirely of polished marble unlike in South Indian temples, where the preferred medium is granite. The style of prayers at North Indian temples is also slightly different, marked by the absence of some South Indian practices (such as the bathing ceremony, priests and the use of coconuts and betel leaves) that have become conflated with Hinduism in South Indian temples.

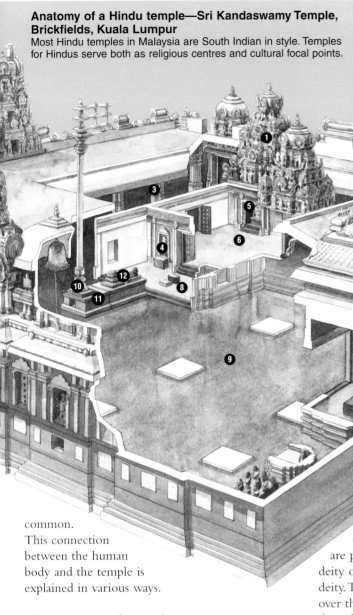

Anatomy of a Hindu temple—Sri Kandaswamy Temple, Brickfields, Kuala Lumpur

Most Hindu temples in Malaysia are South Indian in style. Temples for Hindus serve both as religious centres and cultural focal points.

① *Vimana*

② Each corner of the temple is guarded by a mythological being (*gana*).

③ The corridor represents the skin of the body.

④ The guardians at the entrance to the *garbha-grham* represent the shoulders.

⑤ The *garbha-grham* represents the head.

⑥ *Artha mandapam*

⑦ *Maha mandapam*

⑧ *Snapana mandapam*

⑨ *Sabha mandapam*

⑩ Flagstaff (*kodi-maram*)

⑪ Sacrificial altar (*pali-peedam*)

⑫ Vehicle (*vahanam*)

⑬ *Gopuram*

These sections relate to the six abodes (*atharam*) which are the six points of concentration in yoga.

The vehicle of whichever god the temple is dedicated to faces the *garbha-grham*. Nandi is the vehicle of Shiva.

common. This connection between the human body and the temple is explained in various ways.

The six sections of a temple

A temple has six main sections:

- *sabha mandapam* for music and dance performances and lectures;
- *alamkara mandapam* which houses the chariot or other vehicles and other objects used for special occasions;
- *snapana mandapam* (or *yaga salai*) where special offerings are made;
- *maha mandapam*, a shrine for special images (deities) used in processions and ceremonies;
- *artha mandapam* or the space between all the above and the *garbha-grham* (sanctum sanctorum); and
- *garbha-grham*—the most sacred place in the temple, where the deity to whom the temple is dedicated is kept.

ABODE	PART OF THE BODY	TEMPLE SECTION
Muladharam	thighs	sabha mandapam
Svathishtanam	navel	alamkara mandapam
Manipurakam	stomach	snapana mandapam
Anakatham	chest	maha mandapam
Visutthi	neck	artha mandapam
Aknjai	head	garbha-grham

The flagstaff, sacrificial altar and vehicle

Near the main entrance, in the *snapana mandapam*, are situated a flagstaff (*kodi-maram*), a sacrificial altar (*pali-peedam*) and the vehicle (*vahanam*). These are positioned in a straight line with the main deity of the temple, with the vehicle facing the deity. The flagstaff is as tall as the *vimana* (dome over the *garbha-grham*) and has a small replica of the vehicle at its top. The vehicle for each deity is different. Shiva rides a bull, Vishnu an eagle, Ganesha a rat and Shakti a bull, if she is installed in a Shiva temple, but a lion in a temple built specially for her. As suggested by the placement of the vehicle facing the deity, it is symbolic of the soul totally subdued and always looking towards God. The sacrificial altar is a symbolic one. Near it devotees prostrate themselves and shed all negative qualities before entering the main part of the temple.

Vimana

The *vimana* is the dome over the sanctum sanctorum (*garbha-grham*) of the temple which houses the main deity of the temple. During the consecration ceremony of a new temple or following renovation work on a temple, holy water is poured over the pinnacle of the *vimana*. The *vimana* is also considered to be a symbol of the *linga*—the formless form of God.

Built in 1833, the Mahamariamman Temple in Penang contains fascinating sculptures of the Hindu goddess Mariamman in her many incarnations. The *gopuram* is over seven metres high and features 38 statues of gods and goddesses and four swans, over the entrance. Housed within the *garbha-grham* is a statue of the Goddess Mariamman, whose likeness is taken out in a decorated wooden chariot on a tour of Little India during the Navaratthiri festival.

Hindu festivals

Most holy days are based on the lunar calendar, except for Thai-ponggal and the Hindu New Year. The Hindu almanac (pancangam) provides the date for these festivals. All the holy days are observed in temples as well as at home. Festivals for a particular deity are observed most elaborately in the temples dedicated to that particular deity. Each temple also holds an annual festival of 3–10 days' duration, usually in conjunction with one of the popular festivals, for example the Murugan Temple at Batu Caves, Selangor, celebrates its festival at Thaipusam.

A priest prepares the special pot of rice at Thai-ponggal.

Great attention is paid to cattle during Thai-ponggal festivities; they are washed and decorated.

Thai-ponggal

Thai-ponggal is celebrated on the first day of the Tamil month of Thai (January–February) and is predominantly a domestic festival. *Ponggal* refers to the 'boiling over' of the rice, its cooking and the cooked rice itself. This is traditionally a four-day festival of thanksgiving to the sun and the cattle that have helped with a good harvest. Houses are cleaned on the eve of Thai-Ponggal. On the day, the entrance to the house is decorated with mango leaves, sugar cane and a *kolam* (rice flour decoration).

Sweet rice is cooked in a new pot and offered to the Sun God. He is worshipped with incense and camphor. Then the family eats the rice. On the second day, traditionally, cattle are honoured, with a good wash and their sheds cleaned out. They are decorated with turmeric paste and garlands and allowed a day of rest. They are also fed with *ponggal* made in their honour at their shed. The third day is a day for visiting friends and relatives. Customarily employers distribute gifts to their employees. The third day is celebrated particularly by single women. They make *ponggal* and in offering it to the deity worshipped at home, pray for a good husband.

Festive decorations

Kolam (or rangoli)
At festivals and on auspicious days Hindus create a colourful design on the floor in front of their houses or in a temple. The designs are made from rice flour—coloured on special occasions.

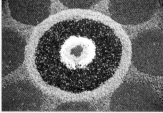

A *kolam* is made to purify the surrounding area.

Kumpam
A pot filled with water and covered with a husked coconut and mango leaves is placed on a banana leaf with rice. A small mound of turmeric paste and grass is added symbolizing Ganesha. The whole *kumpam* is decorated beautifully with flowers and a lamp.

Thoranam
On special occasions a festoon of mango leaves is draped above temple and home doorways. For some events such as weddings this is extended and a banana plant with its flower and young coconuts are added. This festoon is interwoven with young coconut shoots with five slits and folded so that when hung, they look like five-tiered spears inverted.

A special *kumpam* for cattle at Thai-ponggal.

Each year during Thaipusam, a festival of sacrifice and atonement, hundreds of thousands of devotees visit the Murugan temple at Batu Caves, Kuala Lumpur.

Thaipusam

The very popular Thaipusam festival in Malaysia is dedicated to Murugan. It falls on the full moon day of the month of Thai (January–February). This is the day when Shiva revealed his cosmic dance to the sages. According to the Purana (ancient legends), Shakti, as Parvathi, gave Murugan a spear to subdue Soorapadman, the embodiment of the ego that veils the soul. Nearly all Murugan temples in Malaysia hold special prayers and rituals but some, including the Batu Caves temples in Kuala Lumpur, Waterfall Temple in Penang and Kallumalai Temple in Ipoh, are famous for the grandeur of their celebrations which attract hundreds of thousands of devotees.

On the eve of Thaipusam, the sacred image of Murugan is brought to the temple grounds from another temple where it is kept. Devotees follow it on foot, while others wait on the way with trays of offerings. Devotees carry *kavadi* of various sizes with colourful decorations. They usually start at a nearby temple or riverbank and proceed to the temple concerned, to the accompaniment of drums, religious songs and shouts of '*vel vel, vetri vel*' which means 'victorious spear'.

Sivarathiri

This festival (Shiva's Night) is a fast which falls on the 13th night of the waning moon in the Tamil month of Masi (February–March). It is a festival of fasting and special pujas (prayer rituals).

Panguni Utthiram

Panguni Utthiram falls on the full moon day in the month of Panguni (March–April). According to legend, this is the day Shiva was united with Parvathi. This union resulted in the 'birth' of Murugan from the sparks that emanated from Shiva's eyes. In Murugan temples, it is celebrated like Thaipusam.

Tamil New Year

Popularly known as Hindu New Year, this festival falls on the first day of the month of Chitthirai (April–May), when the sun enters Aries, the first sign of the Hindu zodiac.

The house is cleaned and decorated. Silk cloth, gold jewellery, coins, rice and other auspicious objects are placed in the prayer room. New clothes are worn and a vegetarian meal is eaten; worship takes place at home and in the temple, with special pujas. The almanac, containing the monthly predictions for the coming year for each zodiac sign, is read by the priest.

Navaratthiri

Navaratthiri which means 'Nine nights' is celebrated in the month of Puraddasi (September–October) in honour of the goddess Shakti. Images of Hindu deities and saints are arranged on a special dais of nine steps called a *kolu*, with the three shaktis—Parvathi, Lakshmi and Sarasvathi—taking pride of place. A *kumpam* is placed and the Mother Goddess is invited to be present there. Offerings including nine types of grain are also placed there. The morning of the tenth day is considered auspicious for learning

Vaishnavite festivals

Apart from Deepavali with which the two most important incarnations of Vishnu are associated, there are other Vaishnavite festivals.

Sri Rama Navami

Sri Rama Navami meaning 'Rama's ninth' commemorates the birth of Rama on the ninth day of the waxing moon in the Tamil month of Panguni (March–April). In temples dedicated to Rama it is a nine-day festival with a re-enactment of the marriage of Rama and Sita, readings from the *Ramayana*, songs and dance. Special pujas are made.

Krishna Jayanthi

Krishna Jayanthi is a ten-day festival commemorating the birth of Krishna. It is celebrated on the eighth day of the waning moon in the month of Avani (August–September). The Lakshmi Narayan Temple in Kuala Lumpur and the International Society for Krishna Consciousness, which holds a chariot procession, celebrate this festival with great jubilation.

Vaikunda Ekadasi

The fast of Vaikunda Ekadasi falls on the 11th day of the waxing moon in the Tamil month of Markali (December–January). It is similar to Sivarathiri, but before breaking fast in the morning devotees sip water to which leaves of basil, which is sacred to Vishnu, have been added. It is believed the portals of Vaikunda (Vishnu's abode—heaven) open that morning and those who have observed this fast merit a place there.

Vaishnavite devotees carrying the statue of Krishna to the Lakshmi Narayan Temple during the Krishna Jayanthi festival.

and the arts. Nowadays the *kolu* is usually placed in a temple or a (Tamil) school.

Deepavali

This is a major festival in Malaysia—and is now a national holiday—which falls in the Tamil month of Aippasi (October–November). Made up of *deepam* (lamp) and *avali* (row or line) it means 'rows of lamps'. However, it is not a South Indian tradition to light them during the festival. Another difference between northern and southern traditions is that the day of the darkest night is Deepavali day for the northerners while the southerners celebrate the day when the 14th day of the waning moon coincides with 2.5 hours before dawn. On the eve of Deepavali food offerings and prayers are made in honour of deceased family members. Next morning, everyone is anointed with oil and takes a ritual bath. It is believed that Lakshmi is present in the oil and Ganga, the goddess of the River Ganges, is present in the water, cleansing bathers of their sin. New clothes are put on, and daily prayers follows.

There are many legends connected with this festival. A demon king named Naraka oppressed his subjects who prayed to Lord Krishna for deliverance. Krishna fought with the demon and killed him on the eve of the moonless day in Aippasi. The purifying bath and festivities are celebration of the victory of good over evil. Another explanation is associated with the epic *Ramayana*. When Rama returned to his capital, Ayutthya, after 14 years in exile, having defeated Ravana who had abducted his wife, the citizens celebrated his triumphant return by lighting the streets with lamps. The theme of victory over evil is again present. For North Indians this is their New Year. Merchants close annual accounts and ceremoniously open new ones. These are placed before Goddess Lakshmi and worshipped, with requests for a profitable year.

Full moon days

Days when the moon is full are considered suitable for special prayers and celebrations. On the full moon in Kartthikai (November–December) Tamils light rows of lamps outside their houses to commemorate the day when Shiva stood as a mount of fire between Brahma and Vishnu.

Hindu lamps called *ahal vilakku* are a ubiquitous feature of Hindu festivals. Traditionally they are made of clay, are filled with ghee, and use cotton wicks.

Adi-Amavasai

Generally, the moonless day (*amavasai*) of each month is considered especially suitable to fast and pray for the souls of departed fathers. Of these, Adi-Amavasai (in July–August) is the most important.

LEFT: A Navaratthiri *kolu* featuring offerings to the three forms of Shakti.

Hindu rites of passage

The rituals that mark the rites of passage are mainly based on customary observances together with religious practices such as the presence of a priest, the 'sacrificial fire' and recitation of mantras. Since Hindus in Malaysia include people from different parts of India and Sri Lanka, the rites of passage are varied. Hindu texts mention 52 such rites, called samskara. The ceremonies associated with birth, puberty, marriage and death are the most important.

The first haircut
The hair a baby is born with is considered 'defiled' and so it is shaved. Often parents make a vow during pregnancy to have it shaved at a particular temple as an offering to a chosen deity. In such cases, the tonsure takes place on an auspicious day or festival. The cutting is done outside the temple confines. The baby is then bathed, dressed and taken to the temple.

BELOW: In fulfilment of a vow this couple carry their newborn child up 272 steps at the Batu Caves Temple, Kuala Lumpur.

Ear piercing
Both boys and girls go through this ceremony. An auspicious day is chosen and a goldsmith is invited. The house is cleaned and decorated. The maternal uncle arrives with auspicious objects including a pair of gold earrings. The child, already bathed and dressed in new clothes, is seated on the uncle's lap when the ears are pierced. The practice is believed to remove any hereditary defects the child might have acquired at conception.

Before birth

Ceremonies (*valaikappu*) are performed in the fifth and seventh month of pregnancy. The house is decorated and the family brings gifts—including a silk sari, bangles, flowers, saffron powder (*kumkum*), turmeric, fruits and sweets. The expectant mother is bathed, dressed in silk and adorned with jewellery and flowers. She is seated in the hall in front of a *kumpam* (see 'Hindu festivals') and a lamp. An odd number of *sumangali* (married women with living husbands) put bangles on her forearms. Finally the *arathi* (a mixture of water, turmeric and quicklime with a betel leaf and lit camphor oil lamp) is waved in a clockwise motion and the contents emptied outside the entrance to the house. This is believed to avert the 'evil eye' and protect the foetus.

Birth

Despite being a happy occasion, birth is considered ritually impure. Members of the immediate family and close relatives on the father's side do not go to a temple or participate in any religious ceremonies until the period of confinement (from 16 days to a month) is over. The exact time of birth is recorded so that the baby's horoscope may be cast according to the Hindu almanac.

A cleansing ceremony is performed at the end of the confinement period; the house is cleaned and the entrance decorated with a *kolam* and *kumpam*. In the morning the baby's hair is shaved and all members of the family bathe and dress in clean clothes. The priest then comes at the designated auspicious hour. He sets up another *kumpam* and lights a lamp. Sometimes he also lights a small 'sacrificial fire' into which he sprinkles ghee, milk, twigs and flowers as offerings. The parents, with the baby on the father's lap, sit facing the priest, who blesses the jewellery to be worn by the baby. He offers a spoonful of the water from the *kumpam* to each person present. The house is also sprinkled with it for purification.

Puberty

Attaining puberty is considered to be 'the coming of age' of a girl. Traditionally, in most South Indian communities, the maternal uncle is informed and he comes to erect a 'green hut' made of coconut palm fronds. In the meantime the girl is bathed by *sumangali*. She stays in the hut until the official ceremony at the end of her first menstruation.

This practice is hardly found now, especially in Malaysia. Modern housing and schooling do not permit such isolation. However, girls are confined to a particular room or area at least until her menstruation stops. During this period she is fed on nutritious food. On the day of the cleansing ceremony, the house is washed and decorated. The girl sits in front of a *kumpam* and a lit lamp. *Sumangali* blessed with children apply milk to her head and give her a special bath. She is dressed in a silk sari and adorned with jewellery and flowers. Finally the *arathi* (offering of oil lamp) is performed.

Marriage

To Hindus, marriage is not only an auspicious event but a sacrament. It takes an individual from one stage of life to the next where he discharges many responsibilities.

Henna designs for women are traditional for marriage and other ceremonies.

Betrothal

Horoscopes of the groom and bride are compared to see if they are compatible. If they are, the engagement takes place. When couples meet independently horoscopes are not necessary.

On the agreed auspicious day, the bridegroom and his family visit the bride's house with gifts. A silk sari, cosmetics, flowers, fruits, betel leaf, areca nut, turmeric and saffron are placed on trays. Sometimes there are gifts of jewellery. The house is prepared for the occasion with a traditional *kolam* and *kumpam*. Traditionally, the fathers or elders in both the families exchange trays of gifts. The couple exchange rings and the ceremony ends with a feast.

Planting the wedding posts

In the past, marriages took place in a temporary shed or canopy. An auspicious day was chosen to plant the first post, three, five or seven days before the wedding to allow time to complete and decorate the shed. Nowadays, weddings are held in halls. Most large temples in Malaysia have an adjoining hall for this purpose. Nevertheless, the planting the post ceremony is still held. A small branch of a *papal* (*Ficus religiosa*) or *mul murukku* (*Erythrina indica*) tree

is planted in a corner of the compound.

Usually some fresh milk and a small amount of grain are sprinkled and incense and camphor lit.

Nalanggu

This is the application of oil and sandalwood paste. A bride goes through this ceremony twice, a couple of days before the wedding. Auspicious times are chosen. As during the ceremony for puberty, she sits before the *kumpam* and a lit lamp and *sumangali* attend to her bathing rituals. During the second *nalanggu* the bathing is repeated with sandalwood paste and *arathi* only. This is a purification rite.

Marriage ceremony

The bridegroom is led by the best man (the bride's brother) to the marriage dais. He sits near the priest who has set up nine *kumpam* representing the nine planets and another representing Shiva. Near this is a mound of turmeric in which *harialli* grass is stuck. This represents Ganesha, the remover of obstacles.

The priest places a ring of *darbha* grass on the bridegroom's finger, and recites the mantra of intention. Then Ganesha is invoked for the successful completion of the ceremony. At this stage the *kappu* (protective string) is tied around the bridegroom's right wrist and he is given his blessed wedding clothes. After receiving them he leaves the hall to change. Then the bride enters with the bridesmaid, the sister of the bridegroom. After similar ceremonies, she too receives her clothes and leaves.

While waiting, the priest lights the 'sacrificial fire' and when the groom arrives the priest offers grains and fruits to Agni, the god of fire. An important part of the South Indian ceremony is the *patha puja*. The couple wash and apply sandalwood paste to their parents' feet. Later the bridegroom ties the *thali* (sacred pendant) around the bride's neck. Then they walk round the fire, the *kumpam* and a *amni* (grinding stone) placed there seven times, holding hands. During the second circumambulation the bridegroom places the bride's

feet one at a time on the *amni* and slips a silver ring on each of the second toes. Then they sit on the dais and are blessed by relatives and friends. Gifts are also given at this time. A grand feast normally follows.

Funeral rites

As soon as death occurs the body is placed in the hall. An oil lamp with a single wick is lit and placed near the head. The thumbs are tied together with a strip of white cloth, as are the big toes. The mouth is covered. Generally the dead are cremated before sunset on the same day. Eleven *kumpam* (nine for the planets and two for Shiva and Shakti) are placed and, after a puja (prayer), water from these is used to bathe the body which in the meantime has been 'bathed' with turmeric, milk, honey and fruit juices. Then it is dressed, garlanded and placed in a coffin. Religious hymns are sung.

The women walk round the coffin (anticlockwise) three times and place some rice grains in the mouth. This symbolizes their last offering of food. Then 'new clothes' are placed at the coffin. In the meantime, an earthen pot of water and another of red embers are prepared. The sons play an important role in these rites. Usually the eldest son is the *karta* (performer of rites) for the father and the youngest, for the mother. Traditionally, the *karta* is shaven of all body hair.

The coffin is then taken to the cremation ground with the *karta* carrying the water pot on his left shoulder and holding the pot of embers in his right hand. There the coffin is placed on the funeral pyre. The *karta* circumambulates three times, lights the pyre and breaks the pot of water.

The *veddiyan*, who tends the cemetery, sees to it that the cremation is complete. If burial is customary in a family, the grave is prepared and the pot of water broken over it. Everyone who attends the funeral takes a bath before entering their homes.

On the third day after death the *karta*, accompanied by two or four men, goes to the cremation ground. He sprinkles some water on the ashes and collects them with the bones into a new earthen pot containing milk. After prayers, the pot is put into the sea or running water. Prayers are held at dusk for 16 or 31 days and at the end of the period of mourning when the house is cleansed and purification rites are performed.

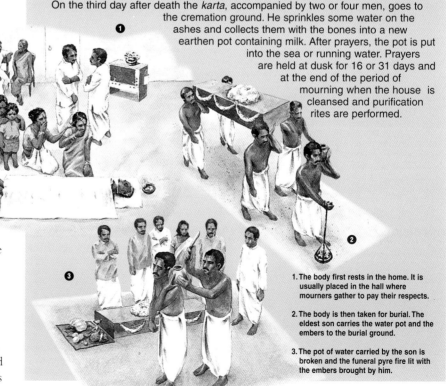

1. The body first rests in the home. It is usually placed in the hall where mourners gather to pay their respects.

2. The body is then taken for burial. The eldest son carries the water pot and the embers to the burial ground.

3. The pot of water carried by the son is broken and the funeral pyre fire lit with the embers brought by him.

Hindu organizations and movements

The Hindu organizations and movements formed in the early years were attempts by Hindus to sustain their religious feelings and maintain their identity in a new land—till they returned to their homeland. With Independence many Hindus chose to remain in Malaysia. The aims of the organizations broadened and now they work to awaken Hindu consciousness among the second and third generation Hindus and to meet the challenges of a multi-cultural, multi-religious society.

The Vivekananda Ashram in Brickfields, Kuala Lumpur, was founded in 1904 to propagate the teachings of the well-known Hindu philosopher and spiritualist Swami Vivekananda. It serves as the foremost Hindu educational centre in Malaysia.

The International Society for Krishna Consciousness mainly concerns itself with distributing publications on Hinduism.

A significant feature of neo-Hindu organizations is the popularization of devotional gatherings as an alternative form of religious expression. The performance of *arathi* (offering of oil lamps) for the guru or deity, *mankalam* (auspicious songs) and *prasadam* (consumption of food offerings) constitute the final phases of congregational worship. Seen below is a visit to Malaysia by a renowned guru from South India, His Holiness Thiruvaaduthurai Athinam, to the Malaysia Hindu Sangam in 2002.

Before Independence

The emergence of Hindu organizations in Malaya can be traced to the late 19th and early 20th centuries when the need for devotional enrichment and scriptural literacy was felt by the immigrant society which was becoming more settled. In particular, the Sri Mahamariamman Temple in Kuala Lumpur and the Selangor Ceylon Saivite Association which set up the Sri Kandaswamy Kovil (Brickfields, Kuala Lumpur) in 1902 were important. The Sri Mahamariamman Temple Devasthanam (temple committee) which also administers two other major temples in Kuala Lumpur, Sri Ganeshar Temple (Pudu) and the Murugan Temple at Batu Caves, fulfilled these needs of the worshippers. Besides these three temples, the Appar Seva Sangam also strove to maintain the Hindu tradition by teaching Saiva hymns used in prayer. Formal temples also held sessions of *purana* (Hindu religious text) reading with explanatory commentaries. Vivekananda Ashram (1904) and the Ramakrishna Mission (1925) disseminated religious knowledge through classes and public lectures by visiting monks and religious leaders.

Closely associated with the acquisition of religious knowledge was the growing interest among middle class Hindus in larger towns to learn classical music and dance. This led to the emergence of cultural societies such as the Sangeetha Abhiviruthi Sabha and the Kalavirithu Sabha in Kuala Lumpur. There is an independent Sangeetha Abhiviruthi Sabha in Ipoh. Besides teaching music and dance, these *sabha* (associations) also exposed their students to the singing of religious hymns.

Post Independence

Following Independence, there was a proliferation of Hindu organizations and movements. These are responsible for the dissemination of religious knowledge and the fulfilment of the devotional needs of all classes of Hindus.

In the meantime, some pre-war organizations became defunct. A good example is the Malaya Saiva Siddhanta Sangam (1922) based at the Athisvaran Temple at Sentul, Kuala Lumpur. It had held classes in Saiva Siddhanta philosophy and even published ancient texts for the benefit of its members. However, most of the organizations still continue their services through public lectures, celebration of memorial days (Swami Ramakrishna Paramahamsa, Mother Sarada Devi and Swami Vivekananda), guru pujas, festivals such as Navaratthiri and other cultural activities. The Arulneri Thirukkoottam was started in 1954 by a group of middle class Hindus in Kuala Lumpur under the leadership of Ramanathan Chettiar, a well-respected scholar in Saiva Siddhanta. It sought to revitalize Hinduism in Malaysia with the infusion of some knowledge in philosophy, through regular group prayers, religious classes and the publication of religious books, while also stressing the need for temple worship.

However, in 1962 the Tiruvarul Tavanari Manram was established. This was an addition to the Arulneri Thirukkoottam and both tried to reach working class Hindus and youth who, the Manram felt, were distancing themselves from their traditions and culture. Some of the young people later settled in different parts of the country and continued the tradition, through new organizations.

Malaysia Hindu Sangam

The Malaysia Hindu Sangam, unlike those organizations already mentioned whose focus was Saivism, has much broader objectives and represents all Hindus in the country (not just the majority Shiva followers). Its membership includes individuals, other Hindu-based organizations and even temples. Formed by a group of educated Hindus (professionals, civil servants and teachers) in 1965, this *sangam* has earned government recognition as attested to by its representation in various bodies such as the National Unity Board, the Marriage Tribunal and the Malaysian Inter-Religious Council.

Included among activities of the *sangam* are programmes to train a pool of local priests and religious teachers, to impart proper religious education to school children with the help of a comprehensive syllabus on Hinduism and to disseminate religious knowledge to Hindus through public lectures and seminars. The success of some of its programmes is evident from the increasing number of Hindus attending religious classes and other religious activities such as verse singing competitions.

Other Hindu organizations

The Hindu Youth Organization was formed in 1957 by a few youths inspired by organizations such as the Christian Methodist Youth Fellowship. It provided an avenue for educated youngsters to get together socially and concentrate on fostering and spreading their religion and culture.

Notable among Vaishnava associations is the Gita Ashram, which focuses its activities on the teaching and spread of the religious philosophy as propounded by the *Bhagavad-Gita*.

The Malaysia Hindu Sangam organizes seminars for the entire Hindu community. It also promotes Hindu culture and arts as seen in the above dance performance.

International Hindu movements

Apart from the organizations which sprang up in Malaysia, there are a number which started as branches of those from India, some of which have now become global.

The foremost among these in Malaysia is the Divine Life Society with its own premises at Batu Caves. Its headquarters are in Rishikesh, India. It

A monument dedicated to Swami Pranavananda, the first local Swami, who was one of the pioneers in establishing the Divine Life Society.

is of special significance to many Malaysians in that the founder, Sri Swami Sivanandaji Saraswati Maharaj, was from South India and had served as a doctor in Malaysia from 1912–24 in Senawang, Negeri Sembilan and Johor Bahru. Upon his return to India he started the movement in 1936

and the Malaysian branch was established in 1954. The first resident monk was Swami Pranavananda, a Malaysian. Though the Veda, Upanishad and the *Bhagavad-Gita* were originally used to emphasize the Hindu way of life, Tamil Saivite and Vaishnavite hymns are also widely used today. It holds religious classes, group prayers (*bhajan* singing), *guru-poornima* (full moon day dedicated to a spiritual guru), a *sadhana* (spiritual practice) week, religious retreats and special prayers on certain festivals and memorial days of Swami Sivanandaji and Swami Pranavananda. Initially, the society attracted the urban middle class Hindus, but in recent years many rural Hindus have joined—a phenomenon in nearly all religious organizations.

Other associations emerged among urban middle class Hindus in the 1970s and gathered their own followers. Examples of such movements are: the Self-Realisation Fellowship, the International Society for Krishna Consciousness, Transcendental Meditation, the Divine Light Mission, the Brahma Kumaris and the Satya Sai Baba Movement.

Hindu temples and religious revivalism

Temples, too, deserve credit for contributing to socio-cultural developments among the Hindus. For example, the Sri Mahamariamman Temple Devasthanam has assumed the role of a Hindu movement. It has been active in conducting religious classes and annual conferences. Its sound financial position, attributed to its management of the Batu Caves Temple in Kuala Lumpur, where the annual Thaipusam festival is celebrated on a monumental scale, provides the means to exert a degree of influence in Hindu matters. This body has been able to reform the religious practices of devotees who went overboard in their observance of religious rituals during Thaipusam.

In the context of religious reform, the Association of Muniswarar Temples, formed in 1974, has effected some significant changes to the mode of worship in temples dedicated to the deity Muniswarar. This deity, hitherto of low standing in the Hindu pantheon, has had its status raised by the association's declaration that Muniswarar (meaning 'the lord of sages') is a manifestation of Lord Shiva, and forbidding the offering of meat and alcohol in the propitiation of the deity. The calendrical festival Sivarathiri, attributed to Lord Shiva, is now celebrated in practically all Muniswarar temples.

Sri Swami Sivanandaji Saraswati Maharaj (1887–1963), the founder of the Divine Life Society. He renounced worldly life and dedicated himself to serving humanity.

Regular classes, with recitations from sacred scriptures, are organized by the Sri Mahamariamman Temple Devasthanam in Kuala Lumpur.

The Satya Sai Baba Movement opened a free medical and dental clinic for the people in Kuala Lumpur.

The Satya Sai Baba Movement

The Satya Sai Baba Movement is based on devotion to Sai Baba, a healer saint from South India. It became popular in Malaysia in the mid-1970s and has a following drawn largely from the urban upper middle class Hindus. An increasing number of Chinese are also devotees and have visited India to receive *darsan* (blessings of the saint). A popular form of worship among followers of this movement is *bhajan* (group prayer), held usually in private homes. It is interesting to note that even Chinese devotees have learnt to sing in Tamil and Sanskrit and conduct their own *bhajan*.

The mode of worship may differ from the conventional form, but Sai Baba devotees continue to celebrate Hindu festivals such as Sivarathiri, Navaratthiri, and Krishna Jayanthi (see 'Hindu festivals').

1. In 1968 the old building of St Joseph's Cathedral in Kuching (shown here on the left) was demolished to make way for a new modern design church.

2. The annual World Women's Day is marked by special services and prayers.

3. The first Anglican church in Malaysia, St George's Church, was built in 1818 by Captain Robert Smith, a military engineer. The church is situated in George Town, Penang.

4. The Tamil Methodist Church Kuala Lumpur has services in Tamil, Telugu, Nepalese and English.

5. Prayer is central to Christian worship and can be either communal or individual.

6. Children at the Bukit Nanas Convent School in Kuala Lumpur set up by the Infant Jesus Sisters in 1899.

7. Batik art by Hanna Varghese, depicting Jesus and his teachings.

WORD OF LIFE

RECEIVE ONE ANOTHER

CHRISTIANITY

The cross is a Roman instrument of execution. Jesus' crucifixion has become a symbol of redemption because Christians believe Jesus was raised from the dead.

Christians make up around nine per cent of Malaysia's population and come from many different denominations. A little over half are Roman Catholics, while the rest are from Protestant groupings, although a small Eastern Orthodox Church also exists. While in Peninsular Malaysia only two to three per cent of the population are Christians, in East Malaysia this figure rises to about twenty to thirty per cent. Most Christians in Sabah and Sarawak are members of the indigenous tribes, such as the Kadazandusun and Iban.

There is some evidence to support the theory that Nestorian Christians were amongst Persian traders in the region as early as the 7th century. The coming of Christianity to Malaysia, however, is generally dated to the period of the Portuguese conquest of Melaka in 1511. The Portuguese were Roman Catholics. Later, under Dutch colonial rule, from 1641, Protestantism came into ascendancy while Catholicism was suppressed. Under British colonial rule, from the 19th century, Protestant missions flourished alongside the spread of Catholicism. With the influx of immigrant Chinese and Indian workers to Malaysia more Christian missionaries were imported to take care of their spiritual needs. In Sabah, for example, the Basel Mission Society began work among migrant Hakka Chinese in 1882.

Now the majority of Christian churches in Malaysia are small and independent churches. Among the larger Protestant churches are the Anglican, Methodist, Presbyterian, Brethren, Lutheran, Baptist, the Assemblies of God and the Salvation Army. While most churches have their roots in foreign missionary activities, some, for example the Latter Rain Church, are completely indigenous to Malaysia.

By the middle of the 20th century, the Roman Catholics had organized themselves into various dioceses under the umbrella of the Catholic Bishops' Conference. The mainstream Protestant churches came together in 1948 to form the Malayan Christian Council (which later became the Council of Churches of Malaysia). The other grouping, comprising pentecostal and charismatic leaning churches, joined together in 1983 to form the National Evangelical Christian Fellowship. In 1985, these three major Christian national bodies came together to establish the Christian Federation of Malaysia.

An integral part of being Christian is membership in a church where, through regular worship and teaching, Christians are called to be disciples of Christ. Just as the historical Jesus went about healing the lepers, giving sight to the blind, forgiving sinners and eating with beggars and outcasts, Christians in Malaysia are challenged to be actively involved in such salvific mission activities. This is why Christians have established numerous social services throughout Malaysia, such as kindergartens and schools, welfare homes for drug addicts, unwed mothers and orphans, and hospitals and clinics for the poor and marginalized. They draw their inspiration from the preaching and teachings of Jesus Christ as discerned through the reading of the Holy Bible.

History of Christianity in Malaysia

Persian and Turkish traders with Nestorian Christian origins were in the region as early as the 7th century. Catholicism was introduced by the Portuguese in the 15th century while Protestantism was introduced with the capture of Melaka by the Dutch in 1641. The decline of the Portuguese and the ascent of the mainly Protestant Dutch in the 17th century led to Catholicism being suppressed. It gained a new lease of life through missionaries under British rule in the 19th century in Peninsular Malaysia and was also introduced in Sabah and Sarawak.

The Dutch built Christ Church in Melaka in 1753. The oldest functioning Protestant church in Malaysia features typical Dutch architecture of the period and has a brass Bible stand with the first verse of St John's Gospel inscribed in Dutch.

The old Christ Church in Stunggang, Lundu (Sarawak), was built in 1855.

Chronology of important events

650	Persian and Turkish traders with Nestorian Christian origins come to the region.
1511	The conquest of Melaka by the Portuguese. This marks the introduction of Roman Catholicism to Melaka.
1545	The arrival of St Francis Xavier in Melaka.
1641	The Dutch capture Melaka and introduce Protestant Christianity to the region.
1786	The founding of Penang by Francis Light and the introduction of Christianity to northern Malaya.
1848	The Borneo Church Mission (the first mission in Sarawak) is set up by Dr (later Bishop) McDougall.
1881	The Roman Catholic Church comes to Sarawak with the arrival of the Mill Hill Missionary Fathers.
1948	The Council of Churches of Malaya and Singapore is formed.
1985	Christian Federation of Malaysia is formed, incorporating the Council of Churches of Malaysia (formerly Malayan Christian Council), Roman Catholics and the National Evangelical Christian Fellowship.

The origins of Catholicism

When Afonso de Albuquerque conquered Melaka in 1511, he brought with him eight military priest chaplains of the Portuguese Military Crusading Order of Christ who introduced Catholicism to the town. However, the beginnings of the Catholic Church in Malaysia are more often associated with St Francis Xavier, the Jesuit missionary who visited Melaka on five occasions. Once the Dutch captured Melaka in the mid-17th century Catholicism was suppressed through deportations and prohibitions on priests.

Despite this, the Catholic community continued to grow, partly through the initiatives of lay groups such as the Confraternity of the Holy Rosary. In 1703, the Dutch came into alliance with Portugal, which allowed for some leniency in the practice of Catholicism.

Priests of the French Societé des Missions Étrangères de Paris (MEP) were invited into the country during the period of British administration in the late 18th and early 19th centuries. They helped found what subsequently became the Catholic Church of Peninsular Malaysia. In Sabah and Sarawak, however, credit is due to the Mill Hill Missionaries for the development of Catholic churches. They were the first English missionary society, set up in England in 1866, with a mission 'to go where the needs are the greatest'. The fathers and brothers of this society were the only priests in the region for many years after their arrival in 1881.

The early development of Protestantism

Protestantism began as a reform movement in the 16th century in Germany under Martin Luther, and gradually spread around the world, developing into a variety of church denominations. Such churches advocate autonomous church government and differ in some doctrinal teachings from the Catholic Church.

When the Dutch, who were fiercely Protestant, captured Melaka from the Portuguese in 1641, they saw an opportunity to check the spread of Catholicism in the Malay Archipelago. Although

suffering repression under the Dutch, a small Catholic community managed to maintain their faith by meeting in secret. This community inter-married with the Portuguese and became a distinct ethnic community which still exists today and which exhibits a hybrid culture—part local and part Portuguese.

With the advent of British colonial rule from the early 19th century, and its expansionist political and economic agenda, a number of Protestant churches were established in Penang, Melaka, Singapore, Kuching and Jesselton (Kota Kinabalu). Key dates in the spread of Protestantism were those of the establishment of Protestant missions throughout the Malay Archipelago: the London Missionary Society (1815), the Anglican Mission in Peninsular Malaya (1818), the Borneo Church Mission (Anglican) in Sarawak (1848), the Brethren (1860), the Basel Mission Society (1882) in Sabah (then North Borneo), the Methodist Mission (1885), the Presbyterian Mission (1881) and the Evangelical Lutheran Church (1907).

By the middle of the 20th century, most of the Protestant church denominations had established themselves, associated with Chinese and Indian migrant communities and with indigenous groups in Sarawak and Sabah. Different Protestant churches existed in various towns and villages. The churches also established many schools in various towns and started a host of welfare homes catering for the poor and needy in many places.

The Church in the 20th and 21st centuries

In the early part of the 20th century, a large number of the Protestant churches became institutionalized and some continued to excel in providing education to thousands through mission schools. In Sarawak and Sabah, the churches were deeply involved in rural development, offering the people health services, agricultural development and community organization. Even today, prominent schools, both Protestant and Catholic in their origins, receive much admiration and support from their alumni, who remain grateful for the vision and dedication of their early school teachers.

The middle of the 20th century was a traumatic period for the country. First there was the Japanese occupation (1941–45), followed by the guerrilla insurgency led by the Communists. It was a period that brought great hardship to the people, and particularly to Christians, as their faith made them easy targets as Western sympathizers. Many church leaders were tortured or imprisoned by the Japanese army. Later, the British colonial administration's attempt to contain the Communist Chinese in 'new villages' and deny them support offered the churches opportunities to provide social services in such villages.

The only Orthodox Church in Malaysia came into being in 1932, made up of Indian Orthodox who had migrated to seek employment in Malaya. Known as the Orthodox Syrian Church in Malaysia, they remain a small community who still retain ties with their mother church in Kerala, India.

The experience of war, followed by Independence in 1957, brought a consciousness to the Protestant churches to develop national leadership to take over responsibility from foreign missionaries. The later part of the 20th century saw the churches come together to share expertise and resources to train local leaders. Bible schools, seminaries and lay development training programmes were established during this period. Protestant churches came together to form the Malayan Christian Council in 1948 (later the Council of Churches of Malaysia) which

The 1960s saw a number of new church buildings erected throughout Malaysia. Here the Bishop of Penang, Monsignor Gregory Yong, sprinkles holy water on the Church of the Holy Spirit, Penang, in 1969.

is an important instrument in fostering Christian unity and encouraging joint cooperation for the good of the churches and the nation.

Until the 1960s the Catholic Church in Malaysia was generally very clergy and European oriented. However, things began to change with the Second Vatican Council (Vatican II); the first ever meetings of bishops from all over the world between 1962 and 1965. Matters discussed included acculturation, lay participation, collegiality, inter-religious dialogue, and the social mission of the Church.

It was not until 1976, when all the bishops and priests of Peninsular Malaysia held their own renewal session, that the Malaysia Church really articulated the ideas generated by Vatican II within the local context. Since then there has been greater participation of the Catholic laity, greater emphasis on inter-religious dialogue and the mission on behalf of justice and peace and more effort in creating an acculturated version of Catholicism in Malaysia.

Missionaries in Malaysia

St Francis Xavier

Apostle of the East, St Francis Xavier (1506–52) is well remembered for his missionary work during the 16th century. He was one of the seven founders of the Jesuits and is considered one of the greatest missionaries in Christian history. St Francis visited Melaka a number of times, each time staying between a few months and a year. He administered to the spiritual needs of the people there. He also established the first school in Malaysia, St Paul's College. Apart from these achievements, he is reputed to have performed miracles such as curing sick children, and prophesized battles to be fought by the people of Melaka. He spent his time in Melaka translating the catechism (questions and answers about Christian doctrine) from Latin into Malay. He died in China but his body was first buried on St Paul's Hill, Melaka. Later his body was taken to Goa. While in Melaka he spent much time attending to the welfare of its people. There are many churches and schools named after him in Malaysia today.

St Francis Xavier's statue in Melaka.

French missionaries

Although the Portuguese introduced Christianity into Malaya they were ousted by the Dutch who did not place as much importance on proselytizing Christianity. Its spread, therefore, slowed. The re-establishment of the Church came at the end of 18th century with the arrival of the Societé des Missions Étrangères de Paris (MEP—founded by Bishop Francois Pallu and Bishop Lambert de la Motte in France in 1659). The French missionaries went first to Siam, and after they were expelled, made their way to Malaya. The first two missionaries to arrive, in 1781, were fathers Garnault and Coude. They settled in Kuala Kedah and later moved to Penang where they founded the Church of Assumption in 1786. The MEP was active in training local converts to become priests and nuns to assume responsibility for running the mission and its churches and organizations. Father Garnault learnt Malay and preached and composed prayers in it. The MEP expanded throughout the peninsula. They set up schools and seminaries and collected funds for La Salle Brothers and Holy Infant Jesus Sisters to set up schools and orphanages. Their work focused on Peninsular Malaya and Singapore.

Convent Light Street, a girls' school, was established by the Holy Infant Jesus Sisters in 1852 in Penang. With an orphanage and boarding house it is the oldest school complex in the country.

Missionaries in Sabah and Sarawak

Dr T. F. McDougall, an Anglican missionary from England, came to Sarawak in 1848. Thomas McDougall was a doctor and in addition to his missionary activities was much in demand for his medical skills. Dr and Mrs McDougall started the mission from scratch, building a church and a mission house with the purpose of instructing new converts and children. Dr McDougall was consecrated Bishop of Sarawak in 1856 and is credited with laying the foundation of the Anglican church in the state. With failing health, McDougall had to leave the tropics in 1867, but he was followed by a succession of Anglican missionaries who helped to spread the Christian faith and set up schools and hospitals among the indigenous communities throughout Sarawak.

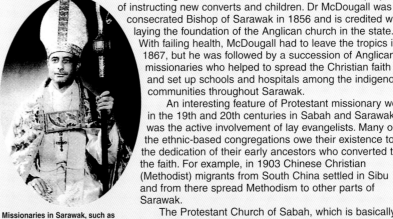

An interesting feature of Protestant missionary work in the 19th and 20th centuries in Sabah and Sarawak was the active involvement of lay evangelists. Many of the ethnic-based congregations owe their existence to the dedication of their early ancestors who converted to the faith. For example, in 1903 Chinese Christian (Methodist) migrants from South China settled in Sibu and from there spread Methodism to other parts of Sarawak.

Missionaries in Sarawak, such as Bishop Cornwall, who was the Bishop of Borneo (1949–62), travelled widely visiting parts of their diocese which were deep in the rainforest.

The Protestant Church of Sabah, which is basically made up of the Rungus people, began with overseas missionary assistance, but by the 1970s was totally led and managed by local lay pastors.

Christian denominations in Malaysia

Christianity arrived on the shores of the nation as part of the European colonial expansion and, more recently, with North American neo-colonialism and globalization. Roman Catholicism developed primarily in the 16th century, especially with the arrival of the Portuguese missionary St Francis Xavier in Melaka. The mainline and older Protestant churches were brought to Malaysia especially in the 19th century while the younger Protestant churches came in the early 20th century, especially between the World Wars, whereas the numerous evangelical and free churches are of recent origins.

St John's Institution was established in 1904 by the La Salle Brothers, with just 40 students. Today the 100-year-old school is one of the most established schools in the country. It is situated in Bukit Nanas right in the heart of Kuala Lumpur.

Mary the mother of Jesus is regarded by Christians as amongst the first disciples of Christ. She is portrayed in the Bible as the faithful mother who was there even when her son Jesus was crucified to death. Roman Catholics have a special devotion to her and honour her by prayers and practices, such as the recitation of the rosary, during which the 'Hail Mary' prayer is recited.

The Catholic Church of Malaysia

Constituting about five per cent of the total population in Malaysia, Roman Catholics number around 200,000 in West Malaysia and 700,000 in Sabah and Sarawak. They are spread across more than 100 parish churches which are grouped by territorial regions called dioceses, each headed by a bishop or archbishop. The bishops come together to form the Catholic Bishops' Conference (CBC) of Malaysia-Singapore-Brunei. This conference is the official voice that speaks on behalf of the Catholic Church in Malaysia. Further, the CBC is a member of the Federation of Asian Bishops' Conferences (FABC). All the bishops of the world are in communion with the Bishop of Rome who is also the Pope, the head of the worldwide Catholic community.

Vatican II Council

What we see of the Roman Catholic Church in Malaysia today owes a lot to the Second Vatican Council, a renewal event which took place in Vatican City from 1962–65. Dominic Verdargon,

who was then Archbishop of Kuala Lumpur, represented Malaysia at this historic event.

Vatican II called for Catholics to be more involved with the world and more in touch with their local contexts. The new way of being Catholic is to be engaged in the lives and cultures of the people, especially the poor and disenfranchised. Catholics also need to be in dialogue with their neighbours of other religions. This is what is called the 'Triple Dialogue', which means that Catholics need to be concerned with the plight of the poor, be involved in their indigenous cultures and be engaged with the religions of Malaysia.

Each local church in Malaysia is run by a priest, with the assistance of a parish council and a variety of commissions. Various groups such as St Vincent de Paul, Family Life and Youth Ministries and Marriage Encounter exist to serve various functions and needs of Malaysian Catholics. Brothers and nuns play significant roles in church life, as do lay Catholics.

The role of the Church in education and welfare

Besides missionary priests who came to found parish churches, religious brothers and sisters (nuns) were instrumental in establishing schools, hospitals, social welfare homes, and other charitable services in Malaysia. The La Salle Brothers and the Holy Infant Jesus Sisters arrived in 1852 from France to open schools such as St Xavier's Institution and Light Street Convent, in Penang. The Canossian Sisters began their ministry in Melaka in 1905, providing education to the descendants of the Portuguese settlement. The Little Sisters of the Poor opened homes for the aged in the 1950s. The Marist Brothers, who had been expelled from China, established Sam Tet School in Ipoh in 1950 and other schools elsewhere in the country to provide Chinese education. The Brothers of Mercy arrived at Skudai, Johor, in 1952 to provide medical services in villages and then went on to set up Fatima Hospital in Ipoh. The Brothers of St Gabriel established Montfort Boys' Town in Batu Tiga, Selangor, in 1959 and later founded another vocational training centre for poor youth in Sabah. The Good Shepherd Sisters opened a kindergarten in Ampang, Kuala Lumpur in 1956 and subsequently established shelter homes for unmarried mothers and battered women. The Franciscan Missionaries of Divine Motherhood set up Our Lady's Hospital in Ipoh in 1965.

Today there are more than 360 mission founded schools—80 mainly Methodist-run schools in Sabah and Sarawak with another 280 mainly Catholic- and Protestant-run schools throughout the country. Today, they adhere to the national curriculum and Christian religious instruction is no longer provided. St John's Institution also runs an AIDS hospice in Kuala Lumpur—the first in the country—and an orphanage in Penang.

A community centre run by the National Office for Human Development under the Archdiocese of Kuala Lumpur. It offers free food to all, irrespective of race, religion and creed. There is also a clinic run by the centre as well as a special needs educational centre.

RIGHT: St Michael's Institution in Ipoh, Perak, one of the most prestigious Christian missionary schools in Malaysia, was established by the La Salle Brothers. Classes began in an old Malay house in 1912 and in 1923 were transferred to its present building designed by a French Catholic missionary.

Protestantism in Malaysia

Protestantism is a generic name to categorize the churches which developed as a result of the reformation inaugurated by Martin Luther and his contemporaries in the 16th century. During the 19th century the following churches were established, mainly through British influence, in Malaysia: Anglican (1809), Brethren (1859), Presbyterian (1881), Basel Christian (1882), and Methodist (1885). The 20th century saw an even greater influx of churches from Europe, America and elsewhere to Malaysia: Evangelical Lutheran (1907), Seventh Day Adventist (1911), Mar Thoma (1926), True Jesus Church (1927), Borneo Evangelical Mission (1928), Jehovah's Witnesses (1932), Assemblies of God (1935), Pentecostal (1936) and many more smaller independent churches.

Revd Trevor Tinda, an Iban Anglican minister, visits a longhouse at Nanga Telingint along the Lemanak River in the Sri Aman division of Sarawak.

Protestant doctrines

Despite certain differences, all Protestants, including those in Malaysia, adhere to three fundamental theological foundations derived from Protestantism when it first began.

- The primary authority of the Bible, which alone provides for the individual Christian the sole source of faith; which is to be interpreted by individual conscience; independent of external regulation by unscriptural church traditions.
- That salvation is available to all believers through individual faith and conviction; attained by the acceptance of redemption accomplished by Jesus Christ's saving death and resurrection; independent of the intermediary role of the Church or the saints.
- That the Church Ministry, as the community of people believing in God, is the teamwork of clergy (bishops, priests and deacons) and lay people (deaconesses, lay readers and others) and is independent of the absolute authority of the papacy.

Protestants proclaim their faith with the words 'Christ is Lord', where the term Lord is reserved for God alone. Thus, to acknowledge Jesus Christ as Lord is to acknowledge that he is supreme and that he occupies a place no one else can occupy. To him and to him alone is full allegiance given.

The Anglican Church

The Anglican Communion is a worldwide fellowship of churches owing their origins to the Church of England. This fellowship of dioceses, provinces and regional churches is in communion with the See of Canterbury. The Anglican Church in Southeast Asia was originally under the jurisdiction of the Bishop of Calcutta, India. The diocese of Singapore, Labuan and Sarawak was formed in 1881, dividing in 1909, 1960 and 1970, when the Diocese of West Malaysia was formed. In 1996 the Province of Southeast Asia, comprising the dioceses of Kuching (100,000), Sabah (40,000), Singapore (figure not available) and West Malaysia (25,000) was established by the Archbishop of Canterbury, making the Anglican Church in the region self-governing. Each diocese is headed by a bishop and the province is overseen by an archbishop.

The Methodist Church

Methodism came to Malaya with the arrival of William F. Oldham in Singapore in 1885. It spread to Borneo in 1900. In 1950, the Southeast Asia Central Conference (comprising Singapore, Malaya, Indonesia and Burma) was formed. In 1968, full autonomy was granted to the Methodist Church in Malaysia and Singapore and in 1977, the Methodist Church in Malaysia and Singapore separated into two churches. Followers number approximately 300,000 in Malaysia.

The Basel Christian Church

In 1882, a number of Hakka Christians emigrated to Sabah (then known as North Borneo). With the help of missionaries from the Basel Mission Society (established in 1815 in Switzerland), they began to build churches in Sabah, the first being built in Lausan in 1886. In 1925, the self-governing and self-supporting Borneo Basel Self-Established Church was formed. In 1964, it was renamed the Basel Christian Church of Malaysia and has approximately 45,000 members.

ABOVE: A banner in St Andrew's Presbyterian Church, Kuala Lumpur.

LEFT: Interior of the All Saints Church, Taiping, Perak. Designed by G. A. Lefroy, the church was built in 1886.

TOP: Kenyah chapel in Ulu Baram, Sarawak.

BOTTOM: The Chinese Methodist (Hokkien) Church, Kuala Lumpur, was opened in 1957.

Christian beliefs and world-view

Christianity began in the 1st century with the person of Jesus of Nazareth. Jesus Christ is God's revelation to humanity, revealing, on the one hand, who God is and, on the other, what it means to be human. He is thus the mediator between God and humankind for, according to Christians, he is at once human and divine. The earthly mission of Jesus did not end with his death, but continues in his disciples through the Church. Christians discern God's will by reading the Holy Bible and prayerfully reflecting upon its teachings in light of the events of the contemporary world.

A painting in St Francis Xavier Church, Petaling Jaya (Selangor), depicting Jesus' journey bearing the cross before his crucifixion.

Faith in God and the Holy Trinity

From its very beginning Christianity showed a deep consciousness of the reality of God. At the root of the Christian belief structure is the affirmation of the one God who is creator of all. Because God is utterly transcendent and thus unknowable, Christians believe that God was revealed to humankind through the person of the Galilean Jesus. We know who God is and what God is like by looking at who Jesus was and what he stood for. Because Jesus was concerned about the salvation (from the Latin word *salus*, meaning to 'make whole') of the peoples of his time, Christians discern that it is God's will that all peoples everywhere attain salvation. This is the 'Good News' (Gospel) which Christians preach. The Church, under the guidance of the Holy Spirit, is charged with continuing this mission of salvation.

The doctrine of the Holy Trinity stands at the centre of Christian faith. It is best summed up as: people are saved by God (the Father), through Jesus Christ (the Son), by the grace of the Holy Spirit (made manifest in the Church today). It describes the three distinct ways the one but triune God relates with humanity.

Faith in Jesus Christ

Belief in Christ is an essential difference between Christianity and the other major religions. The doctrine of Incarnation, a doctrine espousing that the eternal Son of God came down from heaven and became a man (Jesus of Nazareth) to redeem humankind from its sinful condition, is a key element of the faith. The confession of Jesus as Christ, or the anointed one of Yahweh, of whom the prophets foretold and the Jewish world eagerly awaited, became the primary formula of faith of the early Christians. The supernatural factors in the accepted teaching about Christ, however, were problematic from the beginning. For many Christians, Christ's two natures in one person have been an undisputed reality to some; to others a mystery and object of meditation. The definitive statements confirming Jesus as both human and divine can be found in what is known as the 'Chalcedonian formula' of 451 CE. Theological formulations aside, what remains is a notable aspect of Christian religion—a profoundly reverential love for the person of Jesus.

The life of Jesus

Jesus was born in Palestine to the Virgin Mary and Joseph, a poor shepherd, around 1 CE. Christians believe that Mary conceived Jesus through the action of the Holy Spirit. At Christmas Christians around the world celebrate his birth. Jesus spent his life teaching the concept of love for God and of others. He preached, 'Always treat others as you would like them to treat you' (Matthew 7: 12), teaching and healing the sick. He used parables or stories to reach his audience who consisted mostly of the poor and the oppressed. He was crucified by the Romans who ruled Palestine during that period. Jesus is said to have been resurrected after his execution and was seen by many people before he ascended into heaven. His death and resurrection are celebrated at Easter.

Statue of Jesus, son of God.

The Church

If the salvation from God which was begun by Christ is meant for all peoples, it must be continued beyond the earthly death of Jesus. This is where the Church comes in. Constituted by Jesus' disciples, the Church is the visible structure which continues the salvific mission of Jesus. Like Jesus, its mission is to proclaim liberty to captives, recovery of sight to the blind and freedom for the oppressed (Luke 4: 18). This, the Church does not only through proclamation and words, but also through witness, deeds and prophetic action. In teaching 'The Lord's Prayer', Jesus was emphatic that for God's Kingdom to come God's will must be done on earth first just as in heaven. It is not the confession 'Jesus is Lord' (Romans 10: 9) which itself brings salvation, but 'he who does the will of God the Father' (Matthew 7: 2). Hence, the Church, the Christian community, must be about the work of salvation. This is a salvation not only of the afterlife but also before death (saving peoples from sin, oppression, evil and bondage).

The Holy Bible

The Holy Bible is the sacred scripture for Christians and is considered to be 'the Word of God'. The first part of the Bible is the Hebrew Scripture, known by Christians as the Old Testament. It relates the act of God's salvation as seen in Jewish history. The second part of the Bible, called the New Testament, begins with the life of Jesus and

continues through the witness of the early Christians. The four Gospels of Matthew, Mark, Luke, and John are the main sources which depict the life of Jesus. While the original Bible was written in Hebrew, Aramaic and Greek, today it exists in practically all the languages of the world. In 1662 Daniel Bower published the first Malay language New Testament in Melaka. The Indonesian Bible *Khabar Gembira* (Good News) is most popularly used amongst Malay-speaking Christians.

Basic beliefs

Creation
Christians believe that all of creation comes from God. God creates out of nothing for no other reason than because God loves us. The Doctrine of Creation is really about God's relationship with humanity and the relationship of human beings with one another and with the cosmos. Essentially it teaches that God creates only that which is 'not-divine' or 'not-God'. If it were not 'not-God' then it would be God and not a creation.

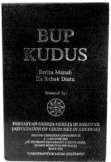

The Bible in the Iban language, spoken by the Iban of Sarawak.

It follows that all creation is not divine and is by nature not perfect, not infinite and subject to committing evil and sin. Creation, therefore, is in need of God's mercy, grace and salvation.

Sin and redemption
The best way to discuss the Christian understanding of sin and redemption is to look at Jesus' teachings through the parable of the Lost Son (Luke 15: 11–32). It begins with a young man who asks his father for his share of the inheritance and leaves home. This is the essence of sin: pride and disowning one's source, God. He squanders his inheritance and finds himself in dire need. This is the effect of sin: pain and suffering. He comes to his senses and decides to return to his father to be treated as a hired worker. This is conversion: remorse and repentance. Upon the young man's return his father embraces him, puts a ring on his finger and celebrates with a feast. This is what redemption is: total forgiveness and unconditional acceptance into God's kingdom of love.

Kingdom of God
The Kingdom of God is central to the entire life and preaching of Jesus. It refers to God's unconditional and liberating sovereign love. In so far as this is already a reality now here on earth it is evidenced where justice and peace reigns, and where people are living honest and decent lives in the service of others and society. The Kingdom of God is also something which awaits fulfilment. It is an eschatological event, still to come (Luke 22: 16), at the end of time. The whole of Jesus' life and message was about actualizing the Kingdom of God. Jesus' command is: seek first the Kingdom of God and everything else will fall into place (Matthew 6:33).

Eschatology: The last things
Eschatology is the study of the last things, namely death, judgement, heaven, hell and the second coming of Christ. Christians believe that the life on earth is but a pilgrimage at the end of which is death. Death, however, is not the end. Jesus will appear again to pass judgement on the nations. People will be judged according to how they lived while on earth. The criteria for this is spelt out in Matthew 25: 31–46. Those who fed the hungry, gave drink to the thirsty, welcomed the stranger, clothed the naked, cared for the sick, and visited the prisoner will be welcomed into God's Kingdom of Heaven. Those who did not will be banished into the eternal fire of hell.

Love thy neighbour
Christianity is a religion which is emphatic about love. This love is not reserved for only one's friends, as even sinners will love those who love them. Instead, Jesus teaches that we should love our enemies, do good to those who hate us, bless those who curse us, and pray for those who mistreat us (Luke 6: 27–36). This is the essence of Christian living, where, in the words of Mother Teresa of Calcutta, we are able to love even until it hurts. Jesus' parable of the Good Samaritan depicts this love. A man was attacked by robbers and left lying by the road. A priest and a religious scholar who passed him didn't help. It was the Samaritan, an outcast and despised person, who rendered help. Jesus instructs us to love the same way an outcast, someone who has always been mistreated, is able to love.

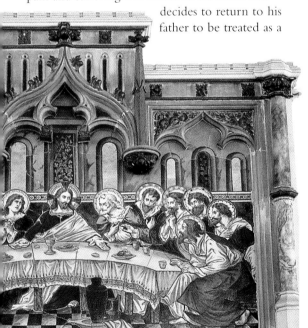

LEFT: The Last Supper which Jesus is believed to have had with his disciples just before his capture and crucifixion is a common theme in church art. This painting is in St Francis Xavier Church in Petaling Jaya, Selangor.

Stained glass windows from St Mary's Cathedral, Kuala Lumpur. God the Father, Christ on the Cross and the Virgin Mary are depicted.

Churches and worship

Given its long history of almost 500 years, Christianity in Malaysia reflects a wide range of church traditions, church architecture, church administration and worship styles. Churches range from large cathedrals with imposing bell towers to simple wooden buildings in rural areas. A modern development in expanding residential areas in cities is the setting up of churches in existing shop lots. The fundamental belief of service to others is shown through relief organizations and community service.

Priests and ministers

In both the Catholic and Protestant traditions the pastor or minister is the leader of the community of faithful. Apart from leading the congregation in prayers and preaching the word of God, priests and ministers celebrate holy communion, baptize infants, conduct marriages,

Bishop Lim Cheng Ean at St Mary's Cathedral, Kuala Lumpur, 2004.

funeral services and regularly reach out to members of their congregation and others in need. They also guide lay people in community service by raising money for the less advantaged or for the Church. Catholic priests also listen to confessions made by individuals.

Dr Brother Cassian Pappu at St John's Cathedral, Kuala Lumpur.

Church architecture

In Malaysia, churches have developed from buildings with traditional Western-style architecture, whether Dutch or English, and classical 'high church' liturgical worship to shop-front churches with an almost ritual-free worship format and vernacular churches with a charismatic, ecstatic worship style. Architecture and worship styles are undoubtedly influenced by the traditions of the respective church denominations within Malaysia, but are also the result of indigenous developments. Given the diversity of ethnicity and culture, it is not surprising that there are many vernacular churches in Malaysia, each using its own language, such as Tamil, Malayalam, Iban, Kadazan, Sengoi, Hokkien, Cantonese, Hakka and Foo Chow. The use of these languages makes Christian worship and education relevant and accessible to the people.

Christian churches are found not only in major cities but also in the smallest villages or townships and serve as centres for Christian worship, spiritual nourishment, education, youth development and social concerns throughout Malaysia.

Bell towers
Bells were traditionally rung to mark important times during the Christian day and for special events such as marriages and at Christmas.

Altar
Rites, including Communion, are conducted at the altar.

Nave
The central space in a church.

Pews
Benchlike seats for the congregation.

Confessional
Catholics go to confession regularly, confessing their sins to the priest and seeking forgiveness.

Seating for the choir

ST. JOHN'S CATHEDRAL

St John's Catholic Cathedral, Kuala Lumpur
Traditionally, churches are built in the shape of a cross, usually with the altar at the eastern end (the direction of the Resurrection).

Individual devotion

Christians believe that the Holy Spirit dwells in each believer. Thus, Christian spirituality can be both personal as well as congregational. Personal worship begins with the individual spending time alone with God in their personal devotion in the privacy of their home or office or whenever a moment of quiet can be found, either in the early morning or in the evening or both.

The devotee may read a short piece of scripture from the Holy Bible and say a prayer. An individual may even sing or hum a hymn or two. Some families have their own family devotions involving the children. These usually include songs, a reading or story from the Bible and saying a simple prayer. This keeps the family focused on God and reminds family members of their duties to God. Family devotions are sometimes fondly referred to as the family altar regardless of whether there is an altar or not. Traditionally, Christians pray before going to bed.

Church services

Larger families of Christians gather in church for congregational worship. Normally, there are at least two gatherings each week, the smaller group meetings (which are often held in the home of a church member on a rotational basis) for prayers and Bible study, and the main Sunday worship. In addition, many Roman Catholics attend Mass in church every morning or every evening. Regardless of church tradition, the Sunday worship in Malaysia includes silent prayer and meditation, singing of hymns, readings from the Bible, a sermon or homily, prayer of confession and intercessory prayers, thanksgiving, the affirmation of faith, holy communion (or Mass in the Catholic Church) and the benediction. The diversity of worship styles is apparent in the sequence in which these various components of the service are performed, the tunes and musical accompaniment of the hymns, the way in which prayers are said—whether sitting, standing or kneeling—the length and emphases of the sermon, the way in which communion is served and understood, and the attire of those who lead the service.

Among the various denominations, worship service styles vary between quiet and loud, passive and active, but the emphasis is on worshipping God and receiving instruction, inspiration, encouragement and wisdom.

In the service of God

Christians believe that their worship of God is not only to be performed by attending church services and praying, but also in how they conduct their lives. The purest form of worship is in doing God's will. Thus, church buildings are also centres for the education and development of children and provide facilities for those in need, such as soup kitchens.

Churches in Malaysia

Churches in Malaysia range from simple wooden buildings to grand cathedrals. Most Christian communities have their own churches. In rural communities the churches are simple, such as those found in small villages. These can be little more elaborate than huts. The cities have large churches built in traditional English styles.

St Mary's Anglican Cathedral Kuala Lumpur, built in 1887, echoes traditional English architectural style.

The oldest functioning Catholic church in Malaysia, St Peter's Church, Melaka, was completed in 1710.

St Michael's and All Angels Church, Sandakan, Sabah. The resplendent church, made from locally-mined granite, was completed in 1913 after 20 years of construction.

Kuala Lumpur's Holy Rosary Church was completed in 1904. The Gothic style church was built by Father Francis Emile Terrien, a French missionary, to cater to the city's then mainly Chinese community.

The St Plechelmus Chapel along the Oya River, near Sibu, Sarawak, ministers to a remote rural community.

Pastoral counselling is available in most churches. Malaysian churches are centres for social work and foster healthy socialization among young and old. Churches emphasize serving all sectors of society, especially those considered to be disadvantaged, such as the disabled, the sick, the poor, and the old and frail. Churches help by constantly raising money to either set up homes for these people or by contributing to existing homes and organizations. One such example which was set up by the Christian community is the Malaysian Christian Association for Relief (CARE) which was born out of the conviction that something must be done for the poor and needy in the country. It was established in 1978, and today offers diversified services such as residential care and community services. Most churches have committees, comprising lay members of the church, to organize events and services which allow them to contribute to their local communities.

Christian rites of passage

The spiritual life of Christians is strengthened by various rites which correspond to the various stages in the development of the individual. Because different Christian denominations and churches recognize or emphasize different rites, it is impossible to describe them all. In general, however, most churches accept the rites of baptism and the Lord's Supper, even if these are understood and performed differently across churches. The Roman Catholic Church's understanding of the Christian rites of passage is outlined below.

The Roman Catholic Archbishop of Kuala Lumpur, Murphy Nicholas Xavier Pakiam, conducting a confirmation ceremony at a church in Kuala Lumpur.

Sacraments and ministries of grace

Rites of passage are generally given the name 'sacraments' or understood as ministries of grace. This concept has been fundamental for understanding the union of God and the human being in the person of Jesus Christ. Sacraments are often described as 'outward and visible signs of inward and spiritual grace'. The grace of Jesus Christ is not merely an internal disposition; it is outwardly manifested in signs and actions.

Roman Catholicism and the Eastern Orthodoxy affirm seven sacraments, while Protestantism affirms only two. The Protestant insistence on only the two sacraments of baptism and the Lord's Supper is based on a firm belief that they were the only ones given explicit warrant in the teaching of Jesus, as discerned from the Bible. Protestants, however, do solemnize some of the other rites, even if not regarding them as sacraments.

The serving of Communion at a Holy Communion ceremony at the Church of the Sacred Heart in Kuala Lumpur.

Baptism

Baptism is a sacrament of Christian initiation that gives the individual new life by which he or she becomes a child of God and a member of the Church. The element used in baptism is water, signifying cleansing. In Malaysia, baptism is normally conducted in a church and performed by a priest or a minister. The essential rite common to all churches is the pouring of water on the head or immersion in water while pronouncing the invocation of the Holy Trinity.

A christening ceremony for the baptism of an infant. Holy water is poured on the forehead and godparents make a vow to care for the child's spiritual growth.

Although the Bible relates baptism for adults only, it was not long before young children, even infants, were being baptized. There are indications that baptism is the spiritual counterpart to circumcision (Colossians 2: 11–12), suggesting that the parallel may extend to its application to infants. In cases of infant baptisms, the Church relies on the commitment and faith of the parents to bring the child up according to Christian teachings. In Malaysia, both infant baptism and adult baptism are practised.

Confirmation

The ceremony of confirmation is a second step in the Christian initiation process, as a follow-up to the sacrament of baptism. It consists of the bishop anointing the forehead with blessed oil and laying hands on the head of the confirmant, while praying for the gifts of the Holy Spirit. These rituals confirm the candidate as a Christian who is constantly in need of God's assistance to live faithfully as a disciple of Christ.

In Malaysia, the sacrament of confirmation is conferred around the age of 15 by the Catholic Church. Confirmation can also be seen as an initiation to mark the transition from childhood to adulthood in the spiritual life. A certain maturity is needed in order to grasp the full meaning of confirmation.

Lord's Supper

The celebration of Holy Communion or Eucharist or the Mass is a commemoration of the Last Supper of Jesus with his disciples. Jesus used bread and wine in this event, often described as the 'breaking of bread'. Christians around the world re-enact this event every Sunday as an expression of remembering not only the Lord's Last Supper but also Jesus' life, teaching, crucifixion, death and resurrection.

The sacrament of penance and reconciliation

Sin is before all else an offence against God. But it is also an offence against one's neighbour. In spite of having been restored to new life through baptism, the temptation to sin remains because of the frailty and weakness of human nature. There is, therefore, a need to be reconciled regularly with God and with one's neighbour. This is the function of the sacrament of penance.

The act of confessing one's sins to a priest is the practice of Catholics. A penance is then set by the priest, which the penitent must fulfil. This penance may be an act of prayer or an act of restitution to the wronged party. The intent is to provide spiritual healing for the soul and aid in conversion towards greater holiness.

In Malaysia the Catholic Church usually holds sacraments of penance and reconciliation on a weekly basis. However, special penitential services are held during holy seasons, especially the time of Advent (the period leading up to Christmas) and Lent (the period leading up to Easter).

Confessionals in a Catholic church. According to church law all confessions must remain confidential.

Christians use various names to describe this celebration. The phrase 'Holy Communion' carries with it the idea of fellowship and sharing. It highlights both the fellowship between Jesus and the church, and also between individual Christians. 'Eucharist' comes from a Greek word which brings forth the theme of thanksgiving. The term 'Mass' derives from a Latin word which connotes a mission of being sent for love and service. All these connotations together aptly describe the meaning and essence of the Lord's Supper.

A typical Sunday service usually includes the recitation of prayers, singing of hymns, breaking of bread, and fellowship. The Bible is also read, following which a sermon is preached by the minister or priest. The bread and wine are then brought to the people who receive them as spiritual food to help nourish their Christian life.

Holy orders/ordination

By virtue of the sacrament of baptism, all Christians are called to holiness and are commissioned to be witnesses of Christ in their lives; through love, service and care for others. There is, however, a special ministry within the Church for people called to serve the Christian community as priests and ministers. The sacrament of holy orders celebrates this ministry. In the ceremony of ordination the bishop lays hands on the head of the candidate for priesthood and says the solemn prayers of consecration; in this way the bishop transfers the power of the orders to the recipient.

A Catholic bishop conducting ordination of two candidates for priesthood.

Preparation for Catholic priesthood in Malaysia takes around seven years of study of philosophy, theology and holy scriptures. This is complemented by studies also of religions other than Christianity (such as Islam, Hinduism, Buddhism) as well as the human and social sciences (psychology, sociology and counselling). These studies are undertaken in seminaries in Penang, Kuching and Singapore.

Anointing of the sick

The custom of praying over those who are sick, laying hands on them and anointing them with oil is a practice from early Christianity. Such practices are

A couple sharing sacred wine as part of their wedding Mass. Most Christians like to have a church service on their wedding day.

Marriage

In the past, marriages conducted by any Christian minister were the only recognized legal form of marriage among Christians in Malaysia. Today, Christian marriages can be conducted legally only by Christian ministers who have been designated as assistant registrars of marriages by the government.

Apart from the exchange of marriage vows, Christian wedding ceremonies in Malaysia often vary from one Christian community to another depending on local customs and ethnic origins. While the exchange of wedding rings is a common feature, the tying of the *thali* (the Hindu sacred pendant tied around the bride's neck in Hindu marriages) by the bridegroom is common among Christians of Indian heritage in Malaysia. In both cases, the ring and the *thali* respectively are blessed with prayers. Amongst Indian Christians, the newly married couple are often also decked with garlands.

Chinese Christians in Malaysia also include some of their own customary practices as part of the wedding ceremony. In particular, the 'tea ceremony' is important whereby the newly married couple offer tea as a sign of their respect and obedience to their parents and elders.

Certain Western features, such as the use of wedding gowns, the giving away of the bride, organ music, particularly *The Bridal March*, have been adopted and can be found in many Christian weddings in the country.

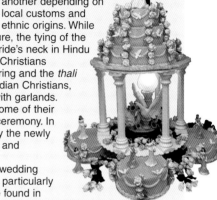

A traditional wedding cake.

Funeral rites

The rites which follow the death of a Christian employ the following themes: the Christian's union with Christ in baptism, the communion of saints into whose community the deceased will be welcomed, the Second Coming of Christ, and the longed for reunion with all the faithful at the end of time.

The funeral rites of Christians in Malaysia generally begin with prayers in the home of the deceased. This is followed by a religious service in church. This may be accompanied by a Mass in the case of Catholics. Most churches have retained a service that includes the preaching of the Christian hope of resurrection and prayers for the mourners.

The final rites are said at the grave and the burial is accompanied by rituals of farewell and committal, prayers of commendation, and the sprinkling of earth over the coffin before it is buried. In recent years cremation has become more common, after which the ashes are interned in a columbarium. Some churches in Malaysia have built a columbarium within the church compound.

ABOVE: Flowers from mourners are common at funeral services. A burial service at the grave side or crematorium follows the funeral service at the church.

RIGHT: Friends and family members may regularly visit the deceased's grave, placing flowers and offering prayers of remembrance.

intended to give the recipient grace and strength during the period of sickness. This sacrament can be conferred wherever the patient is—at home or in hospital. In Malaysia, Catholic lay persons who have been commissioned as extraordinary ministers of holy communion may bring the bread of life—holy communion—to the sick.

Christian festivals

Christian festivals commemorate particular aspects of Christian faith. Special days and seasons in the Christian year commemorate the great acts of God redeeming the world through Jesus Christ. Christmas, which celebrates the birthday of Christ, is undoubtedly the most well-known festival in Malaysia. However, Christians in Malaysia also celebrate other Christian festivals such as Good Friday, the day he was crucified, and Easter Sunday, the day of the Resurrection. In rural communities, especially in Sabah and Sarawak, harvest festivals are very important.

Good Friday 2002. Candles and a statue of Jesus Christ are carried in a procession within the church grounds of St Peter's Catholic Church, Melaka.

The Christian year

The first half of the Christian year is concerned with Christian beliefs, while the second half focuses on Christian duties in response to God's redemptive acts. The divine plan of salvation is based on the Incarnation, Crucifixion, Resurrection and Ascension of Christ and the coming of the Holy Spirit. Accordingly, the most important Christian festivals revolve around these events.

The Malaysian context

Christian festivals have undergone simplification and localization over the years. As a result, many customary ways of observing these festivals have been largely discarded. Some Malaysian Christians, most of whom are first-generation Christians, tend to hold more strictly to the core religious significance of the Christian festivals. In this sense, the observance of Christian festivals in Malaysia can be said to be more theological than cultural in nature.

Lent, Holy Week and Easter

As the Advent season prepares Christians for Christmas, so the season of Lent prepares them for Holy Week, culminating in Good Friday and Easter Sunday. The 40 days of Lent, not counting Sundays

A church service during San Pedro's festival celebrated by the Catholic Portuguese Malaysian community in Melaka.

which are feast days, begin with Ash Wednesday (so named as ashes signify mourning and represent the dust from which God created humanity and the dust to which humanity will return) and span the six Sundays before Easter. This is a season of repentance and voluntary abstinence from certain foods such as meat, alms-giving and acts of devotion. These all signify contrition, mourning and humiliation and being converted to the way of God.

The observance of Lent is in honour of the 40-day fast of Jesus in the wilderness. Churches hold special prayer services in the early morning throughout the Lenten season. The sixth Sunday in Lent, known as Palm Sunday, marks the entry of Christ into the city of Jerusalem, where he was later arrested and crucified. He was greeted with people waving palms. Palm Sunday ushers in Holy Week which marks the last week of Christ's earthly life. This is the most solemn period in the Christian year focusing on the death of Christ by crucifixion.

The Passion, or suffering, of Christ is deeply felt by Christians in the services held during the week. Catholics remember the Passion by meditatively praying the Stations of the Cross, marking the various times and locations where Christ stopped on the way to the Cross. Good Friday marks the day of Christ's Crucifixion. According to scripture, the Crucifixion began at 9 am and ended at 3 pm. Traditionally churches hold services from noon to

Feast of St Anne

For over a century, St Anne's Festival (26 July) has been a significant date in the Asian Christian calendar. An estimated 250,000 visitors from Malaysia and abroad flock to St Anne's Sanctuary at Bukit Mertajam (Penang) for this annual event, which is in honour of St Anne, the mother of the Blessed Virgin Mary. It is a nine-day prayer ritual held at two churches, an old and a new one, dedicated to St Anne, which are just a few metres away from each other on Bukit Mertajam.

St Anne's statue being carried in a procession during the annual feast.

Because of the belief that countless prayers have been answered and petitions granted, this festival also draws pilgrims from other religions. The result is an overwhelming multi-cultural congregation, united by a common devotion to the divine patroness of family joy.

During St Anne's Festival a carnival atmosphere is prevalent. The roads are closed to accommodate the huge crowds. Goods ranging from food to religious souvenirs, flowers, candles, jewellery and brassware are sold along the roads. Parishioners put up food stalls to raise money which goes to various charities and the church building fund.

Major Christian festivals in Malaysia

February /March	During Lent Christians fast and perform other acts of penance in preparation for Holy Week.
March /April	Jesus was crucified on Good Friday. The Resurrection occurred on Easter Sunday, three days later. Easter is regarded as the triumph of life over death.
May	Ascension Day signifies Jesus' return (ascent) to Heaven.
June	Pentecost—the coming of the Holy Spirit is celebrated.
1 December	Advent is the beginning of Christian New Year and the countdown to Christmas.
25 December	Birth of Jesus Christ.

3 pm, as a mark of respect. The last words of Jesus—'Father, forgive them, for they know not what they do'—are often emphasized during the service. Easter Sunday marks his Resurrection three days later. Easter is celebrated with jubilation and hope, Easter cantatas are rendered. Easter eggs, symbolizing new life, are not as prevalent in Malaysia as in the West.

Ascension Day and Pentecost

Ascension Day is observed 40 days after Easter and commemorates Christ's ascent to heaven. Ten days after that comes Pentecost Sunday (Whit Sunday) which is the anniversary of the coming of the Holy Spirit to the apostles, which marks the start of the Holy Spirit's ministry in the church. Pentecost Sunday is traditionally a favourite date for baptism.

Acculturation

In Sabah and Sarawak harvest festivals are of great importance (see 'Rituals and Festivals'). This annual festival is celebrated in Sabah by indigenous groups who were traditionally rice-farming communities. Though it started out as a festival among the largest group in Sabah, the Kadazandusun, other Sabahans now celebrate the festival. Called Tadau Kaamatan in Sabah and Gawai Dayak in Sarawak, churches have special services of thanksgiving, families welcome relatives and friends for meals and children receive gifts from their parents. In rural communities a symbolic offering of a portion of the harvest is made to the churches, thanking God.

Cities and towns all over Malaysia are brightly decorated during Christmas.

Christmas in Malaysia

Advent

The Christian year begins with Advent, which literally means 'important arrival'. Advent is a preparation for Christmas—the birth of Christ, who came to earth to facilitate solidarity between God and humanity. In some churches, especially Catholic, wreaths are used to mark the weeks in the season of Advent. The Advent wreath consists of a circle made out of evergreens and four candles. Usually, a fifth large candle, white in colour, is placed in the middle. The shape of the wreath, the circle, symbolizes the eternal nature of God, while the four candles—three purple, one rose coloured—represent the four weeks of Advent. The light from the candles represents Jesus as the light of the world.

On the first Sunday of Advent, one candle is lit. With each succeeding week, an additional candle is lit, so that by the fourth week all four are alight. The first candle stands for Hope; the second, Peace; the third, which is rose coloured, Joy; while the fourth represents Love.

It is also common during this time to see choirs and church groups visiting orphanages, old people's homes, and hospital wards. Teams of carol singers visit homes and shopping complexes to sing carols.

The choristers at Trinity Methodist Church in Kuala Lumpur.

Christmas

Christmas in Malaysia is celebrated among family and friends. Urban areas such as the greater Klang Valley come alive during the Yuletide season, with bright colourful lights and decorations in homes and business premises, creating a festive atmosphere.

The symbol of Christmas is the nativity scene comprising Christ (child in the manger) surrounded by Mary (his mother) and Joseph (his father) and the shepherds, three kings and farm animals. In Malaysia, this scene is displayed in churches and Sunday school classes and printed on cards and enacted in countless nativity plays by children in churches. The midnight Mass or service is an important event as it was the night of Jesus' birth, and people pray to welcome and adore him.

An enormous 30-metre Christmas tree in Kuala Lumpur's state-of-the-art KLCC shopping centre, 2003. Many legends surround the lore of the Christmas tree. Some suggest that trees are a sign of life and the tree is meant to represent the life of Christ. Others say that the tree symbolizes the Paradise Tree in the Garden of Eden and that the lights on the tree symbolize Christ as the light of the world.

A Christmas delivery at an old people's home in Kuala Lumpur.

Santa Claus is often depicted in decorations in major shopping centres.

Open house

The Christmas tree, decorated with bells, angels and trinkets, is also a favourite decoration in Christian homes. Christmas presents are placed under the tree at home until they are distributed to family members and opened, either on the eve of Christmas or Christmas Day. Churches present Christmas cantatas which tell the Christmas story. Family dinners are held on Christmas Eve. Christmas Day is a public holiday in Malaysia and, as is customary during festivals, Christian families entertain guests in their homes throughout the day, in the spirit of *rumah terbuka* (open house). In a way, this unique practice makes the celebration of Christmas more meaningful, and in line with the spirit of the season. Open houses provide an opportunity for Malaysians of different faiths and cultural backgrounds to socialize with one another. Christmas is the season of peace and goodwill.

Nativity plays at churches and schools portraying the birth of Jesus, such as this one in Sarawak, are commonly performed in the weeks preceding Christmas.

Ecumenical and evangelical Christian movements

Christians in Malaysia have been effective in the church networks they have created. The organizations and movements act as fora for discussing issues pertaining to the unity and mission of the Church. New Christian movements have engendered a more holistic understanding of witness, evangelism and social involvement. These movements have often brought renewed faith and growth in all dimensions of Christian life.

Members of the National Evangelical Christian Fellowship at the 2003 Merdeka Day Prayer Rally, an annual event aimed at stimulating national prayer.

The Ecumenical Movement

The aim of the Ecumenical Movement is the unification of all the Protestant churches and ultimately of all Christians. The word ecumenism refers to the whole inhabited earth conceived as a home. Ecumenism is also sometimes used in a broader sense to include dialogue with other religious traditions.

Council of Churches of Malaysia

The Council of Churches of Malaysia (CCM), formerly known as the Malayan Christian Council (MCC), was officially inaugurated in January 1948.

Members of the Consultative Council for Buddhism, Christianity, Hinduism and Sikhism (MCCBCHS) at a fundraising dinner in 1999.

At the initial meeting, the founding churches were Methodist, Anglican and Presbyterian. Later, they were joined by others such as the Mar Thoma Church; the Lutheran churches; and the Young Men's Christian Association (YMCA). In 1967, the MCC was renamed the Council of Churches of Malaysia and Singapore (CCMS) and was subsequently renamed the Council of Churches of Malaysia (CCM) in 1975.

A number of regional and international events gave local church leaders a vision of what inter-church co-operation could achieve. The formation of the East Asia Christian Conference (EACC) in Bangkok in 1949, and its subsequent meeting in Kuala Lumpur in May 1959, helped put local church leaders in contact with their counterparts in the region. To reflect a broader representation of regional cooperation and ecumenism, EACC was renamed Christian Conference of Asia (CCA). In an effort to establish a local theological institution,

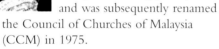

The logo of the worldwide ecumenical movement. The word 'ecumenical' comes from the Greek *oikoumene* meaning 'to inhabit the world'.

Anglicans, Methodists and Evangelical Lutherans jointly initiated Seminari Theoloji Malaysia (STM) in January 1979.

Some of the CCM member churches are: the Anglican Dioceses of Kuching, Sabah and West Malaysia, the Basel Christian Church, the Lutheran Church, the Methodist Church, and the Protestant Church of Sabah.

National Evangelical Christian Fellowship Malaysia

The NECF Malaysia is a national Christian body that represents 2500 evangelical churches in Malaysia. These include the Assemblies of God, Baptists, Brethren, Sidang Injil Borneo (Sabah, Sarawak and Peninsula), Full Gospel Assembly, Full Gospel Tabernacle, Evangelical Free Church, Latter Rain, Hope of God, Salvation Army, independent churches and some mainline denominations such as Presbyterian, Methodist, para church organizations and Bible seminaries. NECF is a member of the World Evangelical Alliance and the Evangelical Fellowship of Asia.

Since its inception in 1983 NECF Malaysia has brought about two decades of evangelical awakening in Malaysia and has drawn together the conservative, traditional, Pentecostal and Charismatic evangelical churches in cooperation and partnership. It is involved in a variety of ministries, including linguistic ministries, through various programmes such as those involving mission, prayer, evangelism, youth, women, leadership development, research and communication.

Christian Federation of Malaysia

After the 1980s, church leaders realized the need for a more broad-based ecumenical body and a unified voice in dealing with the government as well as other religious and secular bodies in the country. Heads of churches from the various traditions came together and established the Christian Federation of Malaysia (CFM). The CFM, inaugurated in 1985,

Churches in Sabah and Sarawak

Due to historical reasons, churches in Sabah and Sarawak have developed, both politically and ecclesiastically, quite separately and independently from Peninsular Malaysia. The Sabah Council of Churches (SCC), formed in the late 1980s, comprises the Catholic, Anglican, Basel, Sidang Injil Borneo (SIB), Seventh Day Adventist, Protestant Church of Sabah (Lutheran), Baptist and Brethren churches. In Sarawak, the Association of Churches of Sarawak (ACS) was formed in the mid-1980s, comprised initially of Catholic, Anglican and Methodist Churches. SIB Sarawak, the Salvation Army and Seventh Day Adventist joined the ACS some time later.

Many of the churches in Sabah and Sarawak are also members of the NECF, including Sidang Injil Borneo Sabah and Sidang Injil Borneo Sarawak.

The Seventh Day Adventist Church's community involvement includes secondary boarding schools in Sabah and Sarawak. The Salvation Army, which made its debut in Penang in July 1938, has a network of services in 30 centres nationwide, including children's and boys' homes in Kuching.

In December 1999 the NECF organized an Emmanuel Celebration at Bukit Jalil Stadium, Kuala Lumpur, which over 60,000 people attended.

brought together three major streams of Christianity—the Roman Catholic Church, the churches affiliated to the CCM and the NECF. True to its objectives, CFM has endeavoured to take joint stands on issues concerning Malaysian society. The CFM plays the role of ambassador for the Christian community and ensures that Christians participate in nation building. It also looks after Christian interests in terms of national integration and fostering goodwill among all Malaysians. The primary challenge facing ecumenism in Malaysia is in relating Malaysian churches to local cultures and traditions. The CFM, being a member of the Malaysian Consultative Council of Buddhism, Christianity, Hinduism and Sikhism (MCCBCHS), serves as a forum for resolving sensitive issues regarding religion and other related matters. It also makes representations to the government on issues affecting the various religions.

The Church has grown to a certain extent in Malaysia in the past few years. According to a survey conducted by the Anglican denomination there was a 44 per cent increase in the diocesan electoral roll in 1995. There are several reasons quoted for such a growth, one of them being the sense of renewal brought about by the Charismatic Renewal Movement and another being the sense of ecumenism. Churches have come together and helped in creating awareness of the religion to the lay people by building new centres or churches. There has been an overall resurgence of the main religions in the country and talks between the government and the various religious bodies especially the MCCBCHS, which comprises the main faiths practised in Malaysia, have allowed for a more tolerant and understanding society.

Evangelical Christian movements

Like many churches around the world, churches in Malaysia have had to adapt themselves to the existence and influence of evangelical Christian movements from as early as the 1930s, though the 1960s were the main period of growth.

Pentecostal Movement

Pentecostalism is an evangelical restorationist movement. It emphasizes the baptism and gifts of the Holy Spirit for the life and mission of the church and indigenous forms of worship and church structure. The Pentecostal Movement, which originated in the United States in 1906, has become the largest and fastest growing segment of Christianity in the world. It has been called Christianity's 'fourth force', alongside Catholicism, Protestantism and the Orthodox denominations.

The modern Pentecostal Movement includes: Classical Pentecostals, Neo-Pentecostals or Charismatic, and Neo-Charismatic and indigenous groups. Although these are Western categories, classical Pentecostal churches in Malaysia reflect more diversity in and contextualisation of beliefs and practices. Pentecostal spirituality has especially appealed to marginalized populations, e.g. overseas Chinese in Malaysia. In recent decades it has also attracted the middle classes and the wealthy.

Pentecostal service at the Glad Tidings Assembly Church in Petaling Jaya, Selangor.

The style of worship among Pentecostals is emotional, musical and revivalist. Speaking or praying in tongues, prophesying, healing, exorcism, 'slayings in the spirit', baptism by fire and holy water are common features observed with great zeal and fervency. This worship style also separates Pentecostals from other mainline Christian denominations. Experience, rather than doctrine, has often been noted as the principal determinant of Pentecostalism. On the other hand, similar to other mainline, evangelical Christian denominations, Pentecostalism tends to adhere to almost all of the other fundamental doctrines of the Christian faith.

What was once known as the Pentecostal Movement has now splintered into numerous diverse, yet overlapping, movements. One of the most important traditional Pentecostal denominations in Malaysia is the Assemblies of God (AOG) with more than 400 churches and many other preaching points. The other notable indigenous church is the New Testament Church started in 1963 by the Hong Kong actress Kong Duen Yee, popularly known as Mui Yee.

Charismatic Movement

The Charismatic Renewal Movement has some of its roots in historic Pentecostalism, and it is now deeply entrenched in most of the mainline Protestant denominations, in Catholicism, and in some Orthodox churches. In contemporary usage, various terms are loosely applied to the Charismatic Movement, such as the 'Renewal Movement', 'Neo-Pentecostal Movement', 'Third Wave Movement', 'Revival Movement' and 'Spirit Movement'.

Although related to Pentecostalism, the Charismatic Movement differs in not being denominationally organized and in its refusal to insist upon speaking in tongues as an essential element of authentic Christian experience. The Charismatic Movement is an informal international and transdenominational fellowship of Christians. By definition it is concerned with *charismata*, the Greek term for 'gifts of grace'.

The terms Pentecostal and Charismatic are frequently used interchangeably and are obviously related. This interchangeability in usage has been unavoidable due to the borderless nature of 'charismatic' theology and expressions. The earlier historical Pentecostal Renewal or Revival movements do share many similarities (although some dissimilarity may be evident too) with modern day charismatic folk Christianity. Common features include speaking in tongues, emphasis on the Holy Spirit, experiencing God, expressive forms in worship (dancing, raising of hands and hopping on the spot) and in the exercise of spiritual gifts.

The Charismatic Movement has been in Malaysia since the 1970s. This 20th-century Pentecostal renewal has impacted every segment of the Christian church with new vitality and fervour. It has certainly provided inspiration and the much-needed spiritual re-awakening among churches and individuals. Two of the pioneers of charismatic ministries in Malaysia were the Full Gospel Assembly (FGA) and Full Gospel Businessmen's Fellowship International (FGBMFI).

As a result of its impact and influence, traditional churches in Malaysia have had to make various adjustments to accommodate charismatic folk Christianity. Many Malaysian Christians view the emergence of charismatic identity as a solution to the problem of Christian unity and believe it helps to overcome ethnic boundaries.

1. The *granthi* (reader of Sikh scripture) reading from the Guru Granth Sahib (Sikh holy book) in a gurdwara.

2. Gurdwara Shahib, Labuan.

3. This 1928 photograph shows Sikh army officers and police, together with the *sangat* (congregation), in Penang transferring the Guru Granth Sahib from Fort Cornwallis gurdwara to the gurdwara of the Sikh police force in Patani Road.

4. Originally, Sikhs came to Malaya to work in the police and armed forces. Some of the first Sikhs brought to Malaya by the British formed the Perak armed force and worked alongside fellow Hindu and Muslim officers. The 1st Battalion Perak Sikhs, comprising only Sikhs, was formed out of this force and existed from 1884 to 1896.

5. The Sikh festival of Vaisakhi being celebrated by Malaysian Sikhs.

SIKHISM

Sikhism was founded in India by Guru Nanak (1469–1539). It is the youngest of the major world religions, with a following of around 22 million people spread over various states in India and a sizeable international diaspora. In India, Sikhs are concentrated in the state of Punjab, where they make up 60 per cent of the population. For this reason, Punjab is frequently referred to as the homeland of the Sikhs.

The largest Sikh populations outside India can be found in the UK, the USA and Canada. In Malaysia, Sikhs number approximately 55,000 and live throughout the country, but in greatest numbers in the Klang Valley.

In Malaysia, Sikhs are represented throughout the professions; however, it is their role as soldiers and police which is most well known. The Sikh religion teaches valour, gallantry and the spirit of sacrifice. As a result, the armies of colonial Britain, modern India and Malaysia have all included many Sikhs.

A large number of Sikhs came to Malaya under the British administration to work in the police and armed forces. In the period after World War I, many Sikhs came to Malaya not just to work in the services but also as traders, moneylenders and in transport businesses.

Sikhism is a religion of strict monotheism. There are no pilgrimages in Sikhism, no rituals and no superstitions. There is also no place for asceticism or monasticism in Sikhism. Sikhs consider human life as an opportunity to fulfil their destiny of becoming a *gurmukh*—an instrument of God to carry out his will through altruistic deeds.

Sikhs believe in the ten gurus. Their teachings are enshrined in the Guru Granth Sahib, the Sikh scripture. The Guru Granth Sahib, compiled and authenticated by the fifth guru, Guru Arjan Dev (1563–1606), was given the status of 'Living Guru' by the tenth guru, Guru Gobind Singh (1666–1708), meaning that the spirit of the guru lives on through it. Sikhs believe that it represents the Word of God.

The Sikh gurus preached devotion to God and love of humanity, expressed through service and sacrifice. At a time when India was being torn apart by caste tensions, sectarianism, religious factionalism and fanaticism, Guru Nanak spread the simple message

Catering to the Sikh community in Malaysia, the *Malaya Samachar* newspaper is published in Punjabi by the Tatt Khalsa organization in Kuala Lumpur.

that 'We are all one, created by the One Creator of all Creation'.

The Sikh community is close-knit. The Sikh temple (gurdwara) is the focal point of religious and social activities. For example, every gurdwara has a *langar* (communal kitchen) where free meals are provided—no one, from any religion, is turned away. The central place to which every Sikh pledges religious allegiance is the Golden Temple at Amritsar, India, which was founded by Guru Ram Das and completed by the fifth guru, Guru Arjan Dev.

The first gurdwaras in Malaysia were set up by Sikhs working in the police force. Currently, there are 119 throughout Malaysia. Their activities are coordinated by the Malaysian Gurdwaras Council, set up in 1988.

History and beliefs of Sikhism

Originating in North India in the 15th century with the life and teachings of Guru Nanak, Sikhism evolved over the next 200 years into the form that is still practised today. Throughout those years ten gurus taught and defended the Sikh faith after which religious authority passed to the Guru Granth Sahib—the most sacred scripture of the Sikh religion. In the mid-19th century, Sikhism came to colonial Malaya.

The evolution of Sikhism

The founder of Sikhism, Guru Nanak, was born in Punjab in 1469. He taught the doctrine of salvation centring on two basic ideas; one about the nature of God, and one about the nature of mankind. The period from 1469 to 1708 is known as the 'Guru

The ten gurus

Guru Nanak, the first of the gurus, began his spiritual quest in 1499. Guru Angad Dev established the equality of the sexes. Guru Amar Das further institutionalized the free communal kitchen known as a *langar* among the Sikhs. The *langar* was open to all, day and night. Guru Ram Das founded the city of Amritsar with the Golden Temple, which became the religious capital of the Sikhs.

Guru Arjan Dev saw political concerns as an essential part of a religious man's sphere of action. This concept was broadened by his successor, Guru Hargobind, as *miri piri*, that religious and temporal concerns were of equal importance. He fought battles with the Mughal state to defend the faith and the society founded by the gurus. Guru Har Rai and Guru Har Krishan played major roles in consolidating the work of their predecessors. Guru Tegh Bahadur defended freedom of worship for people of all faiths.

The religion was given its final form by Guru Gobind Singh, the last of the gurus. He laid down the rules for Sikhs. He also passed on the succession to the Guru Granth Sahib—the holy book—ending the long line of gurus. He said, 'The Guru's spirit will henceforth be in the Granth and the Khalsa. Where the Granth is with any five Sikhs representing the Khalsa, there the Guru will be.'

Guru Nanak (1469–1539)

Guru Nanak was born a Hindu in the village of Talwandi in present-day Pakistan. He began his spiritual quest in 1499 after a religious experience while bathing in a river. During his lifetime he travelled widely, going as far as Baghdad (Iraq). Wherever he went, he engaged the learned of different faiths in discussion and revealed his beliefs to all.

Guru Nanak (1469–1539)

Guru Angad Dev (1504–52)

Guru Amar Das (1479–1574)

Guru Ram Das (1534–81)

Guru Arjan Dev (1563–1606)

Guru Hargobind (1595–1644)

Guru Har Rai (1630–61)

Guru Har Krishan (1656–64)

Guru Tegh Bahadur (1621–75)

Guru Gobind Singh (1666–1708)

Sikh holy days

Before March 1998, the Sikhs used a Hindu calendar to determine their religious days. They now use their own Nanak calendar which started on 14 March 1999 and aligns itself with the Gregorian calendar.

Months	Major festivals/celebrations
December/ January	Gobind Singh's birthday. The tenth Guru, Gobind Singh, founder of the Khalsa, was born in 1666.
February	Holy Maholla. Guru Gobind Singh initiated a Sikh festival of fairs and processions, coinciding with the Indian spring festival of Holi.
April	Vaisakhi. Originally a festival of thanksgiving (harvest festival)—now a celebration of the Khalsa—which traditionally dates to Vaisakhi in 1699.
May	Martyrdom of Guru Arjan.
August	Celebration of the Guru Granth Sahib (Sikh holy book). A remembrance of the completion of the sacred texts.
October	Diwali. A Hindu festival, but adapted to commemorate the release from prison of the sixth Guru, Guru Hargobind. Guru Nanak's birthday.
November	Martyrdom of Guru Tegh Bahadur.

period' and forms the early history of Sikhism. During this time the ten gurus travelled, preached and expanded the religion.

The Sikh religion was given its final form by Guru Gobind Singh, the tenth Guru. On Vaisakhi (harvest festival) in 1699, he introduced the concept of baptism in the religion. Those baptized became part of the Khalsa (army of saint-soldiers). They were to discard caste restrictions, occupational restraints, superstitions and the burden of previous incarnations. Men were given the common surname Singh (lion) and women, Kaur (princess). He also prescribed the five 'k's' for Sikhs: *kesh* (unshorn hair), *kangha* (comb), *kara* (iron bracelet), *kirpan* (sword) and *kachha* (breeches).

From the Punjab to British Malaya

The very first Sikhs to come to Malaya were those exiled by the British after Punjab had been annexed. These individuals arrived in the 1850s. However, the first real wave of immigration, to what was then colonial Malaya, occurred in the 1870s. Around the 1880s, they had settled and established themselves in Kuala Lumpur. Large numbers of Sikhs were brought by the British to enforce law and order in the Straits Settlements and Federated Malay States.

The period after World War I saw an influx of young Sikhs seeking opportunities in trade, transportation businesses, moneylending, security services and other areas.

Sikh organizations, which were strongly influenced by Sikh reform movements active in the Punjab, were founded in Malaya in the early 20th century. These organizations also concerned themselves with Sikh welfare and Sikh identity in Malaya. However, as regional and ideological differences were strong, by the end of World War II few of these organizations remained.

Beliefs and world-view

One God
The Sikh religion is uncompromisingly monotheistic. According to Sikh scripture, God is the sole one who created the myriad universes. He is the truth. He, himself, does not take human form. He is immanent in his creation and yet remains apart from it. He has no hostility and is fearless. His relationship with the universe and man is that of creator and creation. He is benevolent and looks after his creation lovingly. In fact, He is all love, he is indefinable. He has a will, which is altruistic. Everybody is subject to his will, nobody is beyond its scope. A Sikh must, therefore, see God's immanence in all his fellow beings, and love should govern the mutual relationships of all men.

Among God's countless other attributes, he is self-existent, beyond time, and without fear and hate. He is also the ocean of virtues.

The nature of the world
Unlike some other religions of the East which regard the world as *mithya* (illusory), Sikhism accepts it to be real. Sikhism also rejects the belief held by some ascetic systems that the world is a place of suffering or that man is born in this world as a punishment for his sins.

Cosmology and cosmogony
Guru Nanak said that there are hundreds of thousands of netherworlds and innumerable worlds above, and that it is a futile exercise trying to guess their number. Guru Nanak also pointed out that there are innumerable suns and moons constantly travelling immeasurable distances under God's command.

Goal of life
The Sikh ideal is to be a *gurmukh* who aims for the salvation of the entire humanity in his own lifetime and not after death, as in other religious systems. He is expected to discharge all social and political responsibilities wholeheartedly. A *gurmukh* is one who is completely attuned to God's will and whose love for God is expressed in altruistic deeds and community service.

The path
Sikhism considers asceticism, monasticism or withdrawal from life as mere escapism. The Sikh ideal is to be achieved through a family and community life. The gurus preached that worldly activities are no hindrance to spiritual progress. Rather, the worldly aspects of life should be viewed as essential and complementary.

The *khanda* is the symbol of the Khalsa. The central double-edged sword symbolizes the belief in one God and protection against oppression.

Ik Onkaar — There is only One God
Satnaam — Truth is the Name
Karta Purkh — The Creator
Nirbhau — Without Fear
Nirvair — Without Hate

Sikh prayers begin with these words—the *mool mantra*.

Truth
Truth and knowledge are stressed in all faiths. In Sikhism, however, mere knowledge of truth is not considered enough. According to the Sikh gurus, 'Truth is higher than everything. Higher still is truthful living or the practice of truth in life.'

Emphasis on deeds
Love of God has to be translated into love of humanity, since He is immanent in all of mankind. Love cannot be practised in a vacuum. It can be expressed only through altruistic deeds in the service of humanity; hence the importance of deeds in Sikhism.

Equality and justice
Sikhism does not sanction discrimination of any kind as it considers the entire human race to be one brotherhood. God is the Father and all human beings are His children. Women have equality with men in all spheres, social, political and religious.

Justice is a corollary of this equality. A Sikh should be just in his dealings with others, dispense full justice when in authority and fight for justice for the oppressed and the weak. For this, he should be spiritually inspired, morally equipped and physically strong.

The doctrines
A fundamental doctrine of the Sikh faith is the unity of guruship. The ten human gurus and the holy book are one in spirit; all the gurus were animated by the same spirit. The divine words of the gurus (*shabad guru*), revealed through the gurus, are enshrined in the Guru Granth Sahib. Any decision made by a congregation (*sangat*) in the presence of the Guru Granth Sahib which is in accordance with the preaching of the gurus is taken as the decision of a guru (*gurmatta*).

The doctrine of *miri piri* is based on the belief that the spiritual and temporal aspects of life cannot be separated. Sikhism stresses that both are required for balanced growth. The gurus stressed that it is man's destiny to achieve human progress. Sikhs believe that humans are born egocentric. The aim is to progress from this stage to that of *gurmukh*. While a Sikh makes conscious efforts in this direction, through carrying out the altruistic will of God, the gurmukh stage is eventually attained only through God's grace.

Five symbols of the Khalsa
All Sikhs have to wear the five 'k's' as a reminder of their faith.

Kesh (unshorn hair) is a symbol of saintliness. Keeping hair in its natural state is regarded as living in harmony with the will of God.

Kangha (comb) is necessary to keep the hair clean and tidy. Turbans protect the hair and promote a common social identity.

Kara (iron bracelet) symbolizes restraint from evil deeds. It is worn on the right wrist and reminds Sikhs of their vows.

Kirpan (sword) is the emblem of courage and self-defence. It symbolizes dignity, self-reliance, and the capacity and readiness to defend the weak and oppressed.

Kachha (breeches) must be worn at all times and remind Sikhs of the need for self-restraint over passion.

The Langar
Guru Nanak institutionalized the practice of a common kitchen (*langar*) in Sikhism. Here, all are welcome to sit together and share a common meal. There is no distinction made between race, creed or caste.

Members of the Tatt Khalsa Diwan Selangor, Kuala Lumpur, enjoying a meal in the *langar*.

Traditionally, the congregation would sit on the floor, but in modern gurdwaras well equipped *langar* halls are available.

119

Sikh temples and worship

A Sikh temple is called a gurdwara. Wherever there has been a sizeable population of Sikhs, a gurdwara has been built. It acts as the hub of community activities. In Malaysia, there are 119 gurdwaras, both in small towns and the larger cities. The first gurdwara in Malaysia was set up by Sikhs in the police force in Penang in 1881.

The Golden Temple in Amritsar, India, is the spiritual and temporal centre of the Sikh world. The temple was built during the time of the fourth guru, Guru Ram Das.

Origins

The gurdwaras started with the first guru, Guru Nanak. During his tours to various parts of the world, he organized formal congregations of his disciples and set up places where they could meet regularly for prayers and discussions of their problems. These places were called *dharamsala* in the beginning, but later came to be known as gurdwaras, which means 'house of the guru'.

A number of Sikh gurdwaras are considered historic. Among these are the Nanakana Sahib in present-day Pakistan, birthplace of Guru Nanak; the Golden Temple at Amritsar founded by Guru Ram Das and completed by Guru Arjan Dev; Patna Sahib, India, the birthplace of Guru Gobind Singh; and Hazur Sahib at Nanaded in South India where Guru Gobind Singh died.

The *chaur* (fly whisk) is waved over the Guru Granth Sahib as a sign of respect.

Worship and service

Everybody is welcome in a gurdwara, and there are no restrictions on participation. One enters the premises of a gurdwara with bare feet and with the head covered. Sikhs bow down before the Guru Granth Sahib in obeisance, and start their daily work only after reciting a *hukamnama* (hymn) from it or hearing it recited. This first *hukamnama* of the day is displayed at the entrance, and is considered an injunction from God for guidance throughout the day. It must be noted that the reverence shown to the Guru Granth Sahib is not worship of a beautiful book. Rather, it is obeisance to God and his word.

Congregational worship (*sandh-sangat*) in a gurdwara consists of recitation of sacred hymns, singing of hymns (*kirtan*) and congregational prayers at fixed hours. The gurus placed high value on music in praise of God. All hymns in the Guru Granth Sahib conform to and have been arranged under recognized modes of Indian traditional music. In a typical gurdwara, congregational worship is in the form of daily morning and evening services. In the morning, the service starts very early, usually at five o'clock, when the Guru Granth Sahib is ceremoniously installed on a throne (*takhat posh*) erected for this purpose in the hall. A canopy (*chaneni*) hangs overhead to create a regal atmosphere. An attendant waves a *chaur* (fly whisk) overhead symbolizing respect.

The congregation stands facing the Guru Granth Sahib and *ardas* (supplication) is offered. The *ardas* is addressed to God. It can be led by the *granthi* (reader of the scripture) or any senior member of the congregation, male or female, since there is no formal priest class among Sikhs. After offering *ardas*, the congregation sits on the covered floor. The

A Sikh wedding. Weddings and other Sikh functions are centred around the gurdwara.

Takhat posh
Decorated raised platform upon which the Guru Granth Sahib is placed.

Chaneni
This is the richly embroidered velvet or silk canopy that hangs over the holy book.

Guru Granth Sahib
Holy book of the Sikhs. This religious scripture was written during the time of the Sikh Gurus under their direction.

Rumala
An embroidered silk cloth with gold or silver brocade called a *rumala* covers the holy book.

Sangat
The *sangat* (congregation) sits on the floor facing towards the *takhat posh*.

granthi recites a hymn from the Guru Granth Sahib. This is followed by *kirtan* for an hour or two. The service concludes with the *ardas* and the recital of a hymn from the scripture. A sacred sweetmeat called *karah parshad* is distributed.

The evening service begins with recital of special hymns called *rehra* meaning 'the correct path' followed by *kirtan* and ends with *kirtan sohila*, the bedtime prayer, and *ardas*, after which the Guru Granth Sahib is closed and moved to another room in the gurdwara where it rests for the night, leaving the hall vacant for cleaning.

During the daytime, devotees may also come to pay obeisance and make offerings. The *granthi* reads a hymn for them, or they may read a hymn themselves. In some historic gurdwaras such as the Golden Temple at Amritsar, the routine is more elaborate, starting much earlier in the morning and finishing much later. The *kirtan* continues without pause except for three to four hours when floors are washed and carpets cleaned.

The gurdwara in Sikh society

All Sikh functions, collective as well as individual, are generally performed in local gurdwaras. These include naming a child, *amrit* (initiation), engagement, marriage and death rites. Most gurdwaras have a refectory, called a *langar*, where free food is served and sometimes free accommodation is available. Some also have a school, hospital, dispensary and home for the aged attached to them.

The Guru Granth Sahib

While Sikhism is a monotheistic religion it is believed that God is represented by his word conveyed through the gurus and enshrined in the hymns of the Guru Granth Sahib. This holy scripture was originally compiled by Guru Arjan Dev in 1604 CE after which Guru Gobind Singh added to it the later hymns of his father, Guru Tegh Bahadur. He also accorded to it the status of 'guru' when succession of the gurus in human form ended in 1708 CE. Thus the Guru Granth Sahib is installed in every gurdwara as the living and eternal guru of the Sikhs.

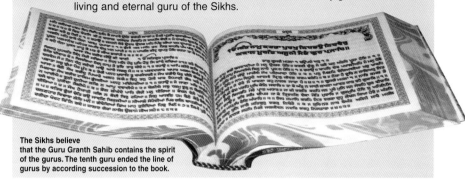

The Sikhs believe that the Guru Granth Sahib contains the spirit of the gurus. The tenth guru ended the line of gurus by according succession to the book.

In Malaysia, some gurdwaras provide instruction in the Punjabi language, which is essential for reciting the hymns in the Guru Granth Sahib. Libraries stocked with religious literature have also been added.

Gurdwaras have played a very important role in Sikh politics. As Sikhism is a faith which recognizes no division between religion and politics, all major political movements by Sikhs in the Punjab have been launched from gurdwaras. The Akal Takht in India, which is a part of the Golden Temple complex, is the highest temporal authority among Sikhs. It is here that major political decisions, considered binding on all Sikhs in any part of the world, have been taken.

In Malaysia, each Sikh religious organization or gurdwara enjoys independent administration. In 1988, a central council of gurdwaras called the Malaysian Gurdwaras Council was established to coordinate the functioning of these gurdwaras.

The Tatt Khalsa Diwan Selangor, Kuala Lumpur, one of the largest religious organizations in the region, provides for the social, cultural and educational needs of the Sikh community.

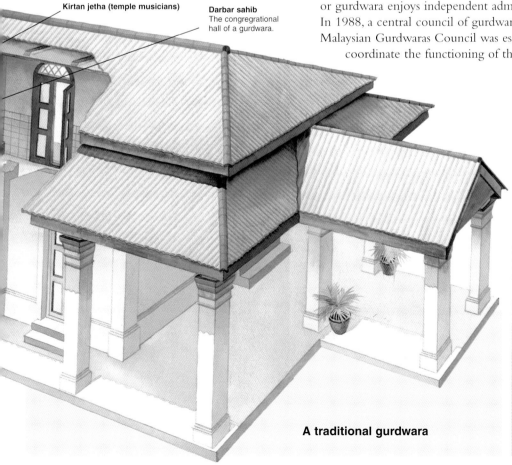

Kirtan jetha (temple musicians)

Darbar sahib
The congregrational hall of a gurdwara.

A traditional gurdwara

Historic gurdwaras in Malaysia

Built in 1890 to serve the needs of Sikhs in the police force, Gurdwara Sahib Police in Jalan Parlimen, Kuala Lumpur, was one of the earliest gurdwaras established in the Klang Valley.

This gurdwara in Penang, now known as the Wadda Gurdwara Sahib, was built in 1901.

1. Gawai Kenyalang (Hornbill Festival) is celebrated in honour of the god of war by the Iban of Sarawak. Previously a precursor to head-taking raids, it is now held at the end of the rice harvest. The climax is when giant carved hornbills are erected on top of poles. Their spirits are believed to transfer messages to the upper world.

2. The Tadau Kaamatan (Harvest Festival) held in May in Sabah and mainly celebrated by the Kadazandusun, is a thanksgiving festival for the bountiful harvest of the season and signifies the beginning of the planting season. The festival is supplemented with appearances of *bobohizan* (high priestesses), cultural performances, agricultural shows, traditional games, the Harvest Queen competition and bull racing, one of the most popular events of the festival.

3. Priestesses participating in the Manawah do Turugan—cleansing of the universe— ceremony in the village of Marabahai by the Tuaran River, Sabah. This ceremony lasts

several weeks and is designed to flush out evil; it is conducted first in homes, then upstream and finally at the beach.

4. A Mah Meri family in Kampung Judah on Carey Island, Selangor, decorate their family outdoor altar (*sangkar*) on the occasion of their annual Hari Moyang (memorial day for ancestors). Food offerings will be placed on the *sangkar* as the whole family gather round it to pay homage to their ancestors or *moyang*.

5. Iban dancing at the Skrang longhouse in the Sri Aman district of Sarawak as part of Gawai Batu (Whetstone Festival)—a festival celebrating the clearing of land ready for planting the new crop of rice. *Batu* refers to the stone used for sharpening tools to clear the land.

6. Iban women in traditional costume at a rice planting ritual ceremony.

INDIGENOUS BELIEFS

In addition to mainstream world religions, other indigenous, traditional beliefs such as those practised by the Orang Asli of Peninsular Malaysia and those of the numerous indigenous groups in Sabah and Sarawak are recognized in Malaysia. Although the beliefs of the Orang Asli and the indigenous groups in Sabah and Sarawak are loosely classified as animism, and generally not recognized by the state, they are not in any way incomplete or less sophisticated. Rather, they are complex and well structured in respect to their ideas about the supernatural world and morality.

These belief systems, in effect, are non-institutionalized religions, usually not regarded as world religions. Followers of these beliefs have no formal institution to administer their activities nor did they have a writing system which would allow the dissemination of information and knowledge. Instead, followers transmitted their teachings, beliefs and values down the generations through a complex oral tradition.

The Jah Hut spirit Juam is believed to protect plantations and live near houses left vacant for a long time. If anyone steals fruit from the plantations Juam will give the thief an upset stomach.

Among these people, these religions are known as traditional or customary religions (*agama adat*). Since the indigenous people are divided into various ethnic groups and live scattered all over the country, the forms and structures of their traditional religions also vary. Some of these religions have their own names and concepts for the supreme being (God) and the pantheon of other deities (supernatural beings). Nevertheless, while these religions do share some common values with other world religions, they also offer a unique perspective on the world; an interpretation and understanding of the world explicitly and implicitly interwoven with their cultural knowledge and ritual practices forming a mosaic of beliefs and practices.

Although the beliefs of the various indigenous groups are varied, there are commonalities. One of the most striking is the influence of the environment in shaping their world-view and religious beliefs system. The groups and their beliefs share a close relationship with nature. Environmental features and physical formations such as rocks, mountains, hills, trees, valleys and rivers are considered sacred. Their whole cultural milieu is centred around cosmological myths that emphasize the sacredness of time, space and place. This close relationship between humans and their environment permeates their entire existence—daily lives are concerned with hunting and food gathering in the jungles which are regarded as quasi-religious activities and are invariably surrounded by taboos. Bad harvests and environmental problems are seen as the gods seeking retribution for some wrongdoing— complex rituals and offerings are made to overcome such situations.

Offerings made to the gods during an Iban padi planting ceremony. All traditional festivals and ceremonies feature offerings of food to the gods.

Indigenous belief systems

The Orang Asli community in Peninsular Malaysia have their own beliefs and traditions dating back hundreds of years, as have the indigenous peoples of Sabah and Sarawak. Although not officially recognized, these beliefs are complex in their own way. These groups are influenced by a myriad of spirits which can bring good or do harm to individuals. Shamans—religious leaders and healers—act as intermediaries between humans and the spirit world.

Semai shaman in Bidor, Perak, invoking his spirit-guide in front of the *balei* (spirit-perch).

Adat

Adat is a collection of accepted rules of conduct by which society is ordered as well as customs and traditions including indigenous religions and associated rituals.

Adat may differ from group to group, but the basic elements remain the same. The primary principle of *adat* is that there should be a balance or harmony between individuals and also between the community and their physical and spiritual environment. It is believed that imbalances between the secular and supernatural worlds result in misfortune, illness and crop failure, amongst others. If the balance is disturbed the environment becomes 'hot'. Restitution must be made to 'cool' the environment and restore balance and harmony. Restitution is made in different ways depending on the beliefs of the particular group.

Modernization and changing religious beliefs have altered *adat*, but the key elements retain their vitality with a number of festivals and rituals still observed by the various ethnic groups in Malaysia.

The Orang Asli

There are approximately 140,000 Orang Asli, divided into the Semang-Negrito, Senoi and Proto-Malays. Orang Asli communities are present in most states in the Peninsula except Perlis and Penang. They are a heterogeneous group of different ethnic groups, adhering to different religions and beliefs. The Orang Asli have gone through social changes ever since they have had contact with outsiders, particularly since the 1800s. In the 20th century, their lives changed markedly due to development and modernization. These changes are reflected in the religions they practise—many have adopted other religions, such as Islam (30 per cent) and Christianity (15 per cent).

Basic beliefs

Most Orang Asli believe in God as a symbol of the ultimate supernatural power. This ultimate power is known as Nyenaang or Jenaang by the Semai; Moyang by the Temuan and Mah Meri; Tohan among the Batek and Che Wong; and Peruman by the Jah Hut. Other deities include the thunder god (Engkuu', Karei or Gobar). If people violate natural laws and commit offences such as incest, the thunder god's anger will be manifested in storms and floods. The Orang Asli also believe in guardian tigers, *naga* (dragons), guardians of the sea and of the world beneath the earth.

Sabah and Sarawak

The indigenous peoples of Sabah make up 60 per cent of the estimated 2.6 million inhabitants and mostly live in rural villages. There are 30 ethnic groups who speak more than 50 languages and 80 dialects. In Sarawak there are about 1,670,000

Beliefs of the Semai

The Semai believe in Jenaang (or Nyenaang) as the ultimate supernatural power. Jenaang created the earth, mankind and all other creatures.

Other deities or helpers of God (angels) are referred to as *maklikat*. Their duties involve helping Jenaang to deliver *kloog* (life) to newborn babies and taking the souls of the elderly to their permanent resting place, Surgaak.

There is a third category of supernatural beings called *nyaniik* (or *daneeh*). Deities in this group include *keramat* (saints), Maai Dengriik (guardian of the earth), *guniik* (good spirits) and bad spirits.

Human beings belong to a fourth category. A final category consists of animals and trees.

indigenous people, 60 per cent of the population. They are divided into 37 known ethnic groups and sub-groups who are mostly situated in the coastal and interior areas.

Basic beliefs

In general, the indigenous peoples of Sabah and Sarawak believe in a supreme being who is the creator of the world, including the spirit world. Human existence is an integrated whole with many worlds, both seen and unseen. The human world needs to live in a symbiotic and harmonious relationship with the different worlds of the plants, animals and spirits. The spirits are benevolent and malevolent. Shamans, intermediaries or ritual specialists are called upon to negotiate any rupture in the relationship. Life is believed to continue in the afterlife for those who do good deeds, while the wicked will suffer even while they are alive. The belief in retribution attributes certain reciprocity for every good or bad action done to others.

Location of the main indigenous groups in Malaysia

- Negritos
  Batek, Jahai, Kensiu, Kintak, Lanoh, Mendriq

- Senoi
  Che Wong, Jah Hut, Mah Meri, Semai, Semaq Beri, Temiar

- Proto-Malay
  Jakun, Orang Kanaq, Orang Kuala, Orang Seletar, Semelai, Temuan

- Areas without indigenous populations

THAILAND

Peninsular Malaysia

BRUNEI | Sabah

Sarawak

INDONESIA

South China Sea

N

0   200 km

- Bajau
- Berawan
- Bidayuh
- Iban
- Kadazandusun
- Kayan
- Kedayan
- Kelabit
- Kenyah
- Melanau
- Murut
- Penan
- Rungus

Some beliefs in Sarawak

The Iban

The Iban are the largest ethnic group in Sarawak. Traditional law and customs (*adat*) are followed to maintain harmony within the community. Many Iban have converted to Christianity and some are Muslims, but ceremonies and rituals are still observed as they maintain ties between families and villages. The Iban traditional belief is that all beings possess separable souls which communicate with gods and spirits through dreams. Cultural and social values are drawn from the Iban's belief that men's souls and those of gods and spirits often encroach upon one another. A number of cults address these beliefs. One example is the padi (rice seeds) cult. Rice is very important to the Iban and elaborate rituals are conducted during the various stages of rice cultivation to supplicate the souls of the padi and thus ensure a bountiful harvest. Other rituals are conducted by shamans when someone falls ill, to recover 'lost souls' entrapped by evil spirits or upon death to ensure a peaceful passage to the afterworld for the person's soul (*semangat*).

An Iban carved *kenyalang* (rhinoceros hornbill) which represents the god of war.

The Bidayuh

The Bidayuh are animists but many have embraced Christianity and some, Islam. Traditional beliefs reflect the importance of maintaining harmonious relationships within the community and with the netherworld. Rituals are the means to maintain this harmony with the spirit world and feature highly within the Bidayuh community. (see 'Rituals and festivals').

The Orang Ulu

The Orang Ulu comprise the Kelabit, Penan, Lun Bawang and 16 other minority groups. Similar to the Bidayuh, Orang Ulu were traditionally animist but are now predominantly Christian. A few are Muslims. They still maintain traditional values such as respect for elders and observe ritual ceremonies associated with rites of passage, the rice harvest or protection from evil spirits.

An Orang Ulu mask used in various rituals.

Iban shamans preparing sacrificial food (*miring*) during a traditional festival (*gawai*). This ritual is associated with every Iban festival.

Shamans of Sarawak

Generally a shaman will be called by a spirit in a dream and very often in the case of the Melanau and Bidayuh, experience a serious illness during which, and after recovery, the patient is identified and initiated as a shaman. Iban shamans are generally men, while amongst the Bidayuh and Kayan, shamans are almost always women. Melanau shamans can be of either sex. Diagnosing illnesses and curing people of their afflictions is the most common function of a shaman today.

Although shamans may experience possession or act as mediums through whom spirits communicate or incarnate themselves, these features are less universally characteristic of shamanism in Sarawak than was once assumed. More general is the undertaking of spiritual journeys to other worlds. Iban shamans (*manang*), for example, are neither possessed by spirits, nor do they act as passive channels through whom spirits communicate with human beings. Rather, during the singing of ritual songs, shamans send out their soul, accompanied by soul guides, on journeys into unseen realms. Here they and their helpers perform a multitude of tasks, such as recovering lost or captured souls, erecting spiritual barriers against malevolent forces, or confronting and possibly slaying spirits. Central to Iban shamanism are ritual songs sung in a poetic form by the shaman in which he narrates an account of the travels of his soul.

Some beliefs and religious practitioners in Sabah

The Kadazandusun

For the Kadazandusun and the Murut, the creator is known as Minamangun and Aki Kaulung respectively. Among the Kadazandusun, four types of spirits exist: *sunduvan* (souls of the living), *tombilvo (*spirits of the dead who sometimes possess humans), *rusod* (spirits of animals and plants) and *logon* (other spirits—good and bad).

Among the Kadazandusun, priestesses (*bobohizan*) play a very important role in the communities. They are called in to heal any break in the natural harmony of the world by offering *sogit* (compensation) to the offended spirit or to the affected community. The *bobohizan* normally expends considerable energy in her negotiations with the evil spirits.

Bobohizan also help the people deal with illness. The *bobohizan* requests her *diwato* (assistant spirits) who reside inside her *komburongo* (a string of dried grass roots) to diagnose the illness—normally traceable to a manifest disrespect towards some plants or animals. Once identified the *bobohizan* undertakes to undo the wrong and apologize on behalf of the patient.

A Lotud *tantagas* (priestess) from the Tuaran district, Sabah.

The Rungus

The Rungus believe in the *osunduw*—supernatural spirits who range from specific and benevolent celestial gods inhabiting the various layers of the upper world (*avan*) to the malevolent terrestrial spirits and demigods (*rogon*), as well as rice spirits (*odu-odu*) of the lower world who are inhabitants (*putana*) of the earth. Some of the more popular gods are the *rusod* who are guardians of the proper order in a household and protectors of its members.

The *bobohizan* plays an important role in the Rungus community as well as that of the Kadazandusun. Their ceremonies share many similarities. The Rungus *bobohizan* perform healing ceremonies through trance which can be spontaneous (*rundukan tomod*). During the trance, the *bobohizan* calls up various *luma' ag* (spirit-guides) to travel to the villages of the *rogon*, bargain for the return of souls in exchange for sacrifice, and return them to the *bobohizan*.

The Murut

The Murut believe in a spirit world inhabited by a variety of *aru* (spirits). *Kamanggas* live in rocks and trees and household objects. Whoever accidentally disturbs a *kamanggas* will be shot with a blowgun and become ill or die. The

A Kadazandusun ceremony called Mangahau, during which ancestral jars (*gusi*) are cleansed by a priestess to appease the spirits of ancestors who are believed to reside in them, Tuaran district, Sabah.

tambailung takes the form of animals which feed on humans. The *lalandou* looks like a tall person and also kills its victims. The *amamalir* deceives its victims, especially children, making them lose their way in the jungle. The Murut also believe in many water spirits. The deepest spots in large rivers are believed to be the abode of the *panandom*, which drowns its victims.

The Murut do not have priests; they believe in personal spirits known as *taniou* who attach themselves to individuals or reside in rocks and pieces of wood. Through dreams they deliver instructions about the location of lost objects. When the individual pays heed to the dream and finds the object, the person becomes a *lumahon* (shaman). *Lumahon* have specialized knowledge and power categorized as *amol*, *umparan* and *sasampui*. The powers of *amol* prevent them from bleeding if stabbed. *Umparan* is the manipulation of curses and is used on people who have acted out of jealousy or greed rather than thinking of the benefit of the community. *Sasampui* is the ability to cast spells.

Rituals and festivals

The combination of beliefs and healing systems involves many major and minor rituals which are associated with healing, agriculture and the seasons although some of these now take a celebratory form rather than a purely religious form. Placation of spirits to give thanks, ask for protection and guidance or to avert their anger is of primary concern, and rituals for different occasions can include animal sacrifices and, almost always, food offerings. Harvest festivals are major celebrations for many groups, while rites of passage are held at important stages of life.

Masks of the Mah Meri spirit Moyang Tinggi (with black headdress), a house protector spirit, are commonly kept in village homes.

Orang Asli rites of passage

All Orang Asli have to go through rituals at important times in their lives. For the Semai, the spiritual needs of newborn babies are looked after by midwives (*bidat*) until the stage when the baby is able to talk fluently and walk independently. During this stage, the midwife will perform a number of rituals to strengthen the *ruwaay* (soul) of the baby. As the baby grows, rituals are performed as necessary.

The Jah Hut and Semelai people are unique among the Orang Asli groups in that they practise circumcision. The circumcision ritual marks the period when a boy becomes a young man. On the day of the circumcision, young boys immerse themselves in the river. This is a cleansing ritual and also provides a numbing effect. There the shaman (*poyang*) will cast his spell to protect the boys from bad spirits. After a few hours soaking in the water, the boys are carried by their fathers and other relatives to the graves of their ancestors. Here they walk around the graves and inform the ancestral spirits about the boys' transition from childhood to adolescence. The boys are then circumcised.

Negrito (Semang) marriages lack the formality of Senoi and Melayu Asli (Proto-Malay) marriages. Traditional Mah Meri weddings involve a number of rituals which can take up to four days and include a cleansing ceremony of the bridal families. At the end of the marriage ceremony of the Temuan of Melaka, a cleansing ritual (bath) called *mandi mayang* cleanses the couple of all bad luck attached to them as single people so that they can begin a new life as husband and wife.

Orang Asli death rituals

The Semai, especially those who live in Pahang, and the Temiar conduct a ritual of singing, music and dancing called *tenamoh* on the 100th day after death. This marks the end of mourning. The Mah Meri, and a few small groups of Temuan, hold memorial days for their ancestors, called Hari Moyang. In the

Top: Orang Asli Jah Hut boys in Pahang being prepared for circumcision by the shaman.

Above: Assistants sprinkle scented water over the shaman during the annual Hari Moyang (Ancestors' Day) at a Temuan village in Bukit Cheeding, Banting, Selangor.

past, when these people were actively engaged in fishing, this annual ritual would coincide with the launching of a *lancang*, a large boat, at the end of the monsoon season. Because the community no longer depends on fishing this ritual has been replaced by a celebration that falls either in February or June every year. It is held on the beach, and the people ask Moyang (guardian of the universe) for blessings and protection from bad spirits. A similar ritual, called Puja Pantai, is performed by another maritime-based society, the Jakun.

Orang Asli harvest and festivities

The Batek perform rituals during the fruit and honey seasons. Some of the Senoi also perform a ritual, called *jiis breeg*, during the fruit season. The Semai and Temiar, involved in swidden cultivation, perform a ritual, followed by festivities, after the harvest season.

Healing and other rituals in Sabah and Sarawak

In Sabah and Sarawak there are many rituals associated with healing of the sick. In Sabah, the Rungus *bobohizan* (high priestesses) frequently perform the *turumuron* ceremony to undo the anger

---

Semai Orang Asli healing rituals
To understand the Semai theory of illness, it is necessary to understand the Semai concept of a human being. They believe human beings consist of four elements: heart soul (*kloog*), head soul (*ruwaay*), shadow soul (*woog*) and body (*broog*). If the *kloog* leaves the body, the person dies.

The second element, the *ruwaay*, resides in the forehead. It is associated with knowledge and illness. *Ruwaay* can leave the body during a trance, sleep and unconsciousness. The third element is the *woog*, the supernatural partner of the body. The last element, the *broog* serves as a container for the *kloog* and *ruwaay*. When a person dies it goes back to its origin, the earth.

In the Semai theory of illness, a person will fall ill if his/her *ruwaay* is lost or has been captured by a *nyaniik* (supernatural being). *Nyaniik* have categories of food such as fish, meat, rice and vegetables and regard *ruwaay* as meat.

Shamans play an important role in Orang Asli healing rituals. They persuade the *guniik* (spirit helpers) to look for the *ruwaay* and bring it back to the patient's body.

of the *rusod* (animal and plant spirits) manifested in the form of illness in the family. For any lingering illness, a less frequent (once in five to ten years) renewal ceremony known as *moginum* is held in which a pig sacrifice is made and where there is feasting and drinking culminating in the *bobohizan* dancing with the *rusod* on a raised platform above the roof of the house.

The Murut have different rituals for different occasions. The *amparawak* ritual placates spirits through animal sacrifices such as chickens, pigs or buffalo. This ritual is offered to protect those starting a project, such as preparing a field for cultivation, or building a house. A sacrifice is made and the blood is smeared on the group starting the project. When *adat* (traditional law) is violated, the village head offers a sacrifice to restore the harmony between the villagers and the spirits. *Amparawak* is also offered when closely related individuals get married as this relationship upsets the cosmos and stops trees from bearing fruit.

In Sarawak, before a funeral, the Iban *manang* (shaman) performs the *serara bungai* (separation of the flowers) ceremony, a symbolic ritual, to ensure total separation between the dead and the living, especially when the dead have returned to interfere with the living, as evidenced by illness, bad dreams or the mysterious disappearance of rice. For bad dreams, the *manang* perform rituals known as *jai mimpi* or *panabar burong,* which neutralize bad omens, and *panabar pemali* to neutralize a violation of taboo.

Rites of passage in Sabah and Sarawak

In Sabah, the *basawangan* is a rite of passage for the first-born among the Murut. The grandparents initiate a gathering of all the in-laws and relatives to introduce the first-born to the family. The guests are requested to offer a gift such as a piece of soap, clothes, gong, or *tajau* (jars). To honour the newly born child, a pig is slaughtered, and the blood is smeared on the child to ensure a long life.

The Rungus and Kadazandusun believe in 'hot' and 'cold' relations; 'hot' being anger, stress and displeasure. Therefore before a Rungus marriage, the *bobohizan* is invited to offer recitation of sacred texts over chickens. The incantations, known as *monogit,* aim to 'cool off' or remove any 'hot' relations or negative elements between the couple and ensure that the newlyweds have a good harvest of crops and raise a family with children who grow healthily to adulthood. The passage of the deceased is aided by a *lumuvas* ceremony to remember the souls and ensure that any lingering souls are sent off to the final resting place in Nabalu (Mount Kinabalu).

The Berawan of Sarawak have an elaborate ritual for the dead. First, a funeral is conducted, except in the case of those who suffered an untimely or premature death. Previously it was taboo to bring these corpses into the longhouse, but this tradition is changing. The second stage *(nulang)* resembles a wake, where the triumph over death is celebrated.

1. Offerings of food are laid out in the gallery of longhouses during *gawai* (festivals) and ceremonies.

2. Iban ritual specialists (*lemembang*) preparing offerings and sacrificial food at a Gawai Dayak festival in Sarawak.

3. An Iban couple in traditional costume prepare for their wedding ceremony in the longhouse.

Harvest festivals

The Tadau Kaamatan of the Kadazandusun of Sabah and the Gawai Dayak of Sarawak are two major festivals associated with harvest season. Although celebrated for various occasions, *gawai* celebrations always include food sacrifice (*miring*), chanting, incantations and dancing by ritual specialists (*lemembang*).

Gawai Dayak is celebrated every year on 1 June as the time to renew bonds of kinship and friendship. Festivities take place in the space across the *ruai* (gallery) of longhouses involving all inhabitants. Another Iban festival is Gawai Batu (Whetstone Festival) in which all tools are collected and blessed with incantations.

Tadau Kaamatan is celebrated annually in Sabah to thank the spirit of the rice (*bambarayon*) during which the community gathers for eating, dancing, drinking of *tapai* (rice wine), dancing the Sumazau (ritual dance), singing and communal sports. A ritual known as *magavau* is the climax of the cycle of rice cultivation when the *bobohizan* calls back the rice spirits who may have got lost and or left behind in the field to feast at a table set with the best rice, *tapai*, eggs, salt and chicken.

Ladies dressed in traditional costume as part of harvest festival celebrations in Sabah.

Nulang marks the start of the period in which the souls journey to the community of those who are dead (*lia de lo leta*).

1. Malaysia's multi-ethnic make-up is evident at this 1993 Hari Raya celebration organized by the Human Values Friendship Group, where Muslims, Buddhists, Christians, Hindus and Sikhs joined in the festivities.

2. At an international ecumenical Christian conference held in Kuala Lumpur in August 2004, Prime Minister Dato' Seri Abdullah Ahmad Badawi was presented with a dictionary of ecumenical terminology by the Rt Revd Tan Sri Dr Lim Cheng Ean, Bishop of the Synod of the Diocese of West Malaysia (Anglican church).

3. During major festivals government ministers hold open houses where people of all races and religions are welcome. Here, leading government members, Deputy Prime Minister Datuk Sri Najib Tun Razak, Datuk Seri Chan Kong Choy, Datuk Seri Ong Ka Ting, Prime Minister Dato' Seri Abdullah Ahmad Badawi, Tun Dr Mahathir Mohamad and others, celebrate Chinese New Year in 2004.

4. Prime Minister Dato' Seri Abdullah Ahmad Badawi being greeted by a Malaysian Hindu, Poomdevi Sellathuray, during the 2004 elections in Seremban.

5. Hari Raya was celebrated jointly with Chinese New Year in 1996. The entrance to a shopping centre displays decorations for both festivals.

INTERFAITH ISSUES

RUKUNEGARA

BAHAWA SA-NYA NEGARA KITA MALAYSIA
mendukong chita₂ hendak

menchapai perpaduan yang lebeh erat di-kalangan
    seluroh masharakat-nya;
memelihara satu chara hidup demokratik;
menchipta satu masharakat yang adil di-mana
    kema'amoran Negara akan dapat di-nikmati
    bersama sechara adil dan saksama;
menjamin satu chara yang liberal terhadap tradisi₂
    kebudayaan-nya yang kaya dan
    berbagai chorak;
membina satu masharakat progresif yang akan
    menggunakan sains dan teknoloji moden;

MAKA KAMI, ra'ayat Malaysia, berikrar akan
menumpukan seluroh tenaga dan usaha kami
untok menchapai chita₂ tersebut berdasarkan
    atas prinsip₂ yang berikut :-

**Keperchayaan kapada Tuhan
Kesetiaan kapada Raja dan Negara
Keluhoran Perlembagaan
Kedaulatan Undang₂
Kesopanan dan Kesusilaan**

The Rukunegara was formally announced by the fourth Yang di-Pertuan Agong Tuanku Ismail Nasiruddin Shah on 31 August 1970.

Perhaps the most formidable challenge facing Malaysian religious life today is to maintain and revitalize the country's pluralistic and multi-religious outlook and keep it at the heart of public life. Historically, Malaysia has the benefit of a long inheritance of shared political and cultural values amongst her people. This is evident in constitutional provision for freedom of religion, the Rukunegara (National Ideology) and in non-governmental interfaith organizations. Whilst the Constitution states that Islam is the religion of the Federation, other faiths are allowed to be practised.

Aware of the power of religion to mobilize the hearts and minds of people, the authorities encourage an atmosphere of tolerance—for all to live by the adage, 'we treat others as we wish others to treat us'. Strengthened by the belief in the oneness of God and the oneness of humanity, leading interfaith non-governmental organizations take the initiative in organizing inter-religious engagements.

Apart from government and organization-supported initiatives, Malaysians work to foster religious harmony and tolerance in their everyday lives. They seek out the commonalities of their religious practices rather than the differences. Where there are differences, then mutual respect and tolerance hold sway. All the commonly held human virtues and the 'golden rule' of treating others as you would wish to be treated yourself are to be found in Islam, Hinduism, Buddhism, Confucianism, Taoism, Christianity and Sikhism. The Ministry of Education has identified 45 universal values to be taught in schools. The aim is to educate Malaysians fully for meaningful inter-religious dialogue.

In Malaysia, interfaith issues are constantly discussed in order to learn from one another and share the universal values which help to strengthen the fabric of Malaysian society. Malaysians appreciate and cherish the meaning of peaceful co-existence amongst people of different faiths as they realize that elsewhere religious conflicts cause untold misery and destruction.

A souvenir from the Malaysian Interfaith Network, giving the 'golden rule' for all religions.

Interfaith dialogue and religious pluralism

One of the distinctive features of Malaysia is the great diversity of its peoples and cultures. Religious pluralism is therefore an existential reality and Malaysians live harmoniously with persons of different religions. Since achieving Independence in 1957, Islam has been the official religion. However, the Malaysian Constitution is also explicit in upholding the freedom of worship and allowing non-Muslims to practise their own religions. In general, the interaction across religions has not only been harmonious but mutually enriching as well.

The members of the MCCBCHS with His Royal Highness the Sultan of Perak, Sultan Azlan Muhibbuddin Shah ibni Almarhum Sultan Yussuf Izzuddin Shah Ghafarullahu-lahu (front row, third from right) in Ipoh, Perak, after a meeting on religious harmony in 1996.

The Rukunegara and Vision 2020

A set of principles known as the Rukunegara (National Ideology) serves as a guide to peaceful and harmonious living in Malaysia. The principles are: belief in God; loyalty to king and country; upholding the Constitution; rule of law; and good behaviour and morality. Malaysia's vision is towards a fully industrialized and developed nation by the year 2020. Vision 2020, launched in 1990, provided the basis for the development of a society within the context of accelerated industrialization and internationalization, anchored in the principles of the Rukunegara. Vision 2020 has nine challenges, the first being moving towards a more moral and ethical society. This is where the various religious communities have responsibility for inculcating universal teachings and values so that Malaysians will develop as spiritual and moral beings able to live harmoniously in a religiously plural context.

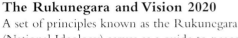

During Chinese New Year, dragon dances can be seen across the country—wherever there are Chinese communities, and especially in the large urban centres.

Interfaith initiatives in Malaysia

In the young nation of Malaysia, organizations and institutions have played significant roles in promoting inter-religious harmony and dialogue. An exploratory inter-religious meeting was held in Kuala Lumpur on 30 June 1956. Initiated by the late Swami Satyananda, founder of the Pure Life Society, the Malayan Council for Interfaith Cooperation was established. This later evolved into the Malaysian Inter-Religious Organization (MIRO).

After the racial riots of May 1969 the government instituted the National Unity Board under a full-time Cabinet minister. Later, the National Consultative Council was established as a forum to discuss, among others, religious issues. These institutions aimed to promote inter-religious and inter-racial harmony through specially formulated governmental as well as non-governmental programmes.

At present, interfaith dialogue in Malaysia is observed at four distinct levels: dialogue of religious leaders; dialogue of scholars and intellectuals; dialogue of movements and non-governmental organizations; and dialogue of the grassroots and common people.

Dialogue of religious leaders

This is the dialogue that takes place primarily amongst the leaders of religious communities, often in view of dialogues with governmental officials. The Malaysian Consultative Council of Buddhism, Christianity, Hinduism and Sikhism (MCCBCHS), officially registered on 6 August 1982, occupies a prominent place in the eyes of the government as a representative body.

While serving mainly as a consultative and liaison body, the MCCBCHS also acts as a watchdog monitoring enactments and policies that affect the religious life of minority religious groups in the country. The first seminar organized by the MCCBCHS was held in 1984 with the theme 'Common Religious Values for Nation-building'.

Through the years the MCCBCHS has also been engaged in dialogue with specific Muslim organizations such as the Institut Kefahaman Islam Malaysia (Institute of Islamic Understanding Malaysia) and the Jabatan Kemajuan Islam Malaysia (Department of Islamic Development Malaysia). All

Grassroots-level interfaith movements

Fostering Inter-Religious Encounters (FIRE)

Founded in Petaling Jaya in March 1998, Fostering Inter-Religious Encounters believes that barriers and conflicts between religious communities can no longer be justified as worldwide desire for peace and understanding has become more evident.

FIRE has organized numerous lectures on the world religions, taught by believers of the respective religions and attended by persons of all religions. It has facilitated informal dialogues amongst persons of different religions to explore issues such as family, women, sexuality, culture, etc. FIRE has also arranged for members of one religion to visit the places of worship of another religious community.

Lasallian Youth Convention

Founded in Ipoh in 1989, the Lasallian Youth Convention is an annual event which brings together student leaders from Lasallian secondary schools throughout Malaysia. The distinctive feature about the group is that it is multi-racial and multi-religious and that the dimension of spirituality occupies the foreground of their activities. This universal spirituality which has its basis in the Rukunegara has been a source of inspiration guiding the youth to greater involvement in social and communitarian projects within their schools and local communities.

of MCCBCHS's activities are aimed at fostering better interfaith relations and understanding.

Dialogue of scholars and intellectuals

A second form of dialogue is that which is more academic and scholarly. The proponents of these dialogues are devout members of the many different religious communities in Malaysia. They engage one another in scholarly exchange in view of promoting greater understanding and appreciation of one another's religion. These activities are also often focused around particular themes affecting persons of all religions, for example, the impact of globalization on religions.

The International Movement for a Just World (JUST) was founded on 1 August 1992 in Malaysia specifically to address some of these concerns. A truly interfaith movement, its members who are adherents of different religious traditions, are predominantly scholars from local universities as well as from abroad. JUST is a strong advocate of civilizational dialogue. Its philosophy is that through dialogue and interaction human beings will discover that the spiritual and moral world-views and values embodied in all religious and cultural philosophies can offer the human race much needed guidance in the common quest for a just world.

JUST publishes a monthly newsletter which deals with the issues facing society in Malaysia and globally.

Local media broadcast religious programmes regularly and allot extra airtime to religion during major religious festivals.

Dialogue of movements and non-governmental organizations

Perhaps the most efficacious form of interfaith dialogue in Malaysia is that which takes place amongst movements and non-governmental organizations on behalf of victims of injustices and oppression. Inspired by their respective faith commitments the members engage in social action in view of facilitating transformation in society. They deal with grassroots problems, ranging from poverty alleviation, industrial exploitation and political oppression to single-parent households and domestic violence to squatter problems and discrimination on account of HIV/AIDS.

While some of these movements and organizations are faith-based, others transcend

religion. Counting amongst the former are the Angkatan Belia Islam Malaysia (ABIM), the Sisters in Islam (SIS), the Buddhist Missionary Society of Malaysia, the Community Action Network (a Roman Catholic graduates' movement), and the Malaysian CARE (a Protestant social services organization).

Examples of movements which transcend religious affiliation are Aliran Kesedaran Negara (ALIRAN, National Consciousness Movement), Women's Development Collective (WDC), All Women's Action Society of Malaysia (AWAM), and Suara Rakyat Malaysia (SUARAM, Voice of the Malaysian People). Even if the primary agenda of many of these groups are social and political action, their activities bring together persons of different religions for dialogue and exchanges.

Dialogue of the grassroots and common people

An important but often unacknowledged form of interfaith dialogue is that which takes place on an everyday basis amongst peoples at the grassroots. This is the natural dialogue which Malaysians are constantly engaged in, such as in their workplace, in schools and factories, in their residential communities, in government offices and hospitals, or while shopping in the market. The fact that there is no religious segregation in public spaces in Malaysia augurs well for interfaith dialogue. People freely associate and mingle with one another, irrespective of religious identity.

A key to congenial interfaith relationship is the willingness of people to accept one another's differences and acknowledge the rights of others, not only to believe differently, but to order their lives according to that belief. The Malaysian media has also helped facilitate this by providing ample coverage of the important religious festivals held in different parts of the country. One of the most distinctive features of religious festivities is the 'open house' tradition where people visit one another's homes to celebrate with the host.

School children performing at an ecumenical rally.

National-level interfaith organizations

Aliran Kesedaran Negara (ALIRAN)
Launched in Penang on 12 August 1977 by seven concerned Malaysians from different ethnic and religious backgrounds, Aliran Kesedaran Negara (Aliran) is a social movement. Its aim is to raise social consciousness and encourage social action that will lead to social justice.

Aliran holds that humanity is the total expression of all the eternal, universal values such as truth, justice, freedom, equality, love, compassion, moderation, tolerance and restraint which lie at the heart of the great spiritual traditions. That is why undergirding Aliran's philosophy is the conviction that realizing the humanity of Malaysians is at once an act of establishing one's loyalty to God and discovering God's divine essence.

Interfaith Spiritual Fellowship (INSaF)
The Interfaith Spiritual Fellowship (INSaF) is actually a 1986 revival of the Malaysian Inter-Religious Organization (MIRO). While associated with the Hindu Pure Life Society, its members come from a variety of religious backgrounds, including Islam. Membership is not confined to religious leaders but, also includes peoples from all walks of life.

With 'unity in diversity' as its motto, INSaF strives to foster national well-being through the promotion of religious harmony. It is dedicated to providing a platform and means for people of different faiths to come together to promote common principles contained in all the religions.

Malaysian Interfaith Network (MIN)
This body was formed in December 2002 comprising of representatives from all the major religions including Islam. It was established to provide a platform of communication for the various interfaith organizations, initiatives and actions in Malaysia.

The five main objectives of MIN are: to promote interfaith understanding, tolerance, respect, appreciation and cooperation; to promote the universal perspective and the common values of all faiths; to promote inner peace, peace with all peoples and peace with the environment; to assist in creating a tolerant, progressive and united nation consistent with the spirit of the Malaysian Constitution; and to network and cooperate with like-minded organizations within and outside Malaysia.

Glossary

A

Ad-din: Religion as a way of life (Islam).

Adat: Custom, code of behaviour within a community, set of norms and rules deriving their legitimacy from traditions.

Advent: The beginning of the Christian year; the four-week period before Christmas.

Akad nikah: Solemnizing of the marriage contract (Islam).

Amparawak: Murut ritual to placate spirits through animal sacrifice; it is performed before the start of a project.

Anbiya: Prophets.

Ang pow: Gift of money given in a red packet, particularly at Chinese New Year (to children and unmarried adults), and at weddings (to the bridal couple).

Anglican Church: A member of the Church of England or affiliated church.

Arathi: Mixture of water, turmeric and quicklime with a betel leaf and lit camphor oil lamp used in Hindu ceremonies.

Ardas: Supplication (Hinduism).

Asar: Muslim afternoon prayers.

Ashrama: The different stages of life (Hinduism).

Aurat: Parts of the body which should be covered in public (Islam).

Azan: Muslim call to prayer.

B

Bambarayon: Kadazandusun rice spirit in honour of which the annual Tadau Kaamatan is held.

Basawangan: Murut rite of passage for first-born babies.

Beidou: Big Dipper constellation; prayed to by Taoists.

Bhagavad-Gita: A section of the *Mahabharata* epic.

Bible: The Christian holy book.

Bilal/muezzin: Person who makes the Islamic call to prayer.

Bishop: A Christian (Catholic or Anglican) priest with spiritual and administrative powers over a diocese.

Bobohizan: Female Kadazandusun priestess.

Bodhisattva: A Buddhist divine being worthy of nirvana who remains with the people to help them to reach salvation.

Brahma: Creator of the world; one of the Hindu *trimurti*.

Buka puasa: Breaking of the Islamic fast.

C

Catechism: Christian instruction by a series of questions and answers.

Catholic Church: The Church which derives its traditions from the ancient undivided Church, with the Pope at its head.

Chap Goh Meh: Chinese Lantern Festival.

Charismatic movement: Christian churches emphasizing communal prayer and the charismatic gifts of speaking in tongues and healing.

Chinese Lantern Festival (Yuan Xiao): Celebration on the 15th day of Chinese New Year. Also known as Chap Goh Meh.

Chinese New Year (Yuan Dan): The beginning of the Chinese lunar calendar; occurs in January or February.

Christian missionaries: Members of a religious (Christian) mission.

Christmas: Christian festival on 25 December to celebrate the birth (around 0 CE) of Jesus.

Church denominations: The various divisions of the Christian Church.

Clergy: Collective body of men and women ordained as religious ministers in the Christian churches.

Confucius: Romanized name of Kong Fu Tze (b. 551 BCE), the founder of Confucianism.

Confucianism: System of beliefs expounded by Confucius which strongly advocates the importance of proper conduct, filial piety and ancestor worship.

D

Dakwah: Islamic outreach.

Dao De Jing (Classic of the Way and its Virtues): The key text of Taoism, written by Lao Zi.

'Datuk' Kong: Chinese Malaysian earth god.

Deepavali: Hindu festival of light which occurs in the Tamil month of Aippasi (October–November).

Dharma: In Buddhism, ideal truth as set forth in the teachings of Buddha.

Dharma: In Hinduism, obligations.

Diocese: A church district under the jurisdiction of a bishop.

Disciple: Personal follower of Christ.

Diwali: Originally a Hindu festival, Diwali has been adapted by the Sikhs as a commemoration of the release from prison of the sixth guru, Guru Hargobind.

Doa: Supplication (Islam).

Duan Wu: Chinese Dragonboat Festival; occurs on 5th day of the 5th moon.

Dukkha: The belief in Theravada Buddhism that all suffering is due to human desire for permanence when everything is impermanent.

E

Easter: Christian celebration of the Resurrection of Jesus Christ.

Ecumenical: Relating to the whole Christian Church and its many divisions.

Eight Immortals: Eight local Chinese heroes, from different regions and times in China.

Evangelist: Preacher of the Christian gospel.

F

Fardhu: Obligatory (Islam).

Fiqh: Islamic jurisprudence.

Five 'k's': Five items which must be worn by Sikhs as symbols of their faith: *kesh* (unshorn hair); *kangha* (comb); *kara* (iron bracelet); *kirpan* (sword); *kachha* (breeches).

G

Ganesha: Elephant-headed Hindu god; remover of obstacles; son of Shiva and Parvathi. Other names: Vinayagar, Pillaiyar, Ganapathy.

Gawai Batu: Iban whetstone festival when all the tools are collected and blessed with incantations.

Gawai Dayak: Iban harvest festival, celebrated on 1 June every year.

Good Friday: The day of the crucifixion of Jesus Christ. His resurrection is celebrated two days later, on Easter Sunday.

Gopuram: Multi-tiered tower over the entrance to a Hindu temple.

Gospels: The first four books of the New Testament.

Granthi: Reader of Sikh scripture.

Guan Gong: Chinese deity whose exploits feature in the classic epic *The Romance of the Three Kingdoms*.

Gurdwara: Sikh temple.

Gurmatta: Decision of a Sikh guru.

Gurmukh: In Sikhism, one who aims for the salvation of the entire humanity in his own lifetime and not after death.

Guru: Hindu or Sikh religious teacher or leader.

Guru Granth Sahib: The Sikh holy book.

H

Hadith: Collected sayings of Prophet Muhammad.

Hajj: Islamic pilgrimage to Mecca, performed during the month of Zulhijjah.

Halal: Permissible (Islam).

Hantaran: Gifts from the bridegroom to the bride (Islam).

Haram: Prohibited, not permitted in Islam.

Hari Asyura: Muslim celebration on the 10th day of Muharram to commemorate the hardships and ordeals faced by Muslims in the past.

Hari Moyang (Ancestors' Day): Annual Orang Asli celebration to honour their ancestors.

Hari Raya Aidiladha: Muslim festival held on 10th day of Zulhijjah when pilgrims gather at Mina, near Mecca.

Hari Raya Aidilfitri: Muslim festival held on the first day of Syawal to mark the end of the fasting month (Ramadhan).

Hari Raya Haji: Alternative name for Hari Raya Aidiladha.

Hari Raya Korban: Alternative name for Hari Raya Aidiladha.

Hari Raya Puasa: Alternative name for Hari Raya Aidilfitri.

Heavenly Duke (Tian Guan): Taoist deity. As the chief representative of Heavenly Will, he examines the conduct of individuals.

Hijrah: Migration of the Prophet (Islam).

Hukamnama: Sikh hymns.

Hungry Ghost Festival (Zhong Yuan): Month-long celebration from 15th day of the 7th moon; a time to repent and forgive sins and perform acts of charity.

I

Imam: Islamic religious officer who leads prayers and conducts religious rites.

Israk Miraj: Day of Prophet Muhammad's Ascension (27th day of Rejab).

Isyak: The obligatory night prayer for Muslims.

J

Jade Emperor: one of the great beings—ruler of the created universe—in Taoism. His birthday is celebrated (particularly by the Hokkien) on the 9th day of the Chinese New Year.

Jenaang: Believed by the Semai to be the ultimate supernatural power; the creator of earth, mankind and all other creatures. Also known as Nyenaang.

Jesuit: A member of the Society of Jesus, a Roman Catholic religious order.

Jubah: Long loose Arabic-style garment worn by Muslim men.

K

Kadi: Islamic judge.

Kalimah syahadah: The Islamic declaration of faith: 'there is no God but Allah, and Muhammad is his Prophet'.

Kamanggas: Murut spirits which live in rocks and trees.

Karma: Principle of retributive justice determining a person's state of life and his reincarnation as the effect of his past deeds.

Khalsa: Sikh community.

Khalwat: Close proximity, cohabitation (Islam).

Khanda: Symbol of the Khalsa.

Khatib: Person who delivers the sermon at Friday prayers.

Khutbah: Sermon given in the mosque at Friday prayers.

Kiblat: Direction in which Muslims pray, facing Mecca.

Kirtan: Singing of hymns (Sikh).

Kolam: Floor decoration of rice flour made on Hindu festival days; also called *rangoli*.

Kuan Yin: Chinese Goddess of Mercy.

Kumpam: Hindu offering of water pot and rice decorated with coconut and mango leaves.

L

Langar: Communal kitchen/ canteen in Sikh gurdwaras.

Lao Zi (604–521 BCE): The founder of Taoism.

Lemembang: Iban shaman.

Lent: The 40-day period of repentance and voluntary abstinence prior to Easter in honour of the 40-day fast of Jesus in the wilderness.

Lumahon: Murut shaman.

M

Maal Hijrah: The first day of the Islamic year; commemoration of Prophet Muhammad's emigration from Mecca to Medina.

Madrasah: Islamic school.

Maghrib: Muslim evening prayer.

Mahabharata: Hindu epic dealing with the conflict between the Pandawa and Korawa clans.

Mahayana: Literally, 'greater vehicle'; a school of Buddhism advocating the attainment of nirvana for the benefit of others.

Manang: Iban shaman.

Mas kahwin: Dowry given by Muslim bridegroom to bride.

Masjid: Mosque.

Maulidur Rasul: Prophet Muhammad's birthday (12th day of Rabiulawwal).

Mazhab: The four Sunni schools of Islamic jurisprudence: Shafii, Maliki, Hanafi, and Hanbali.

Mihrab: Prayer niche in a mosque.

Miri piri: Sikh belief that the spiritual and temporal aspects of life cannot be separated.

Mooncake Festival (Zhong Qiu): Mid-autumn festival marking the successful Chinese rebellion against Mongol rule in 14th-century China.

Mufti: Islamic scholar of *fiqh* who issues legal opinions.

Mukmin: Believer in Islam.

Murugan: Hindu god of heroism; son of Shiva and Parvathi.

Musolla: Muslim place for prayer in a building, often a partitioned room.

N

Nagara: North Indian style Hindu temple.

Najis: Filth; unclean (Islam).

Nasyid: Muslim devotional songs.

Nestorianism: Christian doctrine (attributed to Nestorius) that Christ was two distinct persons, divine and human.

New Testament: Second part of the Bible, relating to the life and teachings of Jesus Christ.

Niat: Intention (Islam).

Nikah: Marriage (Islam).

Nine Emperor Gods: The gods which represent the Beidou (Big Dipper) constellation.

Nine Emperor Gods Festival: The birthday of the Nine Emperor Gods is celebrated on the first nine days of the ninth month of the Chinese calendar.

Nirvana: State of enlightenment in Buddhism.

Nuzul Qur'an: Celebration of the revelation of the Qur'an to Prophet Muhammad on the 17th day of Ramadhan.

Nyenaang: An alternative name for the Semai supernatural power Jenaang.

O

Old Testament: First part of the Bible, relating to the history of the Hebrew people.

Om: The most sacred sound for Hindus; it is the beginning of all Hindu prayers.

P

Pentecostal movement: Christian groups emphasizing the charismatic and fundamental aspects of Christianity.

Planchette divination: spirit-writing; a form of spirit mediation.

Protestantism: Christianity deriving from the principles of the Reformation.

Puasa: Fast/fasting.

Puja: Hindu prayer ritual.

Q

Qing Ming: Tomb Sweeping Day, when graves are cleaned and offerings made to the ancestors. Also known as Cheng Beng, it falls on 5 or 6 April.

Qur'an: Islam's holy book revealed to Prophet Muhammad.

R

Ramadhan: Ninth month in the Muslim calendar, when Muslims fast from dawn till dusk.

Ramayana: Literally 'Rama's wanderings', an Indian epic.

Rasul: Messenger of Allah.

Religious pluralism: A society made up of people of various religions.

Rukun iman: Pillars of the Islamic faith.

Rukun Islam: Pillars of Islam.

S

Sahur: Meal eaten before dawn during Ramadhan.

Samak: To clean oneself according to Islamic practices.

Samatha: Tranquillity meditation in Buddhism.

Samsara: Buddhist and Hindu concept of continual rebirths.

Sandh-sangat: Sikh congregational worship.

Sangam: An organization which embraces all Hindus regardless of which deity they worship.

Sangha: Buddha's enlightened disciples.

Selawat: Blessings for the Prophet.

Sembahyang/solat: Prayer (Islam).

Serban: Cap and scarf wrapped around the head as a turban.

Shiite: One of the two main groups of Muslims; the majority group is the Sunni.

Shiva: One of the Hindu *trimurti*; the destroyer.

Si: Buddhist temples which also house other non-Buddhist deities.

Solat: Prayer (Islam).

Subuh: Muslim morning prayer.

Sun Wu Kong: Monkey God; a Chinese deity considered to have attained enlightenment and become a protector of Buddhism; he is featured in the famous classical Chinese folk tale, *Journey to the West*.

Sunnah: Prophetic traditions.

Sunni: One of the two main groups of Muslims; the minority group is the Shiite.

Sura: Chapter of the Qur'an.

Surau: Small Muslim prayer house.

Syahid: Muslim martyr.

Syariah: Islamic law, or code of ethics relating to all aspects of Muslim life.

Syirik: Polytheism or ascribing partners to Allah.

T

Tadau Kaamatan: Kadazandusun harvest festival, held in May.

Tahlil: Special Islamic prayers said in memory of the deceased.

Takbir: Saying 'Allah is great'.

Tamil New Year (Hindu New Year): Falls on the first day of Chitthirai (April–May) when the sun enters Aries, the first sign of the Hindu zodiac.

Tan: Chinese shrine.

Taoism: Religion founded by Lao Zi (604–521 BCE).

Tarawih: Special Islamic prayers performed after the breaking of fast during Ramadhan.

Tauhid: Muslim affirmation of the oneness of God.

Telekung: Muslim women's white prayer garments.

Thai-ponggal: Four-day thanks-giving festival held from the first day of the Tamil month of Thai (January–February); *ponggal* (sweet rice) is offered to the Sun God.

Thaipusam: Hindu festival dedicated to Murugan which falls on the full moon day of the month of Thai (January–February); the day Shiva revealed his cosmic dance to the sages. Celebrated on a grand scale at Batu Caves near Kuala Lumpur.

Thali: Sacred pendant tied around the bride's neck at Hindu weddings.

Theravada: Literally 'path of elders'; a school of Buddhism that refers to the teachings of Buddha as preserved in early sacred texts, with a spiritual ideal of sainthood.

Thoranam: A festoon of mango leaves draped above Hindu temple and house doorways during festive occasions.

Tian Guan: Heavenly Duke; popular Taoist deity believed to be the chief representative of Heavenly Will whose role is to examine the conduct of individuals.

Tian Heng Shan: Taoism sect which evolved in Malaysia and has spread throughout Southeast Asia.

Trimurti: The Hindu trinity of deities, Brahma, Vishnu and Shiva.

Triple Gem: The object of worship in Buddhism: Buddha, his teachings (*dharma*) and his community of enlightened disciples.

Tudung: Headscarf worn by Muslim women.

U

Ulamak: Islamic religious scholars.

Ummah: Muslim community.

Umrah: Lesser pilgrimage to Mecca.

Upanishad: Sanskrit sacred books.

V

Vaisakhi: Sikh festival, originally of thanksgiving; now a festival of the Khalsa.

Vajrayana: School of Tantric Buddhism.

Valaikappu: Hindu ceremonies.

Varna: Hindu caste.

Veda: Hindu sacred text.

Vinayagar: Elephant-headed Hindu god; remover of obstacles. Also called Ganesha.

Vipassana: Buddhist insight meditation.

Vishnu: One of the Hindu *trimurti*; sustainer of universe, maintainer of order and justice.

W

Wang hantaran: Monetary gift for Muslim bride.

Wayang kulit: Puppet shadow play.

Wesak Day: Commemoration of the birth, enlightenment and death of Buddha.

Wuduk: Minor ablution (Islam).

Y

Yuan Dan: Chinese New Year.

Yuan Xiao: Chinese Lantern Festival (Chap Goh Meh).

Z

Zakat: Obligatory poor tax due from Muslims amounting to 2.5 per cent of wealth accummulated over one year.

Zakat fitrah: Tax paid by Muslims during Ramadhan for distribution to the poor on Aidil-fitri.

Zhong Qiu: Mooncake Festival.

Zhong Yuan: Hungry Ghost Festival.

Zohor: Muslim noon prayer.

Bibliography

Abdul Munir Yaacob and Zainal Azam (2002), *Muslims' Rights in Non Muslim Majority Countries*, Kuala Lumpur: Institute of Islamic Understanding Malaysia.

Ackerman, Susan E. & Lee, Raymond L. M. (1990), *Heaven in Transition*, Kuala Lumpur: Forum Enterprise.

Ahmad, Mushtaq (1995), *Business Ethics in Islam*, Islamabad: The International Institute of Islamic Thought.

Ahmad Sarji (2005), *Malaysia Sebagai Sebuah Negara Islam*, Kuala Lumpur: Institute of Islamic Understanding Malaysia.

Ahmad Sarji and Syed Othman Alhabshi (1999), *The Islamic World and Global Cooperation*, Kuala Lumpur: Institute of Islamic Understanding Malaysia.

Aidit Haji Ghazali (ed.) (1993), *Industrialisation from an Islamic Perspective*, Kuala Lumpur: Institute of Islamic Understanding Malaysia.

Al-Faruqi, Ismail Raji (1986), *The Cultural Atlas of Islam*, New York: Macmillan.

—— (1998), *Islam and Other Faiths*, ed. Ataullah Siddiqui, Leicester: The Islamic Foundation.

Al-Qaradawi, Yusuf (1995), *The Lawful and The Prohibited in Islam*, Kuala Lumpur: Islamic Book Trust.

Ali, Abdullah Yusuf (ed.) (1983), *The Holy Qur'an: Text, Translation and Commentary*, Lahore: Sh. Muhammad Ashraf.

Arnold, T.W. (1961), *The Preaching of Islam*, Lahore: Sh. Muhammad Ashraf.

Asaratnam, S. (1996), *Indian Festivals in Malaya*, Kuala Lumpur: Department of Indian Studies, University of Malaya.

Barret, David B. and Johnston, T. M. (eds.) (2001), *World Christian Encyclopaedia*, 2 vols, Oxford & New York: Oxford University Press.

Blythe, Wilfred (1969), *The Impact of Chinese Secret Societies in Malaya: A Historical Study*, London: Oxford University Press.

Bowen, John R. (1993), *Muslims through Discourse*, Princeton: Princeton University Press.

Bunnag, Jane (1973), *Buddhist Monk, Buddhist Layman*, London: Cambridge University Press.

Cheu Hock-Tong (1988), *The Nine Emperor Gods: A Study of Chinese Spirit Medium Cults*, Singapore: Times Books International.

—— (ed.) (1993), *Chinese Beliefs and Practices in Southeast Asia*, Subang Jaya: Pelanduk Publications (M) Sdn Bhd.

Choudhury, Golam W. (1994), *Islam and the Modern Muslim World*, 2nd edn, Kuala Lumpur: WHS Publications Sdn Bhd.

Conze, Edward (1957), *Buddhism,* Oxford: Bruno Cassire Press.

Couillard, Andre-Marie (1980), *Tradition in Tension: Carving in a Jah-Hut Community*, Penang: Penerbit Universiti Sains Malaysia.

Council of Churches of Malaysia (1997), *Celebrating 50 Years of United Witness and Service: 1947–1997*, Petaling Jaya: Council of Churches of Malaysia.

Cox, Harvey (1995), 'Christianity' in Sharma, Arvind (ed.), *Our Religions,* San Francisco: Harper.

Das Gupta S. B. (1957), *Aspects of Indian Religious Thought*, Calcutta: Mukherjee.

Dentan, Robert K. (1968), *The Semai: A Non-Violent People of Malaya*, New York: Holt, Rinehart and Winston.

Dhammananda, K. Sri (1998), *What Buddhists Believe*, Kuala Lumpur: Buddhist Missionary Society.

Endicott, Kirk M. (1979), *Batek Negrito Religion: The World View and Rituals of a Hunting and Gathering People of Peninsular Malaysia*, Oxford: Clarendon Press.

Esposito, John L. (ed.) (1983), *Voices of Resurgent Islam*, New York: Oxford University Press.

—— (ed.) (1987), *Islam in Asia*, New York: Oxford University Press.

—— (ed.) (1995), *The Oxford Encyclopedia of the Modern Islamic World*, New York: Oxford University Press.

Fabella, Virginia and Sugirtharajah (eds.) (2000), *Dictionary of Third World Theologies*, New York: Orbis.

Ferguson, Sinclair B. and Wright, David F. (eds.) (1988), *New Dictionary of Theology*, Downers Grove: Inter-Varsity Press.

Freeman, Derek (1970), *Report on the Iban*, London: Athlone Press.

Gauhar, Altaf (1978), *The Challenge of Islam*, London: The Islamic Council of Europe.

Hamidullah M. (1968), *Introduction to Islam*, Lahore: Ashraf Printing Press.

Hastings, James (ed.) (1915), *The Encyclopedia of Religion & Ethics*, London: Watts & Co.

Ho, Daniel K. C. (1996), 'The Church in Malaysia', in Athyal, Saphir (ed.), *Church in Asia Today: Challenges and Opportunities*, Singapore: Asia Lausanne Committee for World Evangelization.

Hong, Evelyn (1987), *Natives of Sarawak: Survival in Borneo's Vanishing Forest*, 2nd edn, Kuching: Institut Masyarakat.

Howell, Signe (1984), *Society and Cosmos: Chewong of Peninsular Malaysia*, Singapore: Oxford University Press.

Humphreys, Christmas (1978), *Buddhism*, Middlesex: Penguin.

Hunt, Robert, Lee Kam Hing and Roxborogh, John (eds.) (1992), *Christianity in Malaysia: A Denominational History*, Subang Jaya: Pelanduk Publications (M) Sdn Bhd.

IKIM (2003), *Journal of Islam and International Affairs*, Kuala Lumpur: Institute of Islamic Understanding Malaysia.

International Institute of Islamic Thought, The (1989), *Toward Islamization of Disciplines*, Herndon: The International Institute of Islamic Thought.

Islam, Abm. Mahbubul (2002), *Freedom of Religion in Shariah: A Comparative Analysis*, Kuala Lumpur: A. S. Noordeen.

Islamic Foundation, The (1979), *Islamic Perspectives: Studies in Honour of Sayyid Abul A'la Mawdudi*, Leicester: The Islamic Foundation.

Jennings, Sue (1995), *Theatre, Ritual and Transformation*, London: Routledge.

Juli Edo (1988), *Agama dan Perubatan Semai*, Tesis Sarjana Falsafah, Bangi: Universiti Kebangsaan Malaysia.

Kadir H. Din (ed.) (1993), *Development and the Muslims*, Bangi: Universiti Kebangsaan Malaysia.

Kanitkar, V. P. (Hemant) and Cole, W. Owen (1995), *Hinduism*, London: Hodder & Stoughton Ltd.

Karim, Wazir-Jahan (1981), *Ma Batisek Concepts of Living Things*, New Jersey: Athlone Press.

Keeley, Robin (ed.) (1982), *Handbook of Christian Belief*, Herts.: Lion Publishing.

Kholi, S. S. (1992), *The Sikh Philosophy*, Amritsar: Singh Brothers.

Khurshid Ahmad and Zafar Ishaq Ansai (1979), *Islamic Perspectives*, Leicester: The Islamic Foundation.

Klein, F. A. (1985), *The Religion of Islam*, London: Curzon Press.

Knitter, Paul (1995), *One Earth Many Religions: Multi-faith Dialogue and Global Responsibility*, New York: Orbis Books.

Laderman, Carol (1991), *Taming the Winds of Desire: Psychology, Medicine and Aesthetics in Malay Shamanistic Performance*, Berkeley: University of California Press.

Lester, Robert (1973), *Theravada Buddhism in South East Asia*, Michigan: University of Michigan Press.

Ling, Trevor (1976), *The Buddha*, Middlesex: Penguin.

Lingenfelter, Sherwood G. (1990), *Social Organisation of Sabah Societies*, Kota Kinabalu: Sabah Museum and State Archives.

Lings, Martin (1983–94), *Muhammad: His Life Based on the Earliest Sources*, Lahore: Suhail Academy.

Liow Woon Khin, Benny (1989), 'Buddhist Temples and Associations in Penang', Kuala Lumpur: *Journal of the Malaysian Branch of the Royal Asiatic Society*, Vol 62, Part 1.

Liu Ruixiang and Lin Zhihe (1993) (translated), *The Classic of Filial Piety*, Jinan: Shandong Friendship Press.

Mahathir Mohamad (2000), *Islam and the Muslim Ummah*, Subang Jaya: Pelanduk Publications (M) Sdn Bhd.

Mohamad @ Md Som Sujimon, (compiler) (2003), *Monograph on Selected Malay Intellectuals*, Kuala Lumpur: International Islamic University Malaysia.

Mohd Taib Osman (ed.) (1997), *Islamic Civilization in the Malay World*, Kuala Lumpur: Dewan Bahasa dan Pustaka and the Research Centre for Islamic History, Art and Culture, Istanbul.

Moor, E. (1968), *The Hindu Pantheon*, Varanasi: Indological Book House.

Muhammad Khalid Masud (2000), *Shatibi's Philosophy of Islamic Law*, 2nd edn, Kuala Lumpur: Islamic Book Trust.

Nik Mohamed Affandi bin Nik Yusoff (2002), *Islam & Business*, Subang Jaya: Pelanduk Publications (M) Sdn Bhd.

Norhashimah Mohd Yasin (1996), *Islamisation/Malaynisation: A Study on the Role of Islamic Law in the Economic Development of Malaysia 1969–1993*, Kuala Lumpur: Islamic Book Trust.

Ong Seng Huat (1998), *Two Hundred Years of Penang Hakka*, Penang: Penang Hakka Association.

—— (1999), *History of Teochews in Malaysia*, Petaling Jaya: Yi Pin.

—— (2000), *Investigation into Chinese Popular Festivals*, Petaling Jaya: Yi Pin.

—— (2001), *Introduction to Taoism*, Kuala Lumpur: Malaysian San Cheng Taoism Religion Association.

—— (2001), *Malaysian Chinese Cemeteries and Burial Culture*, Kuala Lumpur: Xiao En Cultural Endowment.

—— (2002), *Studies on Doctrine of Filial Piety*, Kuala Lumpur: Xiao En Cultural Endowment.

—— (2002), *180 Years of Hui Chew Chinese in Penang*, Penang: Penang Hui Chew Association.

Osman Bakar (1997), *Islam and Civilizational Dialogue: The Quest for a Truly Universal Civilization*, Kuala Lumpur: University of Malaya Press.

Rahula, Wapola (1978), *What Buddha Taught*, London: Gordon Fraser.

Rajentheran, M. and Manimaran, S. (1984), *Adat dan Pantang Larang Orang India (di Malaysia)*, Kuala Lumpur: Penerbit Fajar Bakti Sdn Bhd.

Roseman, Marina (1991), *Healing Sounds from the Malaysian Rainforest: Temiar Music and Medicine*, Berkeley: University of California Press.

Roxborogh, John (1987), *The Charismatic Movement and the Churches*, Kuala Lumpur: Aldersgate Prayer Fellowship.

—— (1991), *A Common Voice: A History of the Ecumenical Movement in Malaysia*, Petaling Jaya: Council of Churches of Malaysia.

Russell, Sue A. (1999), *Conversion, Identity, and Power: The Impact of Christianity on Power, Relationships and Social Exchanges*, Oxford: University Press of America.

Samuel, Wilfred J. (2003), *Folk Charismatic Christianity*, Kota Kinabalu: Sabah Theological Seminary.

Sandhu, K. S. (1969), *Indians in Malaya: Some Aspects of their Immigration and Settlement 1785–1957*, Cambridge: Cambridge University Press.

Sather, Clifford (2001), *Seeds of Play, Words of Power: An Ethnographic Study of Iban Shamanic Chants*, Kuching: Tun Jugah Foundation and Borneo Research Council.

Seyyed Hossein Nasr (1984), *Science and Civilization in Islam*, Kuala Lumpur: Dewan Pustaka Fajar.

Sidhu, Saran Singh (2003), *Sikh Gurdwaras in Malaysia & Singapore: An Illustrated History 1873–2003*, Kuala Lumpur: Sikh Naujawan Sabha Malaysia.

Singh, Daljeet (1994), *Essentials of Sikhism*, Amritsar: Singh Brothers.

Siti Fatimah Abdul Rahman (ed.) (2002), *The Impact of Globalisation on Social and Cultural Life: An Islamic Response*, Kuala Lumpur: Institute of Islamic Understanding Malaysia.

Soo Khin Wah (1990), *A Study of the Cult of Mazu in Peninsular Malaysia*: Contributions to Southeast Asian Ethnography, No. 9, Columbus: Ohio State University.

Sunquist, Scott W. (ed.) (2001), *A Dictionary of Asian Christianity*, Michigan: William B. Eerdmans.

Syed Othman Alhabshi and Aidit Ghazali (1994), *Islamic Values and Management*, Kuala Lumpur: Institute of Islamic Understanding Malaysia.

Syed Othman Alhabshi and Syed Omar Syed Agil (1994), *The Role and Influence of Religion in Society*, Kuala Lumpur: Institute of Islamic Understanding Malaysia.

Tabbarah, Afif A. (1998), *The Spirit of Islam*, New Delhi: Islamic Book Service.

Tan Chee Beng (1985), *The Development and Distribution of Dejiao Associations in Malaysia and Singapore: A Study on a Chinese Religious Organization*, (Occasional Paper No. 79), Singapore: Institute of Southeast Asian Studies.

Taufik Abdullah and Sharon Siddique (1986), *Islam and Society in Southeast Asia*, Singapore: Institute of Southeast Asian Studies.

Thameem Ushama (1995), *Methodologies of the Quranic Exegesis*, Kuala Lumpur: A. S. Noordeen.

Thomas, P. (1956), *Hindu Religion, Customs and Manners*, Bombay: Taraporevala Soris & Co. Private Ltd.

Von Denffer, Ahmad (1985), *Ulum al-Qur'an: An Introduction to the Sciences of the Qur'an*, 2nd edn, Leicester: The Islamic Foundation.

Walters, Albert Sundararaj (2002), *We Believe in One God? Reflections on the Trinity in the Malaysian Context*, Delhi: ISPCK.

Weaver, Mary Jo (1991), *Introduction to Christianity*, Belmont: Wadsworth.

Williams, John Alden (ed.) (1961), *Islam*, New York: Washington Square Press.

—— (1994), *The Word of Islam*, USA: University of Texas Press.

Winstedt, Richard (1961), *The Malay Magician: Being Shaman, Shiva and Sufi*, London: Routledge and Kegan Paul.

Winzeler, Robert L. (ed.) (1993), *The Seen and the Unseen: Shamanism, Mediumship and Possession in Borneo*, Monograph Series, Vol. 2. Williamsburg: Borneo Research Council.

Yousif, Ahmad F. (1998), *Religious Freedom, Minorities and Islam*, Kuala Lumpur: Thinker's Library Sdn Bhd.

Yusuf al-Qardawi (translated by Kamal El-Helbawy) (1995), *The Lawful and The Prohibited in Islam*, Kuala Lumpur: Islamic Book Trust.

Index

Picture Credits

A. Kasim Abas, pp. 28–9, plains of Mecca and Arafah; p. 125, *kenyalang*. **AKG Photo**, p. 9, woodcut of Confucian scholars. **Abdul Samat Musa**, p. 42, Islamic law enactment booklets. **Ahmad Sarji**, p. 34, Ahmad Sarji. **Amitabha Buddist Society**, p. 64, Amitabha. **Ar-Raudah Media**, p. 31, CD. **Ariel Tunguia**, p. 4, girl making offering; p. 10, *akad nikah*, Federal Mosque; p. 21, Sunni Muslims; p. 23, Muslim men in prayer, worshipper; p. 34 *ketupat*; p. 35, meat distribution; p. 37, main dome, *mihrab* wall, Masjid Tengku Tengah Zaharah, Masjid Asy-Syakirin, Masjid Bukhary; p. 38, Tabung Haji Mosque, *surau*; p. 39, village mosque, educational centre, housing estate, *akad nikah*, meals after prayers; p. 42, JAKIM; p. 47, LUTH building, Bank Muamalat; p. 48, PERKIM building; p. 49, JIM office; p. 51, IKIM, IKIM radio, YPEIM building; p. 55, halal restaurant, traditional slaughter at market; p. 61, lady with incense; p. 63, Kek Lok Si temple, Buddhist devotees; p. 103, St Francis Xavier's statue; p. 130, dragon dance; p. 132, walking on hot coals. **Arkib Negara Malaysia**, p. 15, Sultan Alaeddin Suleimen Shah; p. 62, Chinese gentlemen; pp. 70–1 Chinese temple; p. 129, Rukunegara. **Auger, Timothy**, p. 5, Masjid Ubudiah; p. 105, All Saints Church; p. 109, St Michael's and All Angels Church. **Azmi Dato' Mohd Rais**, p. 43, *syariah* lawyers. **Berita Publishing**, p. 53, front cover of *Jelita*. **Bernama**, p. 42, imam leading prayers; p. 49, USIA building; p. 50, ceremony at 2003 OIC summit; **Bowden, David**, pp. 10–1, Muslim schoolboys; p. 26, paying *zakat* at the mosque; p. 27, *tarawih* prayer; p. 38, *madrasah* sign; p. 41, gable; p. 53, Prime Minister's office. **Buddhist Gem Fellowship**, p. 69, monks; pp. 128–9, Hari Raya celebration; p. 130, members of MCCBCHS. **Buerger, Dianne**, p. 52, ceiling fan. **Chai Kah Yune**, p. 39, Malay village; p. 75, convex

mirror; p. 80, sweetmeats; p. 87, Ganesha. **Council of Churches of Malaysia**, p. 6, interfaith meeting; p. 100, World Women's Day prayers, Christian batik art; p. 114, MCCBCHS dinner, logo; p. 128, ecumenical Christian conference; p. 131, ecumenical rally. **Cross, Martin**, p. 40, Putra Mosque; p. 44, modern *pondok* school; p. 53, Kolej Perubatan Di Raja Perak; p. 98, Vivekananda Ashram. **Davison, Julian**, p. 7, Terengkera Mosque. **Dewan Bahasa dan Pustaka**, p. 45, schoolbooks. **Divine Life Society**, p. 99, monument to Swami Pranavananda, Sri Swami Sivanandaji Saraswati Maharaj. **EDM Archives**, p. 1, young girls reading Qur'an; p. 2; motif; p. 7, Orang Ulu burial post; p. 8, wood sculpture; pp. 8–9, Masjid Kampung Laut; p. 9, Arabic prayer compass; p. 12, prayer mat; p. 13, fragment of Arabic *dirham*, tombstone, coin, Terengganu Stone, gravestone; p. 15, kris; p. 16, Sultan Abu Bakar Mosque; p. 22, calligraphy; p. 23, *sura*, Qur'an, Hadith; p. 30, motifs; p. 31, Qur'an; p. 33, Muslim burial; p. 35, greeting cards; p. 36, Masjid Kampung Laut; p. 44, Hadith; p. 63, clan house; p. 87, *wayang kulit* puppet; p. 100, Bukit Nanas Convent School; pp. 100–1, Tamil Methodist Church Kuala Lumpur; p. 102, Christ Church in Sarawak; p. 107, Iban bible; pp. 116–17, Sikh Native State guides; p. 118, Gurus (all). **Elisha Abdul Halim**, p. 52, schoolchildren. **Federal Information Department Malaysia**, p. 18, Tunku Abdul Rahman Putra; p. 19, Zainal Abidin bin Ahmad; p. 31, Qur'an reading competition; p. 34, *Tokoh Maal Hiraj* winners (all except Tan Sri Dato' Seri (Dr) Ahmad Sarji bin Abdul Hamid; p. 40, Yang di-Pertuan Agong. **Federal Information Department Sarawak**, p. 37, State Mosque Sarawak. **Freesoul Photography**, p. 80, tea ceremony, wedding dinner. **Gallery of Colour**, p. 61,

Wesak Day celebration; p. 73, Taoist devotee; p. 74, spiral incense; p. 76, Chinese lanterns; p. 77, Photor Kong, turtle buns, walking on hot coals, Qing Ming; p. 78, dragon, guardian lion; p. 79, Cheng Hoon Temple; p. 90, festival procession, priest in inner sanctum; pp. 90–1, Murugan; p. 91, ghee lamp; p. 94, priest at Thai-ponggal, cow at Thai-ponggal, *kolam*; p. 95, oil lamp; p. 96, naming ceremony; p. 101, praying; p. 112, church service; pp. 112–13, Good Friday procession, X'mas tree; p. 113, X'mas decorations, Santa Claus. **George S. K. Chiew**, p. 76, procession. **Goh Seng Chong**, p. 4, stained glass window; p. 9, conch shell, Anglican Bishop; p. 10, performing *doa*; p. 37, Masjid Tun Abdul Aziz; p. 44, computer lab; p. 47, Takaful Nasional building; p. 49, ABIM office, Taman Sri Petaling Mosque; p. 55, halal and non-halal sections in supermarket; p. 57, mother with daughters; pp. 64–5, scenes from the Buddha's life (all); p. 66, beads, Buddhist devotee; p. 67, Thai Buddhist altar, Buddhist devotee lighting joss sticks; p. 71, Zhong Wan statue; p. 72, Monkey God; p. 76, Jade Emperor; p. 78, offerings in temple; p. 91, fruit and flower offering, washing the deity; p. 92, Lakshmi Nayaran temple; p. 104, community centre; p. 107, stained glass windows (all); p. 108, Dr Brother Cassian Pappu, Rt Revd Lim Cheng Ean; p. 110, confessionals; p. 119, *kesh*, *kachha*. **Gregory, Annette**, p. 110, communion, confirmation ceremony; p. 111, wedding ceremony, funeral service. **Haji Jalal**, p. 41, Conference of Rulers meeting. **Haks, Leo**, p. 16, Kampung Hulu Mosque. **HBL Network Photo Agency (M) Sdn Bhd**, p. 6, Wesak Day; p. 7, Nine Emperor Gods festival; pp. 10–1, Muslim woman, Masjid Zahir; p. 11, Islamic Arts Museum dome; p. 20, National Mosque; p. 28, the Kaabah; p. 51, OIC conference delegates; p. 53, Palace of the Golden Horses; p. 64,

Mahayana monks; p. 70, temple doors; p. 77, oranges; p. 88, *vimana*. *Herald*, p. 111, ordination ceremony. **HSBC Bank Malaysia Berhad**, p. 46, banking pamphlets. **International Islamic University Malaysia**, p. 45, Prof. Dr Mohd Kamal Hassan, students, IIUM campus. **International Society of Krishna Consciousness**, p. 95, devotees carrying Krishna statue. **International Movement for A Just World**, p. 131, pamphlet. **ISTAC**, p. 53, ISTAC building. **JAKIM**, p. 35, lecture in mosque; p. 49, YADIM building; p. 55, halal logo, modern slaughter methods; p. 131, religious television programme. **Jacobs, Joseph**, p. 68, Ven. Dr K. Sri Dhammananda; p. 89, Shiva and Parvathi, Durga, decorative temple figures; p. 90, Brahmin priests; p. 119, *kangha, kara* and *kirpan*. **KasehDia Publication**, p. 54, halal food guide. **Lau, Dennis**, p. 105, Kenyah chapel; p. 113, nativity play; p. 125, Orang Ulu mask. **Lee Sin Bee**, p. 8, dome from Benut Mosque; p. 24, *bilal*; p. 25, prayer positions; p. 85, oil lamp; p. 88, trident; p. 91, camphor lamp. **Lembaga Tabung Haji**, p. 28, circumambulation, stone-casting ritual; p. 29, pilgrims, tents. **Lim Joo**, pp. 26–7, Gotong Royong. **Malayan Banking Berhad**, p. 46, banking pamphlet. **Malaysian Buddhist Association**, p. 68, logo, Ven. Kim Beng, Ven. Chuk Mor, Cheng Huah Kindergarten; p. 69, Malaysian Buddhist Institute. **Malaysian Chinese Muslim Association**, p. 49, MACMA function. **Malaysian Hindu Sangham**, p. 98, Thiruvaaduthurai Athinam; p. 99, cultural performance. **Malaysian Interfaith Network**, p. 129, golden rule guide. **Malaysian Timber Council**, p. 21, laboratory technician. **Methuen: London, 1913**, p. 17, Daing Lehut from *H.H. The Ranee of Sarawak* (Margaret Brooke). **Mohd Yunus Noor**, p. 34, signboard. **Money**